Practicing Primitive

Practicing Primitive

A Handbook of Aboriginal Skills

By Steven M. Watts

Gibbs Smith, Publisher
Salt Lake City

Published by
Gibbs Smith, Publisher
P.O. Box 667
Layton, Utah 84041

Orders: 1.800.748.5439
www.gibbs-smith.com

Edited and designed by David Wescott
Printed and bound in U.S.A

Many of articles in this book were previously published in the *Bulletin of Primitive Technology*. The publisher bears no responsibility for their accuracy or content. Neither the publisher or author bear responsibility for the results of any project described herein or for the reader's safety during participation. Caution and common sense are recommended for every activity. For additional information, refer to *Primitive Technology I: A Book of Earthskills* and *Primitive Technology II: Ancestral Skills.*

Library of Congress Cataloging-in-Publication Data

Watts, Steven M.
Practicing primitive: a handbook of aboriginal skills / By Steven M. Watts.
p. cm.
ISBN 1-58685-299-X
1.Indians of North America—Industries. 2. Indians of North America—Implements. 3. Indian weapons—North America. 4.Flintknapping. 5.Pottery craft. 6.Hand weaving. 7. Implements, utensils, etc. I. Title.

E98.I5.W37 2005
680'.89'97—dc22

2004058961

Dedicated to:

my parents
Olin and Daphine
who allowed me to
wonder and to wander

and to:

the "girls at home"
Cindy and Starwalker
whose support was unswerving
for a husband and father
consumed with an idea
which often kept him
preoccupied and away from home.

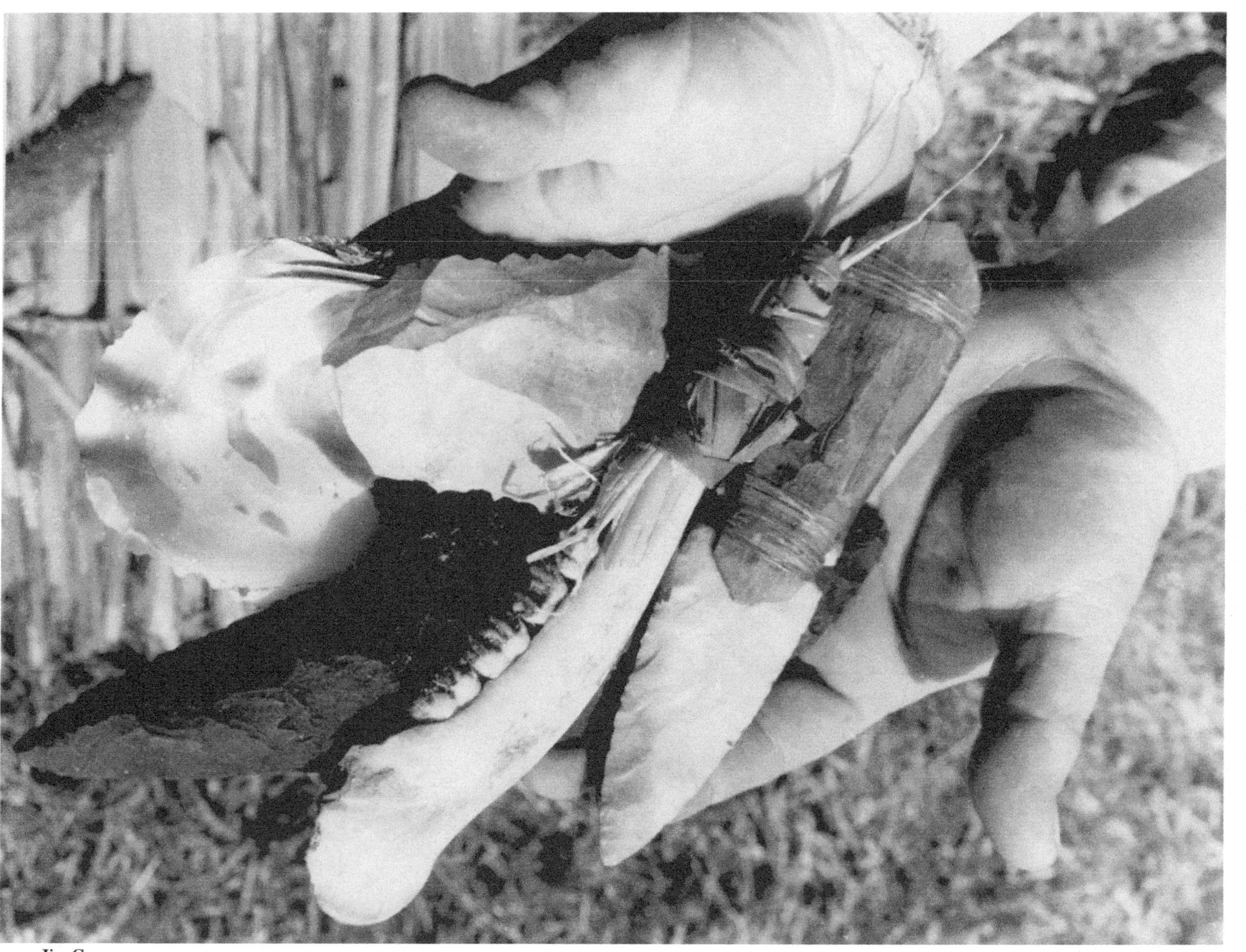

Jim Green

Table of Contents
(for a world before tables)

Michael Eldredge

Acknowledgments

It is almost impossible to be too grateful for family, friends, teachers, students and life itself. Not to acknowledge others, is to lessen one's self. There is no way I can recognize all who have contributed to this journey, but I hereby acknowledge and thank the following:

David Wescott - friend, teacher, colleague and confidant, who made this project and so many others possible.

Dr. Errett Callahan - mentor and friend whose accomplishments in, and dedication to primitive technology and experimental archaeology stand as examples for us all.

John White, Ancient Lifeways Institute - whose inspired teaching demonstrates the continuity of the past and the present.

Members of the education staff at the Schiele Museum of Natural History (1984 - present) - but especially to three individuals:

Michael Eldredge, my "right hand man", who was there from the beginning, encouraging me and offering help and support every step of the way.
Suzanne Simmons, our "head woman", whose faith in and dedication to the Aboriginal Studies Program is immeasurable.
Kay Moss, my office mate for six years, who served as a sounding board and role model.

Dr. Ann Tippit, Director of the Schiele Museum and Dr. Alan May, Curator of Anthro-pology - for their belief in the value of replicative experiences and experiments in our attempts to better understand the past.

Alan Stout, Museum Director when I arrived - who made the Aboriginal Studies Program possible; and Dr. David Brose - who followed him and allowed it to continue.

Members of the southeastern archaeological community who see the value of primitive technology to archaeology - Dr. Janet Levy, Dr. David Moore, Dr. Albert Goodyear, Dr. Bruce Rippeteau, Tommy Charles, Chris Judge, Archie Smith, Nena Rice, Dr. Randy Daniel, Ruth Wetmore, Bob Pace, and Dr. William Marquardt.

Scott Jones and Jack Cresson - who exemplify the bridge between archaeology and primitive technology.

My interns and apprentices - Denise Ashman, Tracy Barbee, Kate Carter, Henry Colomb, Jessica Hoffmire, Angel Honeycutt, Meredith Hovis, Alex Kilgore, Marianne Knap, Michelle Moore, Cyndi Rapenske, Susan Richards, Richard Rosenfeld and Donna Tully - for their hard work, dedication and (above all) loyalty.

Mike Peters, "quartermaster" - who works tirelessly behind the scenes, sacrificing time, energy and money to the cause.

My colleagues in the primitive technology and traditional skills field - David Holladay, Mark Butler, Norm Kidder, Alice Tulluch, Peg Matthewson, Jim Riggs, Maria Sideroff, John and Geri McPherson, Scott Silsby, Scooter Cheatham, Darry Wood, Cody Lundin, Eustace Conway, Mike and Carrie Ryan, Steven Endholm, Tamara Wilder, Matt and Michelle Richards, Bob Perkins, Keith Grenoble, Dick Baugh, Doug Elliot, Jeff Gottlieb, Thomas Elpel, Paul Campbell, Larry Olsen, Evard Gibby, Ben Kirkland, Tim Baker, Rob Withrow, Barry Keegan, Bart and Robin Blankenship, Ben Pressley, Mac Maness, Mors Kochanski, Kirk Drier, Lynx Shepherd, Han de Hass and many others who inspired me in my work.

The Advanced Aboriginal Studies Group and all my students, far and near - who keep me teaching and learning. I do it for myself, but you are the catalysts.

Members of the Catawba Indian Nation and the Eastern Band of Cherokee - who have opened their doors and their hearts to share with me their living traditions.

Cindy Watts, Starwalker, Jonathan and Skye Reed, Olin and Daphine Watts, Earle Lane and Willard Busby - without a supportive family I could not have persevered.

Wilson and Chuck Noland - "You never know what the tide may bring."

Thanks to all who travel this path with me.

Michael Eldredge

Credits: Many of the articles found in this volume were previously published in: *The Bulletin of Primitive Technology* (issues 1-27), *Primitive Technology: A Book of Earth Skills, Primitive Technology II: Ancestral Skills* (David Wescott, ed.), *Backwoodsman Magazine* (Charlie Richie, ed), *South Carolina Antiquities (SC* Archaeological Society), *Woodsmoke: Collected Writings on Ancient Living Skills* (Richard and Linda Jamison, eds.) and *Primitive Wilderness Living and Survival Skills* (John and Geri McPherson).

Photographs: Photos not credited in the text were most likely taken by Michael Eldredge, Mike Peters, Steve Watts, David Wescott, Suzanne Simmons, John Lathem or Jim Green. Cover photo by Mike Peters, back cover photo by Suzanne Simmons.

Pre Face

> ***"The learning and practice of aboriginal skills can help us all get in touch with our own roots, no matter what our particular heritage may be (Asian, Australian, Native American, European, African, etc.). Here in North America, we look to the Indian Peoples and the ancestors of these people to teach us the skills that are 'native' to this place. Yet, if we go back far enough into our own pasts, we discover that we are all aboriginal peoples at some time in some place. The 'stone age' is the great common denominator of humanness. Primitive' ('first') skills are our shared inheritance."***
>
> **Steve Watts, 1985**

You and I are related. We share a genetic and technological lineage which began deep in Mother Africa many millennia ago. Our bodies, our brains and our behaviors bear the marks of this long journey through time.

In your hands you hold a bundle. **Practicing Primitive: A Handbook Of Aboriginal Skills** is a collection of words and images put together over a twenty-year period in a search for hands-on communication with that stone age past. These words and images are artifacts of my attempts to share that connection with others.

Some were meant for publication at their conception. Some were designed specifically for use by my students. And, some were simply the results of self-expression and introspection. Gathered together here, they are yours to open and to use - skills to be practiced and ideas to be pondered.

Yet, like relics removed from their archaeological context, they have little meaning in and of themselves. They are tools meant to point beyond themselves to a greater understanding and appreciation of our shared prehistoric heritage. They are signposts on a journey - markers on a trail.

Beyond the light of the fire, the shadows of our ancestors beckon.
They are us . . .
you and I . . . related.

1

Our Ancestors . . .
Ourselves

John Lathem

The future is not to be found in the past. Yet, we know that the outermost bud on the uppermost branch is fed by the deepest root. Ninety-five-plus percent of our history as humans cannot be ignored. "Written " by scavengers, hunters, gatherers and early agriculturists; the story of the Stone Age is our story.

Primitive technology is a way into that story. We are drawn to it as to a fire . . . and there we find the others.

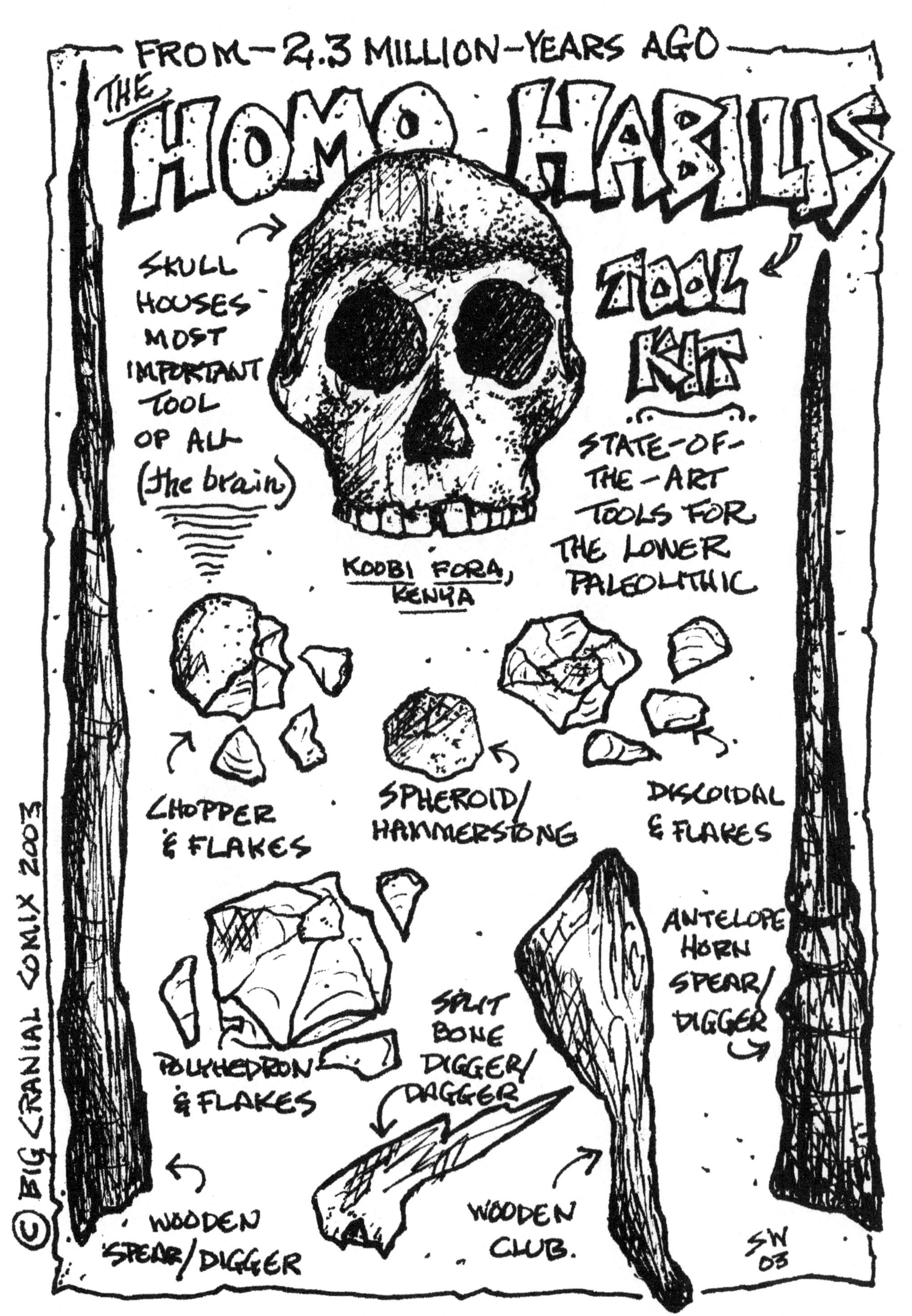
FROM—2.3 MILLION—YEARS AGO
THE HOMO HABILUS
SKULL HOUSES MOST IMPORTANT TOOL OF ALL (the brain)
TOOL KIT
STATE-OF-THE-ART TOOLS FOR THE LOWER PALEOLITHIC
KOOBI FORA, KENYA
CHOPPER & FLAKES
SPHEROID/ HAMMERSTONE
DISCOIDAL & FLAKES
ANTELOPE HORN SPEAR/ DIGGER
POLYHEDRON & FLAKES
SPLIT BONE DIGGER/ DAGGER
WOODEN SPEAR/DIGGER
WOODEN CLUB.
SW 03
© BIG CRANIAL COMIX 2003

The Lower Paleolithic

2,500,000 Years Ago
In the grasslands of Mother Africa

More and more often now, they came down from the trees. Driven by a rising curiosity which surfaced again and again in an ever expanding brain. Down . . . down to the ground with its tall grass. Risking it all . . . for food and fascination.

Armed with cleverness and the ability to stand alone with eyes above the swaying seedheads, they ventured out. Pushing back the boundaries of their unknowns, moving further and further into the dark domain of the Big Cats. They watched from hilltop, boulder and sandy rise. They knew the sabertooth's gifts . . . the Power and the Edges.

The power of shoulders, legs and paws to climb, and run and grab and hold. The power of jaws to crush and splinter. A power far beyond their own. And the edges . . . teeth and claws to stab and rip, to sever and slice. Edges . . . edges of power far beyond their own.

Only on the ground could they have discovered the Key. Only here . . . the place between Ape and Man . . . here within their sight, within their grasp, lay . . . the Stone. Lifting it up, they forged their futures and wrote our pasts. Striking one against another, they exposed the keenness within. Talisman and tool were born in the same instant. The Power and the Edge was now theirs.

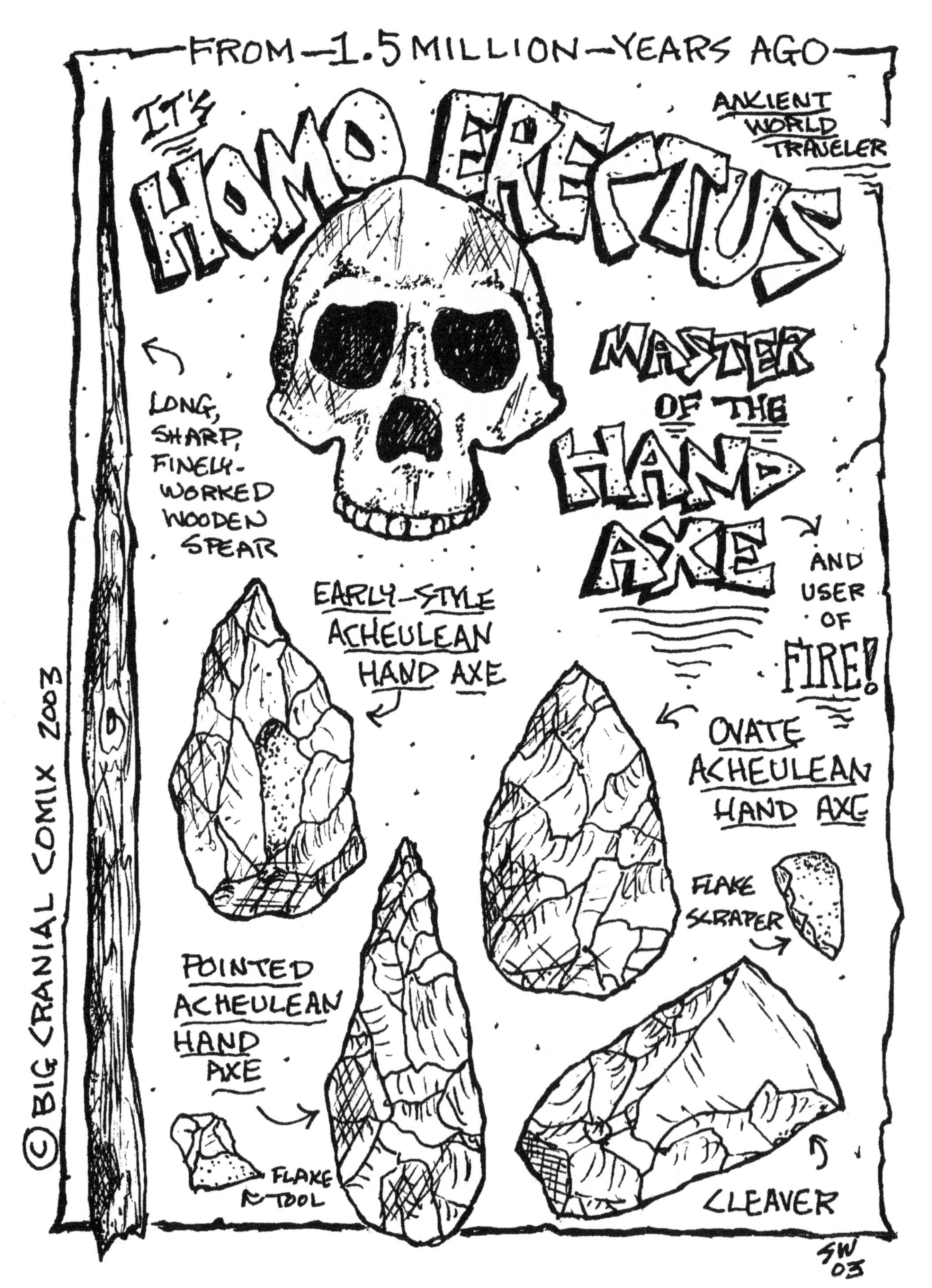

FROM—1.5 MILLION—YEARS AGO
IT'S
HOMO ERECTUS
ANKIENT WORLD TRAVELER
MASTER OF THE HAND AXE
AND USER OF FIRE!
LONG, SHARP, FINELY-WORKED WOODEN SPEAR
EARLY-STYLE ACHEULEAN HAND AXE
OVATE ACHEULEAN HAND AXE
FLAKE SCRAPER
POINTED ACHEULEAN HAND AXE
FLAKE TOOL
CLEAVER
© BIG CRANIAL COMIX 2003
SW 03

The Middle Paleolithic

60,000 Years Ago
The Ice Age in Central Europe

The wind seemed to grow more powerful . . . putting a strain on the old worn auroch hide that sealed the entrance to the cave. Two of the hunters rushed forward to brace the support poles. Strong hands pulled hard against the frayed rawhide lashings . . . making them fast once more. It was a tiring end to an exhausting day

The morning had been spent in the laborious digging. The frozen ground did not yield easily to the onslaught of wooden levers and scapula hand spades. But, it was necessary. The old one deserved the deepest possible resting place. Her last days had been spent in the company of a pain that came from far within . . . a pain that had finally carried her into the Land of the Past.

They laid her there with her finest basket by her side. The strongest of her digging sticks rested near at hand. Her wolfskin bag was packed . . . the lacings drawn tight . . . the shell cup securely attached.

Her scrapers and backed knives were resharpened one last time . . . the Edges. Edges she would need to cut through the darkness . . . and begin the journey beyond.

The Upper Paleolithic

30,000 Years Ago
Northern Europe, on the edge of perhaps the largest forest this world has ever seen

From the late Pleistocene up to the Roman/Christian/Iron Age invasion, this sea of trees grew from the Atlantic to the Pacific . . . from Scotland, across northern Europe, across Asia, and through Siberia to Beringia. Perhaps no one person ever traversed its whole range. Only remnants of this ancient forest remain today.

Deer . . . moving quietly through the evergreens. Their breath, and the breath of the hunters who stalk them, visible now in the early morning cold.

continued . . .

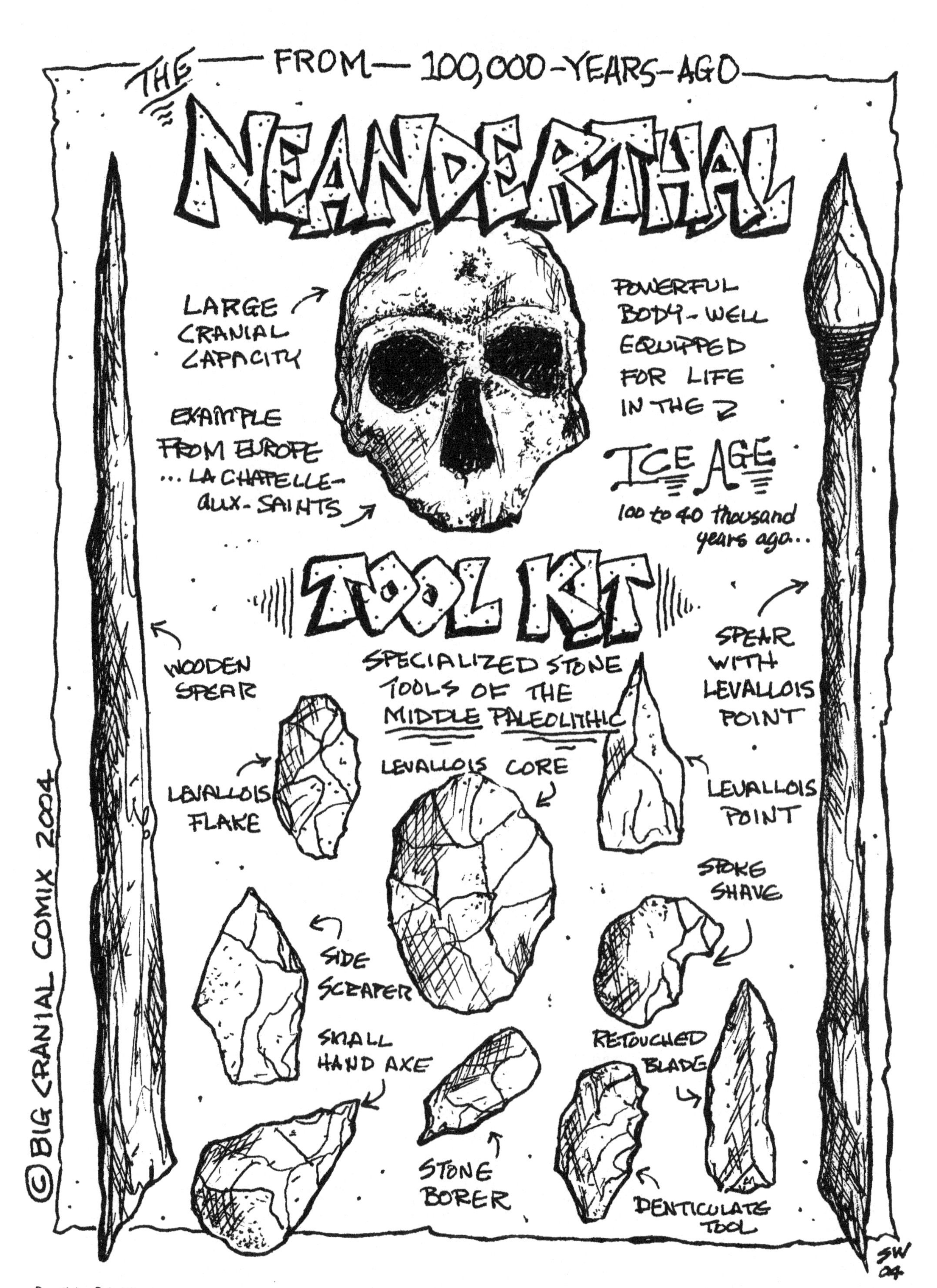
THE
FROM 100,000 YEARS AGO
NEANDERTHAL
LARGE CRANIAL CAPACITY
EXAMPLE FROM EUROPE ... LA CHAPELLE-AUX-SAINTS
POWERFUL BODY - WELL EQUIPPED FOR LIFE IN THE
ICE AGE
100 to 40 thousand years ago...
TOOL KIT
SPECIALIZED STONE TOOLS OF THE MIDDLE PALEOLITHIC
WOODEN SPEAR
SPEAR WITH LEVALLOIS POINT
LEVALLOIS FLAKE
LEVALLOIS CORE
LEVALLOIS POINT
SPOKE SHAVE
SIDE SCRAPER
SMALL HAND AXE
RETOUCHED BLADE
STONE BORER
DENTICULATE TOOL
SW 04

The Head Man looked back at his men. Some were barely men at all. Their neck thongs held only one or two ornaments . . . only he and one experienced other wore the claws of the Great Cat. Their long, soft-tanned shirts and leggings of deerskin made no sound at all as they moved. The glints of their laurel leaf knives were hidden within sheaths of bark. The paint on their faces and weapons was the color of the earth itself
These men were hunters all . . . yet, there was more.
They were fathers, husbands, sons and Clan brothers.
Some he had taught as young boys. One had taught him.
Each had a special gift . . .
the artist, the dreamer, the master blade maker.
He thought back . . . as he looked back . . . back to the night before.

Last night the hunters gathered by the f ret For a long time the only sounds were the popping sparks and the "click, click" of antler-tipped tools chipping away the final flakes that would bring the stone spear points to their most lethal keenness . . . the Edges. Edges that would bring the Deer to their hearths. With their thoughts focused, they polished their antler spearthrowers (decorated with the carved images of Deer).

This was a special fire. The fire of Winter Solstice. The fire to bring back the sun from its long journey South along the horizon. The fire (like the trees which keep their green) gave promise of regeneration . . . a promise of returning Deer . . . rebirth . . . on-going life . . . like the antlers which are shed only to grow again.

Last night was special. It was the night the Antlered Man appeared. Stepping from the darkness into the wreath of the fire's light, he stood tall with the smell of musk all around him. The embodied Spirit of the Woods and the Hunt (his regal crown of antlers towering over a body covered with earth and evergreen) had come to strengthen their arms, clear their eyes, and guide their spears. Lifting the giant rack from his head, he hung it in the branches of a tree. There, white as snow against the boughs, he left it as a promise. There would be food, clothes, tools, weapons and . . . life ahead in the cold, dark months to come.

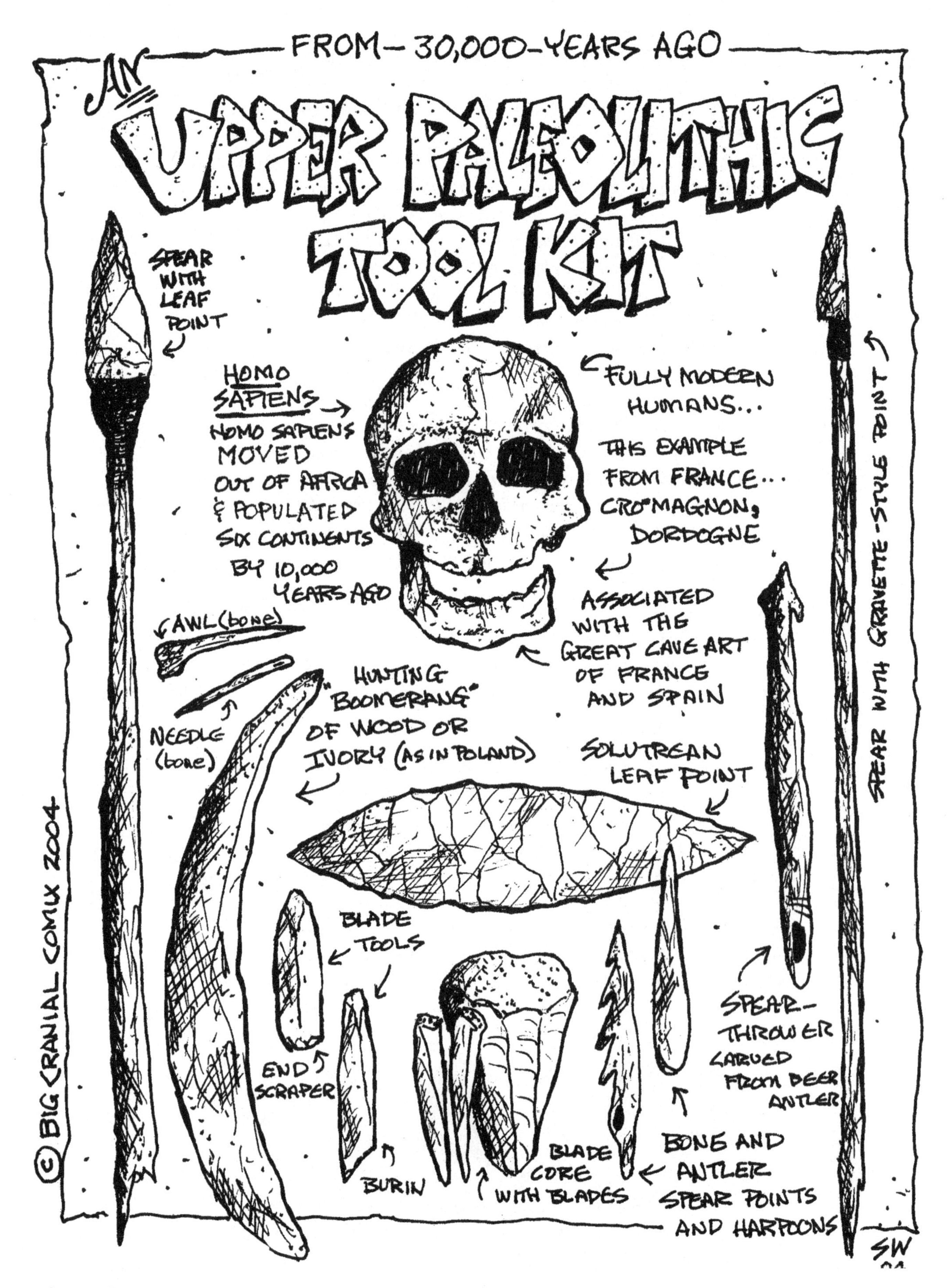
FROM—30,000—YEARS AGO
AN
UPPER PALEOLITHIC
TOOL KIT
SPEAR WITH LEAF POINT
HOMO SAPIENS
HOMO SAPIENS MOVED OUT OF AFRICA & POPULATED SIX CONTINENTS BY 10,000 YEARS AGO
FULLY MODERN HUMANS...
THIS EXAMPLE FROM FRANCE... CRO-MAGNON, DORDOGNE
ASSOCIATED WITH THE GREAT CAVE ART OF FRANCE AND SPAIN
AWL (bone)
NEEDLE (bone)
HUNTING "BOOMERANG" OF WOOD OR IVORY (AS IN POLAND)
SOLUTREAN LEAF POINT
SPEAR WITH GRAVETTE-STYLE POINT
BLADE TOOLS
END SCRAPER
BURIN
BLADE CORE WITH BLADES
BONE AND ANTLER SPEAR POINTS AND HARPOONS
SPEAR-THROWER CARVED FROM DEER ANTLER
© BIG CRANIAL COMIX 2004
SW

The Mesolithic

9,000 Years Ago

A birch-forest camp at the marsh's edge in the British Isles

This would be the last great cultural expression of the hunter-gatherer lifestyle in that part of the world before the pastoral/agricultural revolution hit.

"Willow . . . Willow, they have returned! Tonight there will be music!"

Four days was not so long, but the weather had turned bad.
A cold rain could mean trouble for a fast-moving, lightly-equipped
band of hunters. Had they sought shelter in the remains of
last year's camp? The bark there would still be strong, but
the poles were several seasons old.

No matter . . . they were home.
All of them. The moosehide bundles on
Their backs were heavy with meat.

That meant that more was cached in the tree platforms
by the river. Tomorrow, Willow will lead the women's
party to retrieve the rest.

And there . . . there in front . . . her only son,
returning safe and sound from his first man's
journey past the Edge into the Deep
Woods. It wasn't so long ago
that she had given him up to the care of her brother.
She had cried for many nights, but had known that it
was time. Now he walks proudly beside his uncle . . .
his new bow (still braced) clinched tightly
in his fist. No longer a boy, he held his head high,
the wind catching the Hawk's feathers tied in
his hair for the first time.

Tonight . . . there will be the comfort of a fire surrounded
by all. The flames' edges will cut the cold. Red Deer
will talk of the hunt, while old Sparrow tightens the
head of his drum. (Already he sings the song in his own head.)

continued . . .

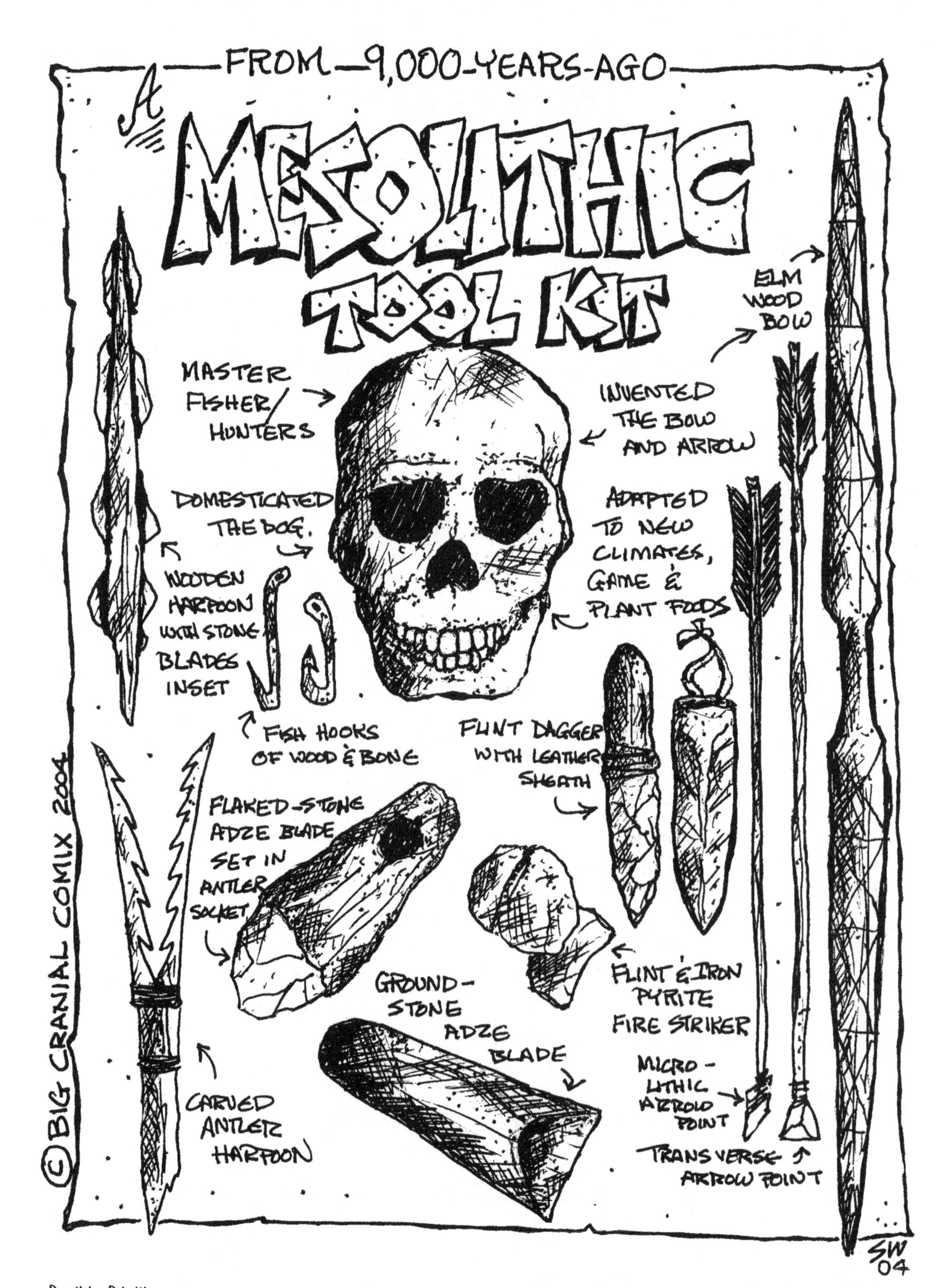
FROM 9,000 YEARS AGO
A MESOLITHIC TOOL KIT
MASTER FISHER/HUNTERS
INVENTED THE BOW AND ARROW
ELM WOOD BOW
DOMESTICATED THE DOG.
ADAPTED TO NEW CLIMATES, GAME & PLANT FOODS
WOODEN HARPOON WITH STONE BLADES INSET
FISH HOOKS OF WOOD & BONE
FLINT DAGGER WITH LEATHER SHEATH
FLAKED-STONE ADZE BLADE SET IN ANTLER SOCKET
GROUND-STONE ADZE BLADE
FLINT & IRON PYRITE FIRE STRIKER
MICRO-LITHIC ARROW POINT
TRANSVERSE ARROW POINT
CARVED ANTLER HARPOON
© BIG CRANIAL COMIX 2004
SW 04

*Tonight, Willow will have eyes only for her son.
It seems that not enough winters have
passed for him to be sitting at the hunters'
place on the North Star side of the fire.*

*His father would be proud were he here to see.
Taken before his time, he will seem (on this night)
to live again. Tomorrow, she will pass on her
husband 's four polished antler beads . . . beads
that were passed to him by his father . . . and his
father before him.*

*But, tonight . . . in gratitude and in memory . . . she
will burn an offering of Birch and Marrow.
And, tonight . . . at last . . . she will sleep.*

The Present

*Today, the Big Cats no longer compete with us for food
and territory, as now, we struggle to protect the dwindling numbers
of their descendants. The threats of contemporary life more
often walk on two legs . . . on dark streets, in brightly lit corporate
corridors, and even in the warm familiar glow of our
neighborhoods and homes. Our "boundaries of the unknown "
take the form of microbes that defy our cleverness, and poisons
we drink and breathe but cannot see.
And, the "dark domains" of the twenty-first century
lie not in the tall grass, but rather in our own
interior landscapes still so uncharted.*

*Here, far down this path through time, we continue to seek
the Power and the Edges. Longing still to expose the keenness within . . .
railing against the impotence and numbness which too often surrounds
us. The Big Cats are gone, but We and the Stone remain.*

SW-1993

2
The Stone Age Edge

Mike Peters

Beginning around 2.5 million years ago our ancient ancestors discovered the power of a sharp edge. By fracturing certain kinds of rocks in a particular way they created humankind's first stone tools - simple flakes and choppers used to cut meat, shape wood, and dig for food and water.

From that time until about 5,000 years ago, stone, bone, wood, and shell tools were the constant companions of all of our ancestors. These were the tools that shaped our world for more than 95% of our history.

SW - 1992

STONE TOOL BASICS

Functions, Features, Form and Fracture

"The right tool for the right job" is perhaps a very ancient bit of wisdom. Define the task, then find or create the needed tool using the proper stone type, methods and techniques of manufacture. Although many stone tools are multifunctional (or can be easily modified to be so) few can function well outside their "Task" category. You will no more butcher a deer with a hammerstone than you would hammer a nail with a razor blade.

Tasks Required	*Tool Models:*	*Tool Types:*	*Stone Types:*	*Manufacturing Techniques:*
Smashing, Bashing, Crushing, Grinding, Hammering, Pounding, Clubbing, etc.	Heavy and Blunt	Hammerstones, Nutting, Mulling and Grinding Stones, Stone Mauls, etc.	Medium and Fine Grained Stones –(From sandstones to basalts)	Expedient Gathering, Pecking and Grinding, Rough Flaking, etc.
Chopping, Hewing, Butchering, Ground Breaking, Hacking, etc.	Heavy and Sharp	Ground Stone Axes, Flaked Stone Axes and Choppers, Hoes, Adzes, etc.	Hard—Fine Grained, Stones, Cryptocrystaline, Stone (quartz, flint, chert, etc.)	Pecking and Grinding, Bipolar and Direct Percussion, Pressure Flaking, etc.
Slicing, Cutting, Saw, Trimming, Piercing, Drilling, Engraving, Scraping Carving, etc.	Light and Sharp	Modified and Unmodified Flakes and Blades, Bifaces, Projectile Points, Scrapers, Drills, Gravers,	Flints, Cherts, Quartz, Quartzite, Obsidian, etc.	Bipolar and Direct Percussion, Pressure Flaking, Notching Techniques, etc.

Bipolar Percussion
Illustrated at the Point of Impact

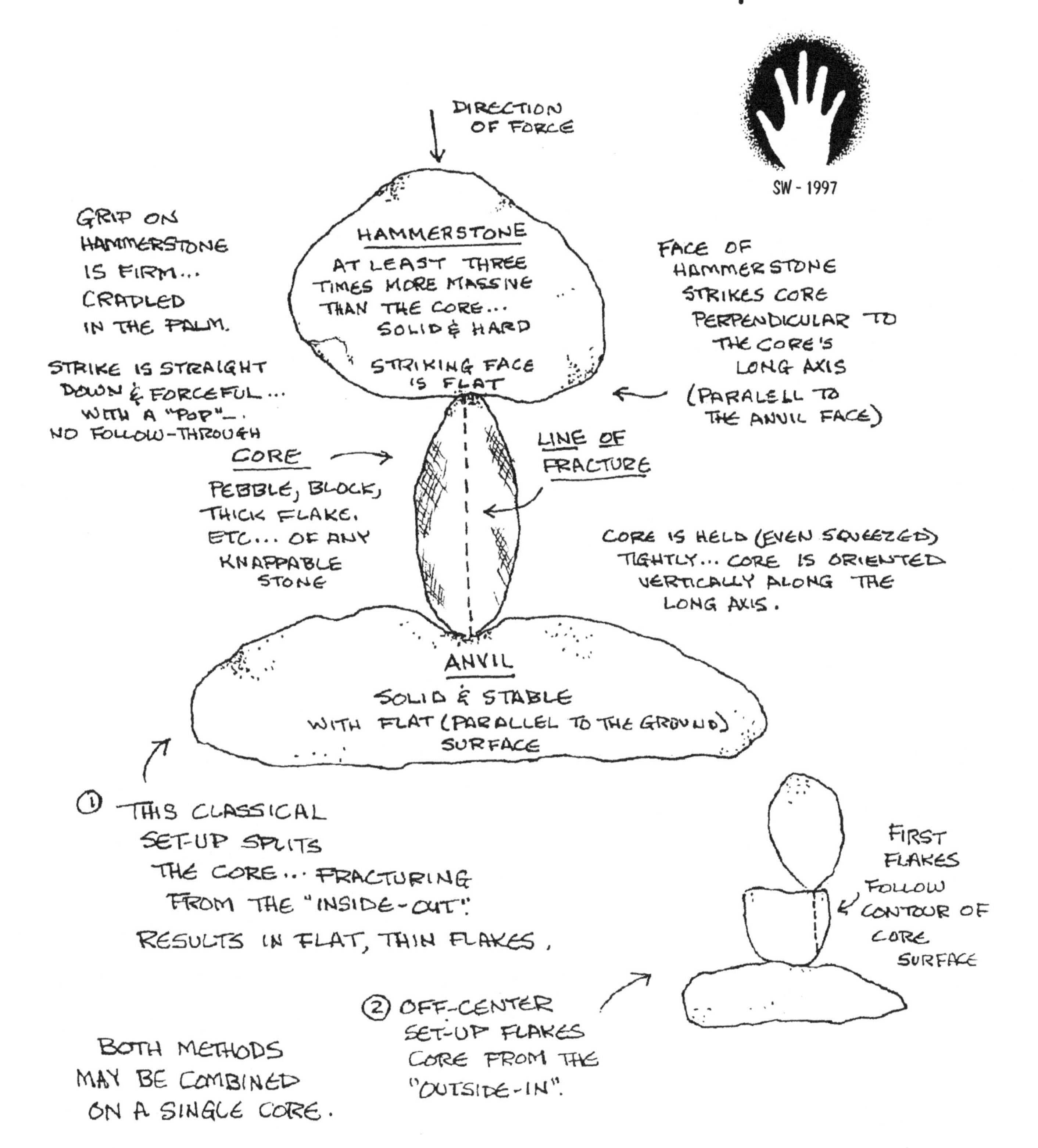

Striking Flakes from a Core Using Direct Percussion

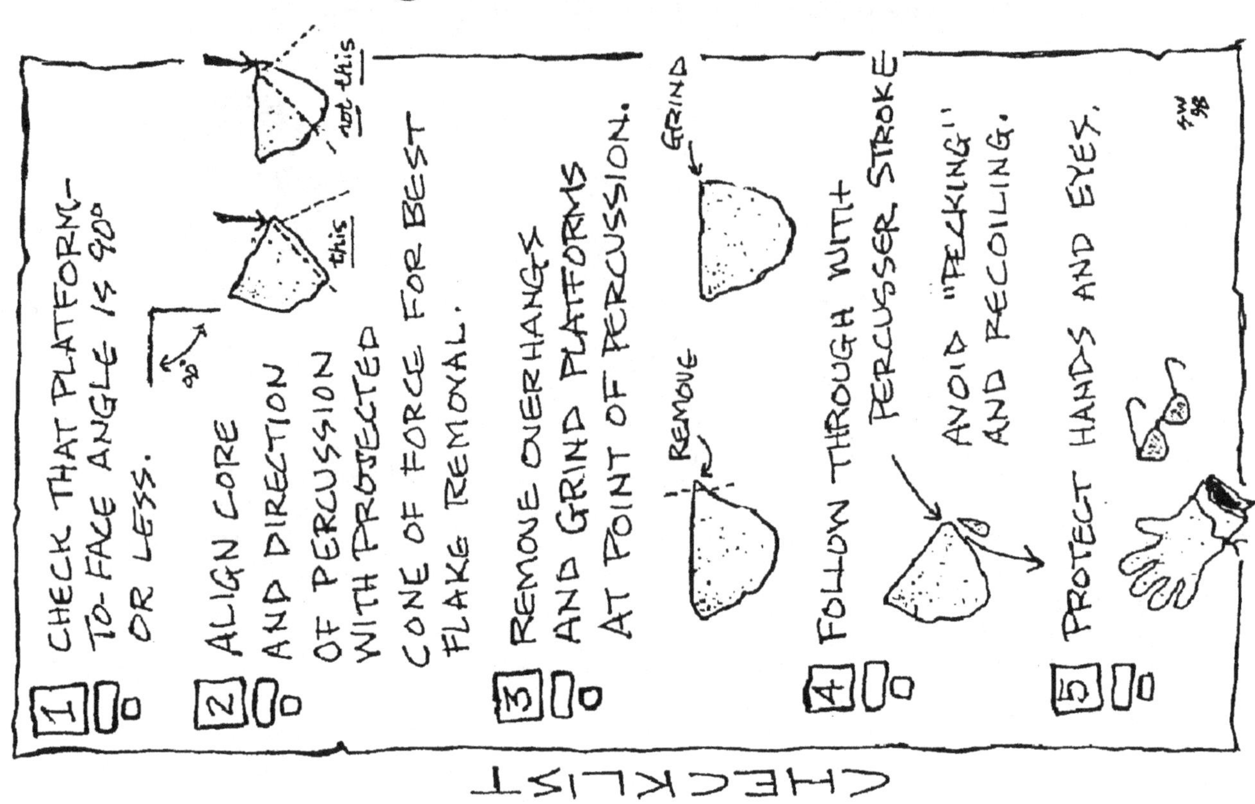

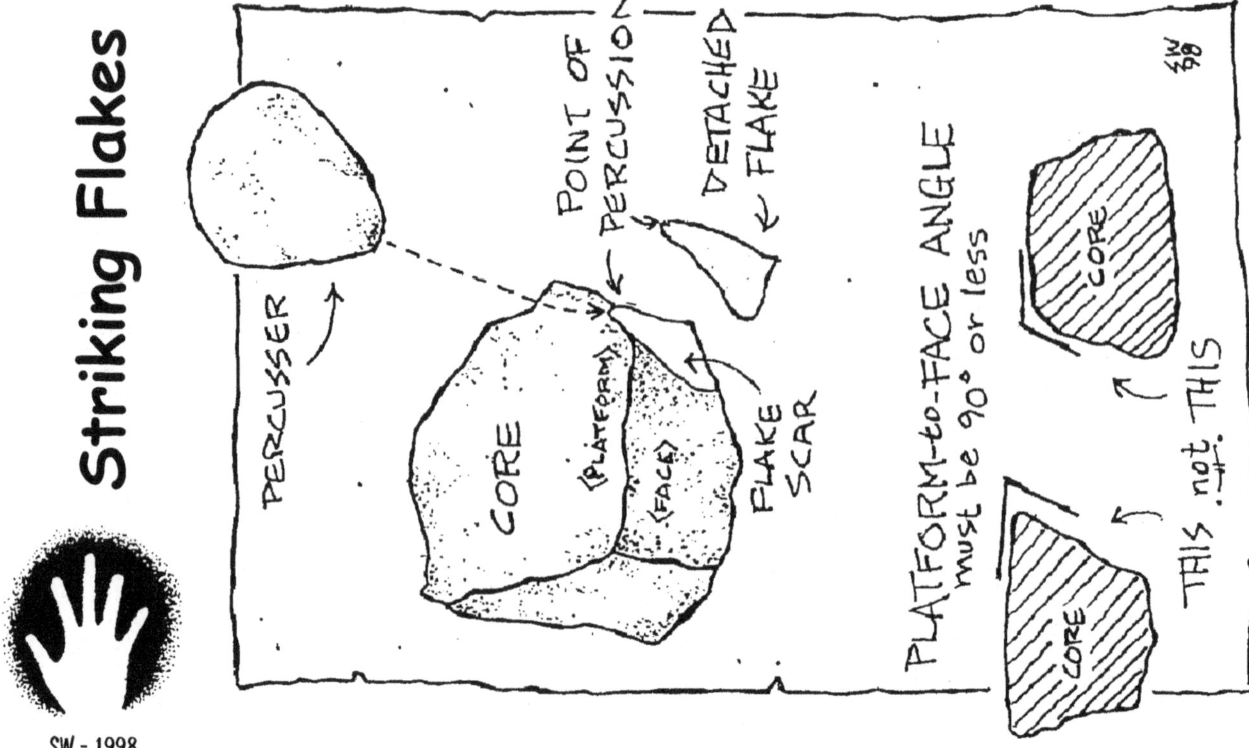

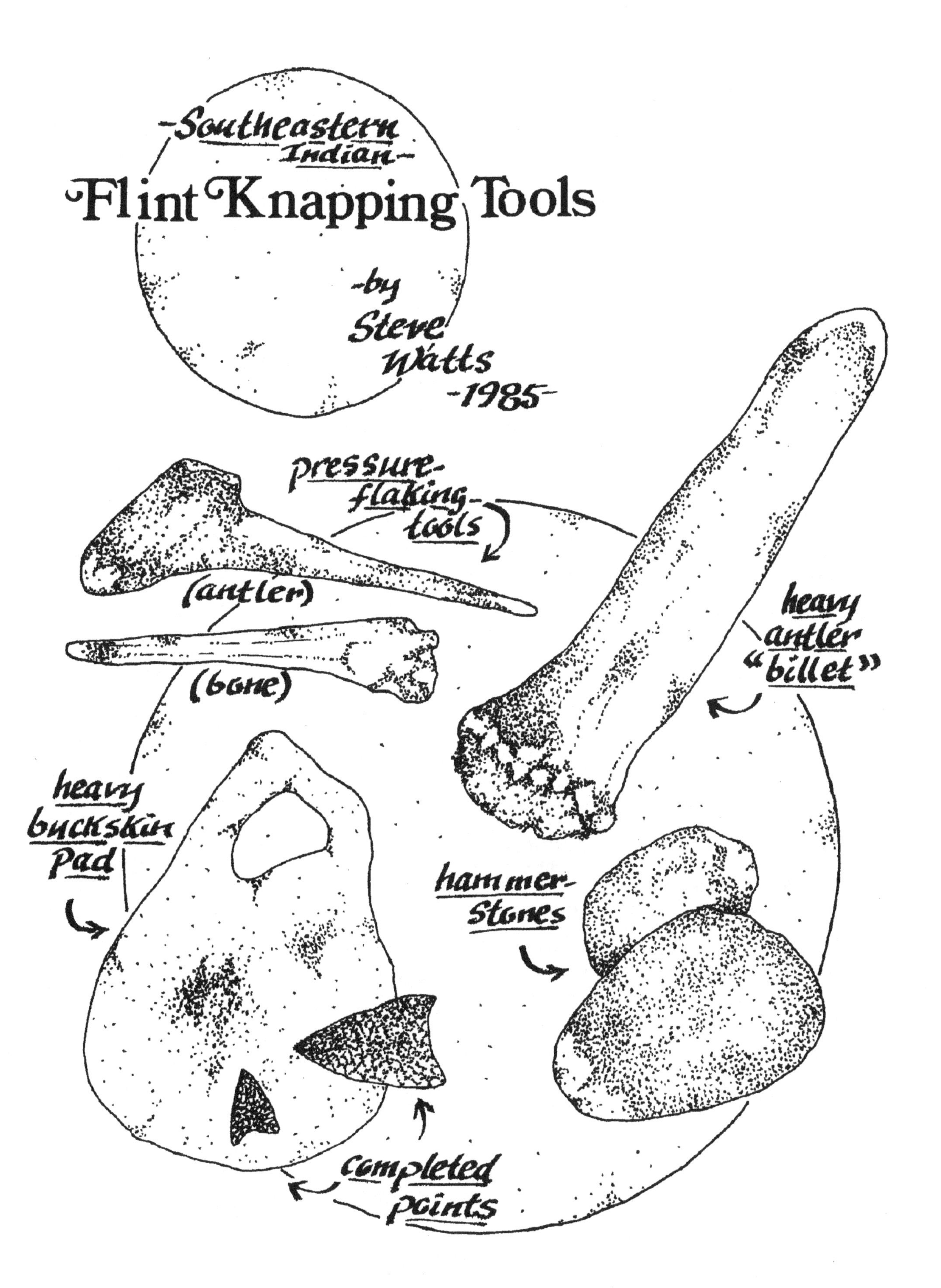
-Southeastern Indian-
Flint Knapping Tools
-by Steve Watts -1985-
pressure-flaking-tools
(antler)
(bone)
heavy antler "billet"
heavy buckskin Pad
hammer-Stones
completed points

A Quick Guide To
Classic Old-World Paleolithic Chopper and Handaxe Forms

The classification of the oldest or Paleolithic cultures is mainly based on the succession of stone industries found in north-west Europe, notably in France, where the early researches were carried out. Now that detailed studies have also been made in other parts of the Old World, it is possible to present a general picture of the evolution of culture in Paleolithic times.

Kenneth P. Oakley, Man The Tool Maker

Oldowan Choppers

These choppers (with their associated flakes) are among humankind's oldest tools. Close to 2 million years ago, African *Homo habili* created unifacial (flakes on one side) and bifacial (flakes on both sides) edged cutting/hacking/chopping tools from large pebbles and small cobbles (stones average about 3" around) of lava, quartz and quartzite.

Both bipolar and hard hammer direct percussion techniques were used. Sometimes as few as 3 or 4 flakes were struck to create the cutting edge, with most of the tool's surface remaining unaltered.

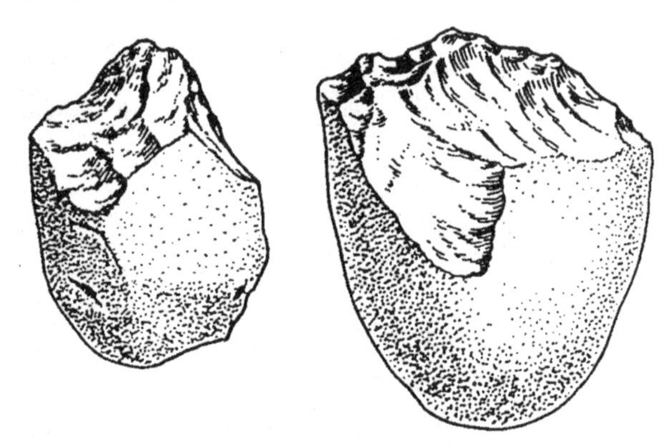

YEARS	PERIOD	GROUP	INDUSTRY
	Neolithic		
10,000			
	Mesolithic		Magdalenian,
12,000			Solutrean,
			Aurignacian,
40,000	Upper Paleolithic	*Homo sapiens*	Perigordian, and others
125,000	Middle Paleolithic	*Homo sapiens (Neanderthals)*	Mousterian
2,000,000	Lower Paleolithic	*Homo erectus*	Acheulean Abbevillian
3,000,000		*Homo habilis*	Oldowan
		Australopithecus	No Tools
4,000,000			

Abbevillian Handaxes

Our early *Homo erectus* ancestors created larger bifacial handaxes (averaging 6-7" long and 4-5 "wide) called "Abbevillian" in Europe and "Early Acheulian" or "Chellan" in Africa. "These tools represent the dawn of the hand-axe culture".

Most often knapped on all edges, from nodules or cobbles - these tools exhibit deep, relatively short flake scars. The resulting cutting edges are sinuous. Cortex bearing surfaces may remain on one or both faces and at the base.

Acheulian Handaxes

Acheulian handaxes were the tools of choice for *Homo erectus* and continued to be used to some extent into the Middle Paleolithic.

Prepared platforms and soft hammer percussion techniques become more evident as we examine later Acheulian examples. Made from nodules, cobbles or large spalls - these tools, are typically almond-shaped in plan view, exhibiting straight cutting edges with relatively smooth and symmetrical lenticular cross-sections. Mid-Acheulian axes may retain cortex surfaces on the butt end, while later forms often exhibit fully-flaked margins and faces.

Acheulian handaxes are found throughout the Old World - Africa, Europe and Asia.

---

*For an introduction to classic treatments of handaxe forms see - **Tools Of The Old And New Stone Age** by Jacques Bordaz (1970), **The Old Stone Age** by Francois Bordes (1968), **Man The Tool Maker** by Kenneth P. Oakley (1957). For a more recent treatment see **Making Silent Stones Speak** by Kathy Schick and Nicholas Toth (1994).*

Illustrations on pages 18-19 from Bordes, 1968.

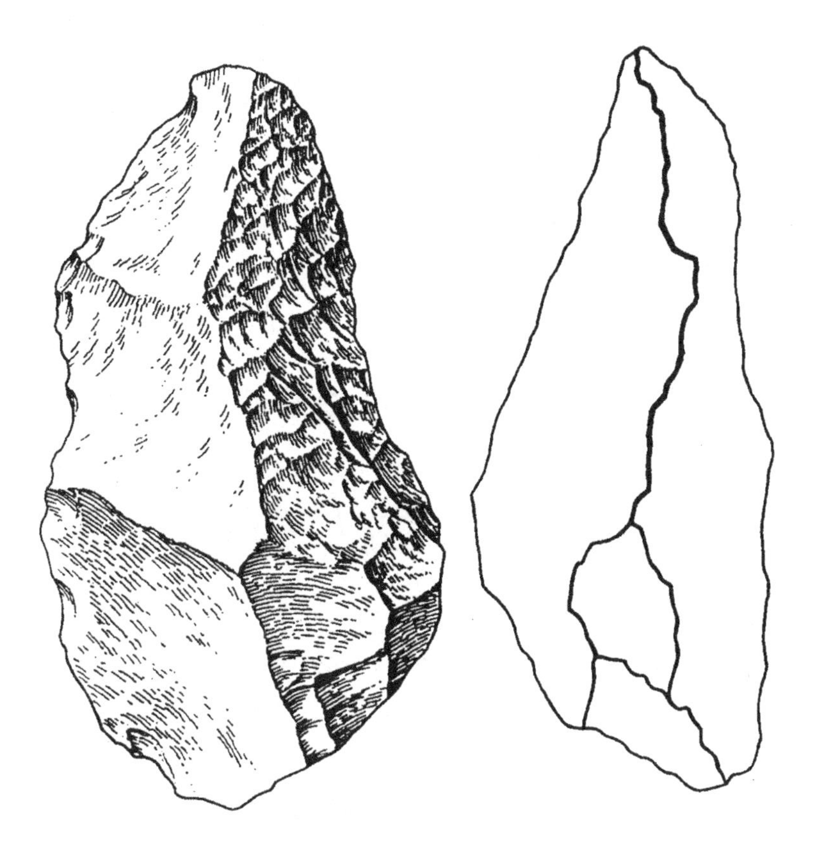

Abbevillian Handaxes

(not actual size)

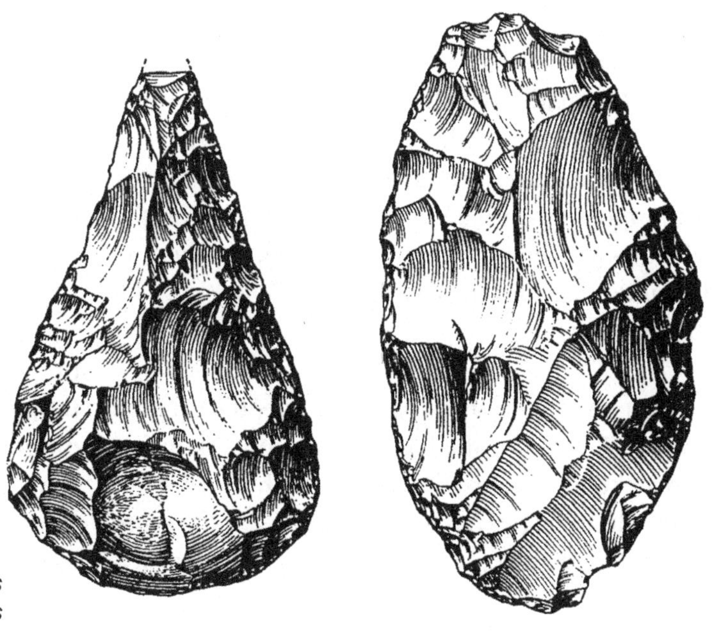

Acheulian Handaxes

(not actual size)

Handaxemanship

". . the advantage of the hand axe lies not in its suitability for any one particular task, but in its usefulness for any number of tasks . . ."
L. H. Keeley,
***Experimental Determinations of Stone Tool Uses*, 1980**

"Old World Handaxes: The Birth of the Biface" was the theme of the sixth annual Knap-In at the Schiele Museum in Gastonia, North Carolina (August 4-6,1995). Using both cast and original Old World African and European handaxes for inspiration, forty-six knappers from seven eastern states (plus a stray Californian) explored their Lower Paleolithic tool heritage. Working mostly in tough North Carolina metarhyolites and Virginia quartzites, participants produced a variety of replica and near-replica Acheulian handaxes.

Adding information to the inspiration, Scott Jones of Media Prehistoria and the University of Georgia-Athens presented *The Handaxe-Maker's Tale: Confessions of a Reluctant Handaxe Knapper*. Errett Callahan also presented some of the latest information (including a cast) on the magnificent handaxes from the Late Acheulean site of Kalambo Falls, Africa. He also reviewed some of the most up-to-date writing being done on the subject - a soon to be published paper, *Defending Acheulean Technology: An African Perspective* by Stephen Edwards.

Sunday was set aside as an experiential/applied session. Twenty of the handaxes produced during the weekend were used to accomplish a variety of tasks. Though referred to as handaxes (or the more quaint, "fist hatchets"), it has long been suggested that these tools served a variety of functions. In the bush, the handaxe might have been the perfect tool for *Homo erectus* - as is suggested by over 1,000,000 years of use. It was certainly portable enough for a people without pockets, and with the addition of a percusser (found or carried) it could serve as the core for a multitude of flake tools. We tried it out as a knife (skinning and butchering), pick (digging a hole), anvil/hammerstone (bone breaking and brain extraction), axe (manufacturing a digging stick), a ritual object and a weapon (hunting hay bales at twenty yards). Refer to photos on pages 26 and 27.

In all tasks, our replicas performed admirably - being best suited to knife and digging functions. Most of the edge-wear analysis that has been done on prehistoric handaxes suggest soft tissue use - though some are beaten and battered, suggesting digging and chopping functions as well. In fact, though viewed (correctly, I believe) as a multi-functional tool, some handaxes may have evolved toward some specialization - with big thick diggers and smaller thin, knife-like cutters appearing in the archaeological record. Some thoughts on both the general and specialized forms are presented here (See illustrations pages 21-24).

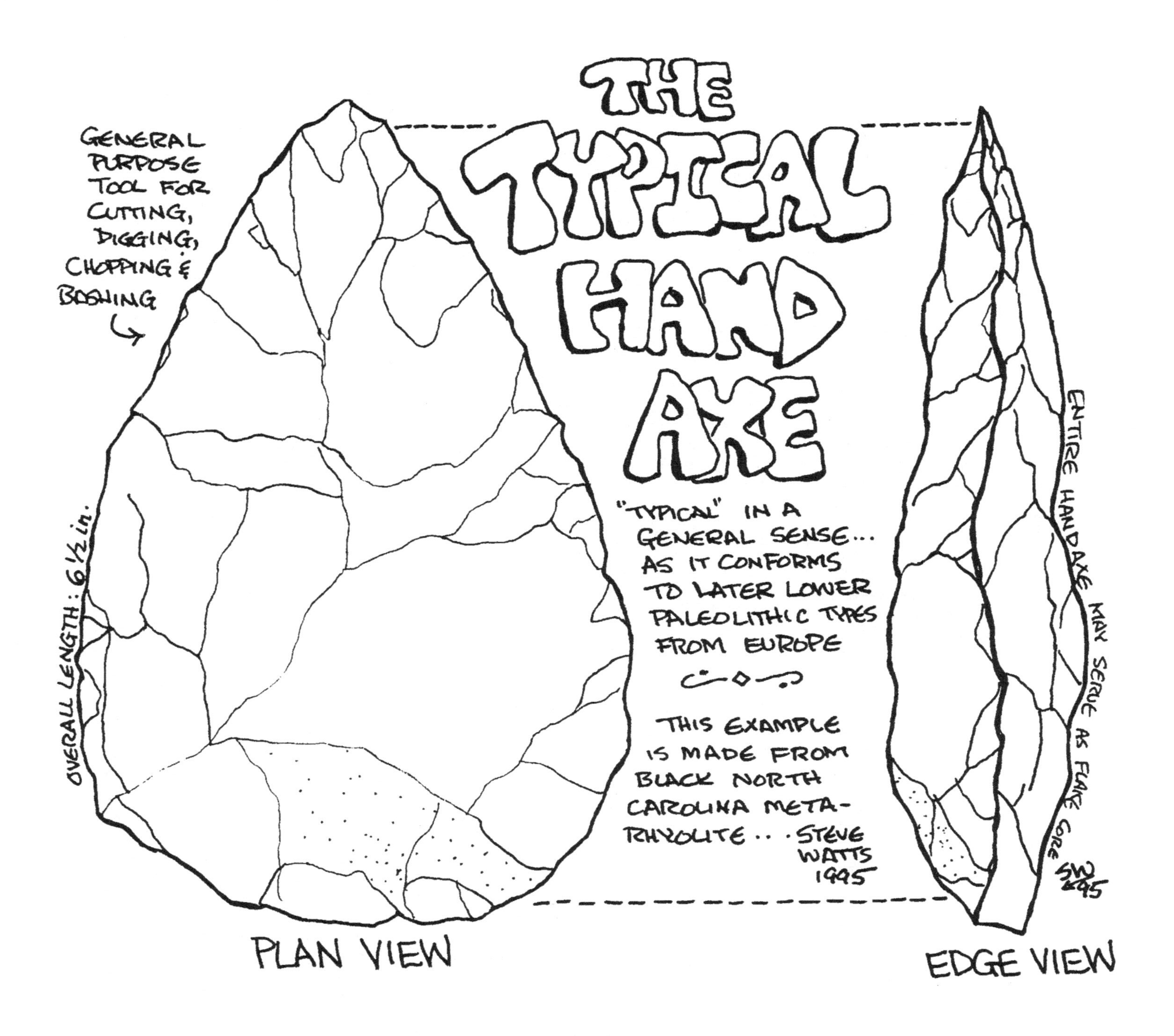
THE TYPICAL HAND AXE
GENERAL PURPOSE TOOL FOR CUTTING, DIGGING, CHOPPING & BASHING
OVERALL LENGTH: 6 1/2 in.
"TYPICAL" IN A GENERAL SENSE... AS IT CONFORMS TO LATER LOWER PALEOLITHIC TYPES FROM EUROPE
THIS EXAMPLE IS MADE FROM BLACK NORTH CAROLINA META-RHYOLITE... STEVE WATTS 1995
ENTIRE HANDAXE MAY SERVE AS FLAKE CORE
SW 1995
PLAN VIEW
EDGE VIEW

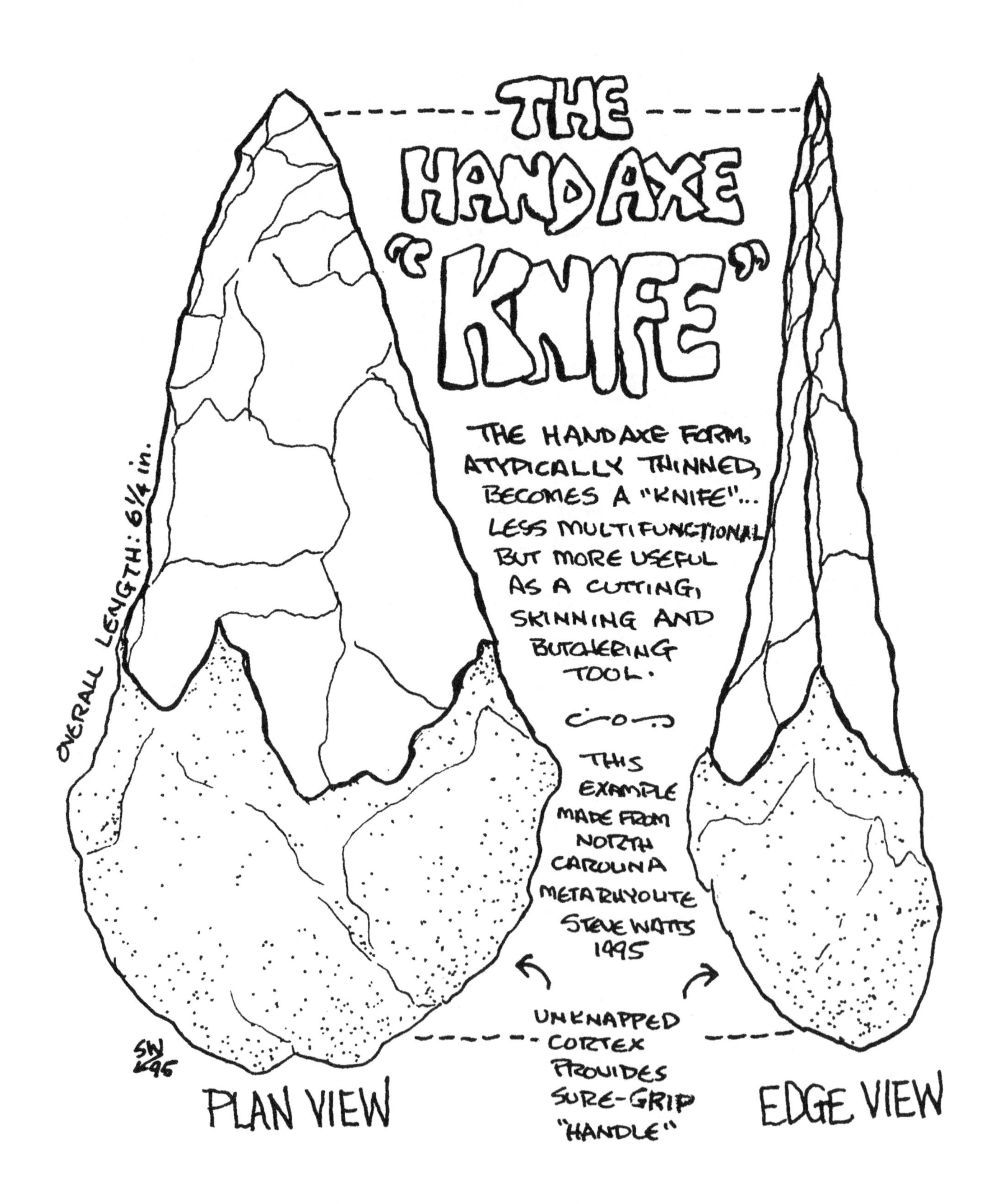
THE HANDAXE "KNIFE"
THE HANDAXE FORM, ATYPICALLY THINNED, BECOMES A "KNIFE"... LESS MULTIFUNCTIONAL BUT MORE USEFUL AS A CUTTING, SKINNING AND BUTCHERING TOOL.
THIS EXAMPLE MADE FROM NORTH CAROLINA METARHYOLITE
STEVE WATTS 1995
OVERALL LENGTH: 6¼ in.
UNKNAPPED CORTEX PROVIDES SURE-GRIP "HANDLE"
SW 6/95
PLAN VIEW
EDGE VIEW

HAND AXE
"PICK"
ALL HANDAXES COULD/CAN BE USED FOR DIGGING.
BUT, SOME SEEM TO BE DESIGNED SPECIFICALLY FOR SUCH.
A GOOD "PICK" HANDAXE HAS A STRONG TIP AND IS ALMOST AS THICK AS IT IS WIDE.
THIS EXAMPLE IS MADE FROM BLACK NORTH CAROLINA META-RHYOLITE...
STEVE WATTS 1995
OVERALL LENGTH: 7 3/4 in.
STRONG "BACKED" MEDIAN RIDGE
SW 95
PLAN VIEW
EDGE VIEW

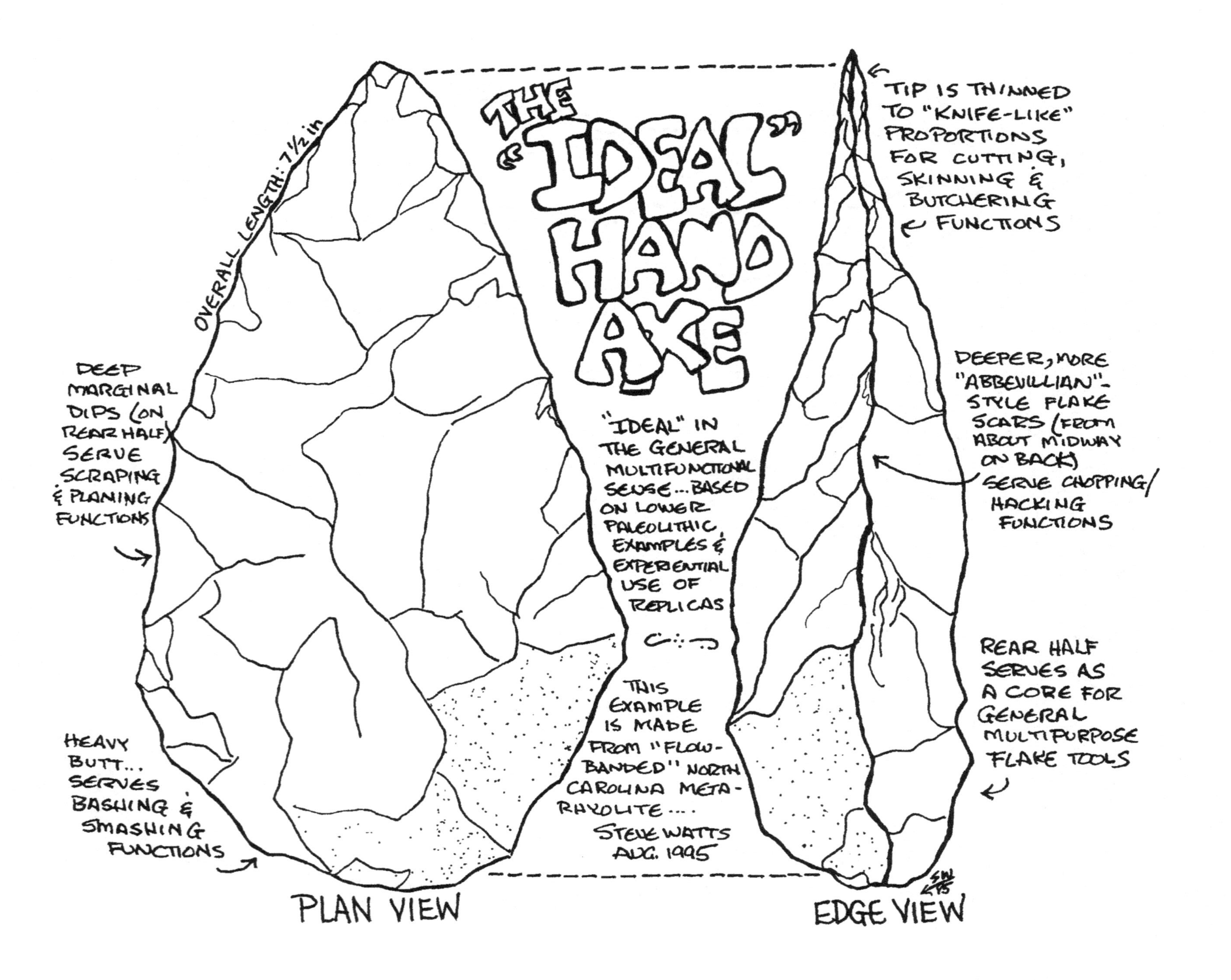
THE "IDEAL" HAND AXE
TIP IS THINNED TO "KNIFE-LIKE" PROPORTIONS FOR CUTTING, SKINNING & BUTCHERING FUNCTIONS
OVERALL LENGTH: 7½ in
DEEP MARGINAL DIPS (ON REAR HALF) SERVE SCRAPING & PLANING FUNCTIONS
"IDEAL" IN THE GENERAL MULTIFUNCTIONAL SENSE... BASED ON LOWER PALEOLITHIC EXAMPLES & EXPERIENTIAL USE OF REPLICAS
DEEPER, MORE "ABBEVILLIAN"-STYLE FLAKE SCARS (FROM ABOUT MIDWAY ON BACK) SERVE CHOPPING/HACKING FUNCTIONS
THIS EXAMPLE IS MADE FROM "FLOW-BANDED" NORTH CAROLINA META-RHYOLITE...
STEVE WATTS AUG. 1995
HEAVY BUTT... SERVES BASHING & SMASHING FUNCTIONS
REAR HALF SERVES AS A CORE FOR GENERAL MULTIPURPOSE FLAKE TOOLS
SW 95
PLAN VIEW
EDGE VIEW

Knapping Memo

SLOW DOWN
THINK
PLAN

PREPARE PLATFORMS
WATCH THE CENTERLINE
REMOVE THE HUMPS
AVOID THE DIPS
SUPPORT THE PIECE
THIN
STRAIGHTEN THE EDGE

SLOW DOWN
THINK
PLAN

RELAX
ENJOY
CONTROL THE CONTOUR
SEEK THE SYMMETRY
PREPARE PLATFORMS

SLOW DOWN
THINK
PLAN

David Wescott

The author percussion knapping at Wagner Basalt Quarry, Arizona.

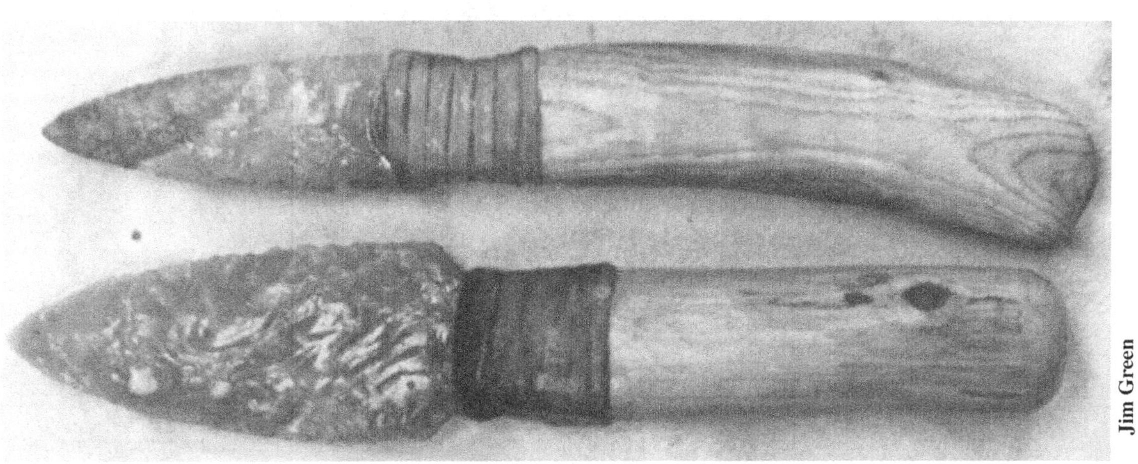

Jim Green

Old World Handaxes

The handaxe as pick/shovel: Jack Cresson heads the hole digging. (Note: No fingers were lost in the application.)

The handaxe as bashing/prying tool: Opening the skull and removing the brains.

From the Sixth Annual Knap-In at the Schiele Museum in Gastonia, North Carolina August 4-6,1995

Replica handaxes used in the various applications.

Photos by Tom Hall

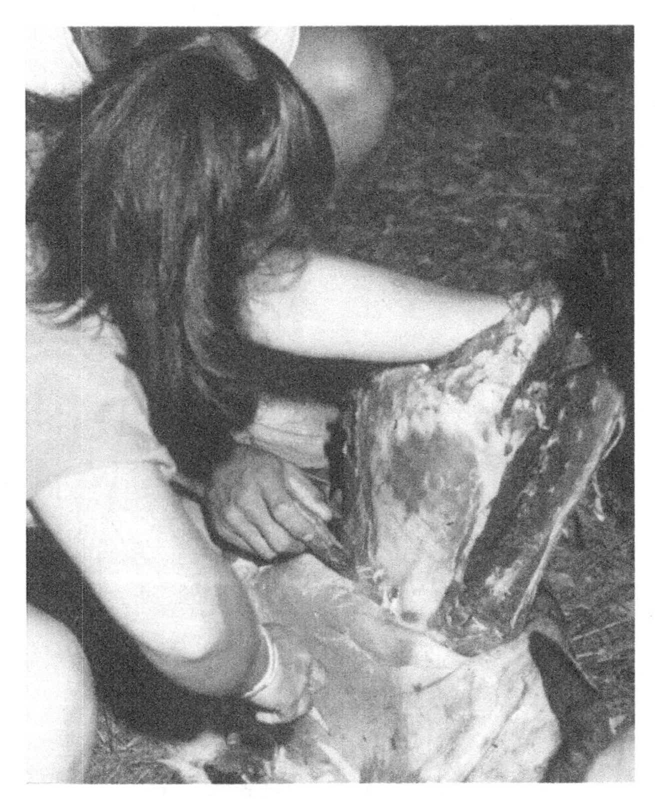

The handaxe as knife: butchering and skinning.

Rocky Culbertson working on a large metarhyolite handaxe.

The handaxe as hammerstone and anvil: bone breaking and marrow extraction.

This photo essay is from the applied session of the Sixth Annual Knap-In at the Schiele Museum in Gastonia, North Carolina (August 4-6,1995). Each year the knap-in follows a central theme so that everyone is investigating a common project with a variety of facets. The theme for '95 was "Old World Handaxes: The Birth of the Biface"

The handaxe as axe: manufacturing a digging stick (oak).

Some Uses for the Versatile

Leaf Point

Steve Watts, 1999

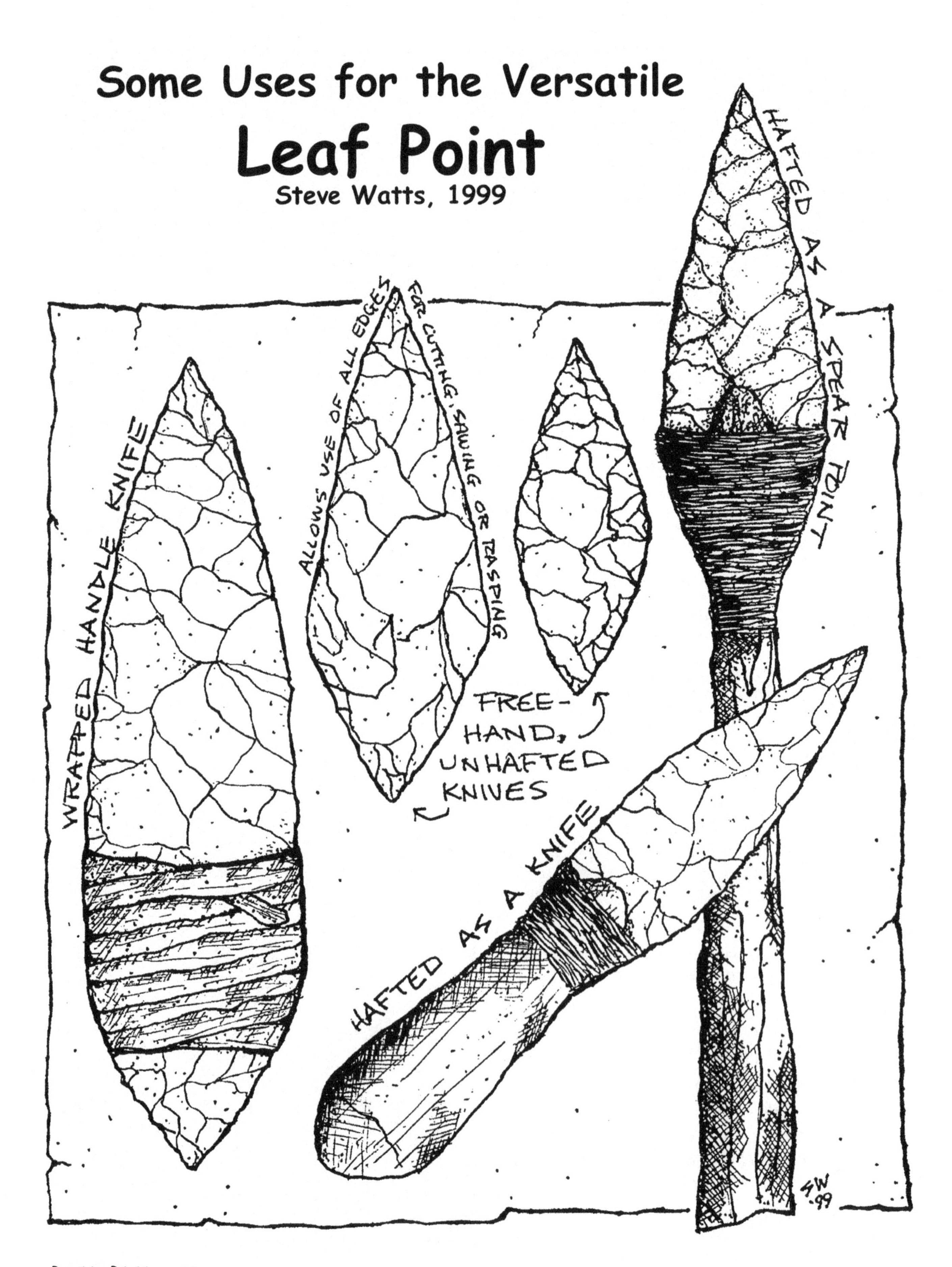

Four Spears

Steve Watts, 1998

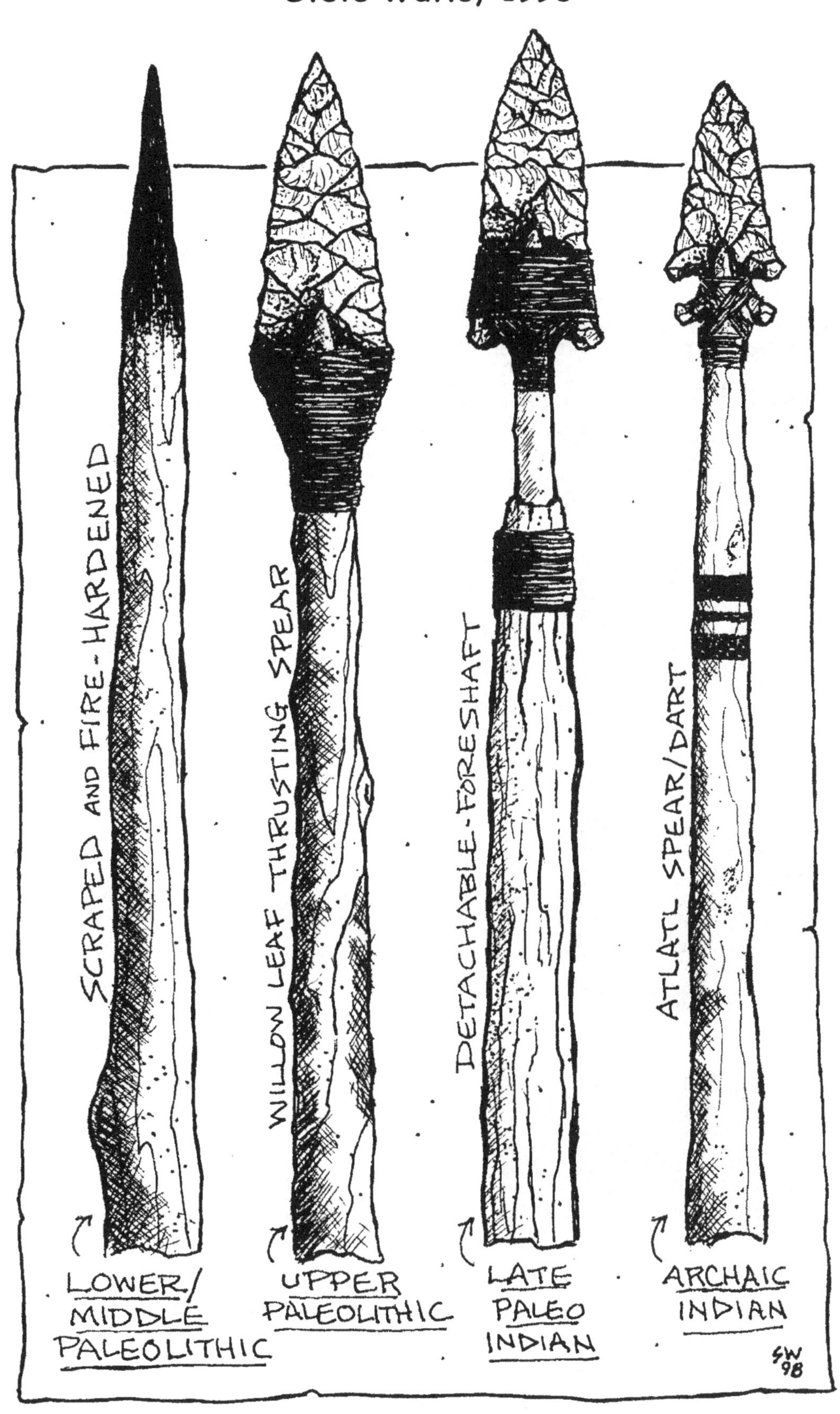

Australian-Style Blade Knives

Steve Watts, 1998

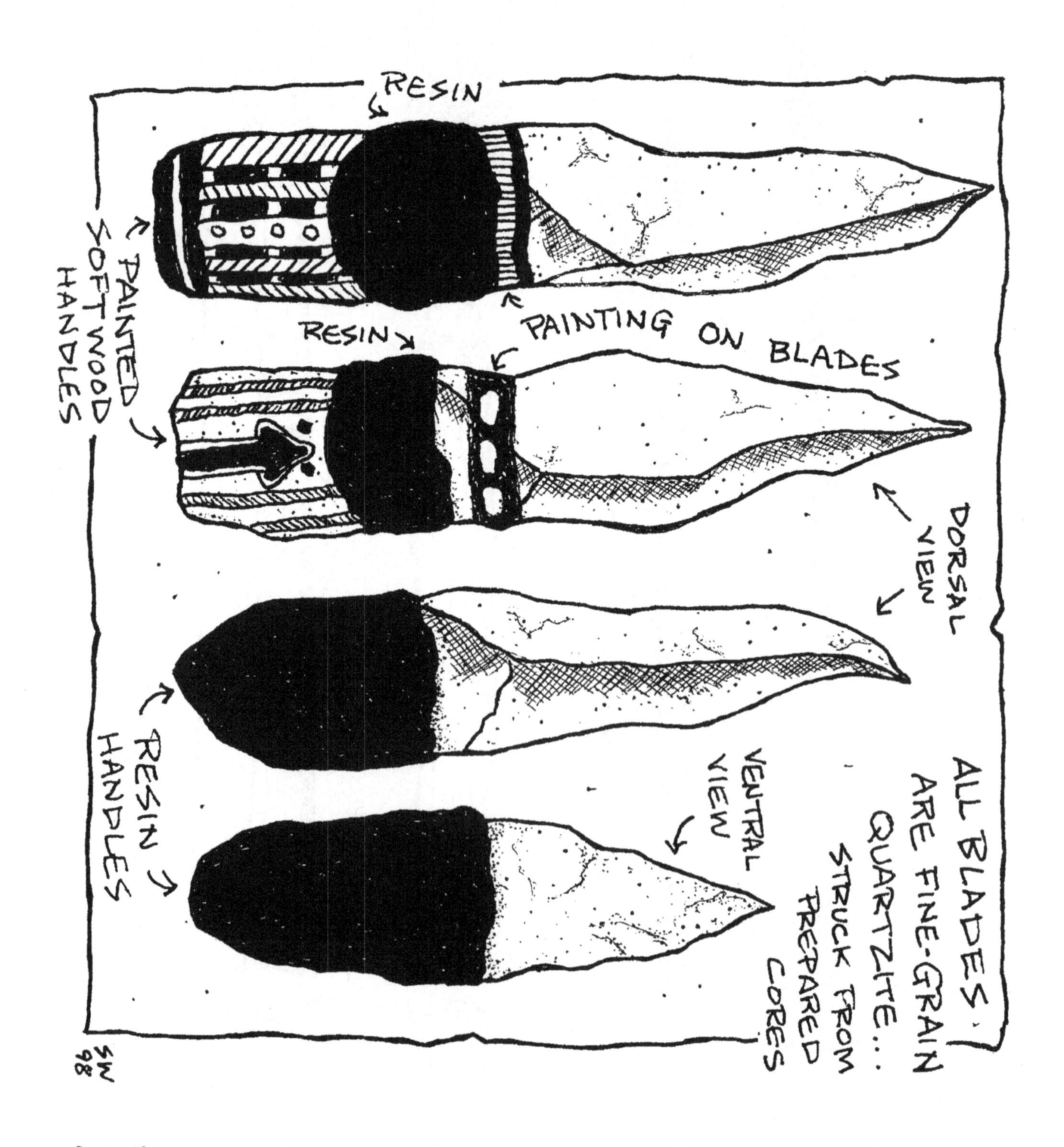

SW - 1995

A Short History...of the Short History...of a Slate Knife

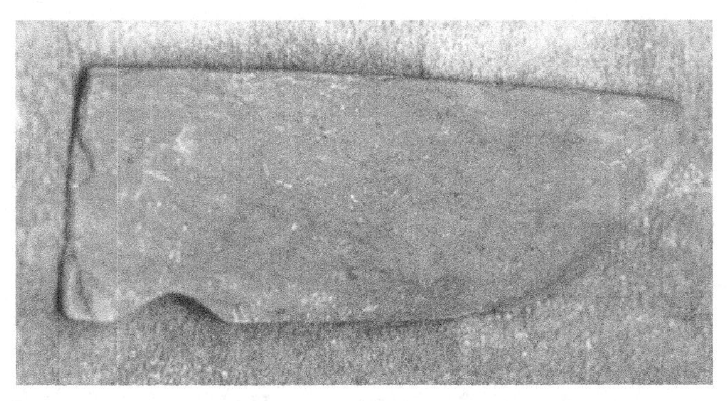

Green slate knife, shaped, ground, pressed into service and recorded through simple documentation.

This knife was manufactured in Arivaca, Arizona in a friend's front yard on New Year's Day, 1995. Made from a very soft green slate, it was quickly formed and ground.

During the next seven days, this knife journeyed with David Wescott, David Holladay (of Boulder Outdoor Survival School), Bill Broyles (Twentieth Century Fox Studios) and myself south into Sonora, Mexico . . . to the coast of the Sea of Cortez, the homeland of the Seri Indians . . . and back. Although quickly made, and of inferior grade material, this knife rode out the trip (in either my shirt pocket or day pack) and served a variety of functions both modern and aboriginal in style. About half-way through the trip my affection and concern grew for this little soft-edged thing, and I manufactured a palm leaf sheath for the remainder of the adventure.

Wescott, Holladay, Broyles, myself and our Seri guide, Hernesto Millano Villas Lobos all used the knife for one or more functions.

Modern-Style Uses:

• Spreading peanut butter . . . (Don't laugh. I originally doubted this knife's ability to accomplish such. After the first successful spreading I for one, was elated. Many other spreadings followed.)
• Cutting bread . . . With either a wooden or plastic cutting board to protect the edge.
• Cutting a variety of plastic wraps, plastic bags and box tops.
• Cutting out the foil seal in the dried milk can. Slicing cheese. Slicing cooked ham. Dicing onions.

Aboriginal-Style Uses:

• Dicing prickly pear cactus pads.
• Cutting/mashing avocado.
• Cleaning fish.
• Processing leaves for cordage fibers. The most extensive use of this knife involved the cutting, scraping, and cleaning of fibers from both Yucca and Snake Plant. Both the blade edge and "notch" were utilized.
• Butchering Sting Rays . . . We spear-fished for sting rays to use for fish bait. This was the most challenging task for the knife. Sting ray skin is exceedingly tough, slippery, tough, slimey, tough (and did I say tough).

Plan View of the "Arivaca Knife" (full size)

Solid line represents knife outline on day of manufacture 1/1/95

Dotted lines represent changes in knife cutline due to wear and/or damage as of 1/8/95

Drilling Mechanisms

Methods...Actions

Punching...pushing/pecking (points)
Cutting...rotating (blades)
Scraping...rotating or obverse/reverse action (edges)
Burning...obverse/reverse action friction (blunts)
Abrading...grinding/rubbing (blunt/flat surfaces with floating or fixed abrasives)

Delivery Systems...Examples

Hand-Held...perforators, finger drills, palm drills, reamers
Hand-Spun...shaft hand drills
Cord-Driven...bow drills, strap drills
Inertia-Driven...pump drills, top drills

SW - 1995

Primitive Technologies Involved in the Manufacture of a Pump Drill

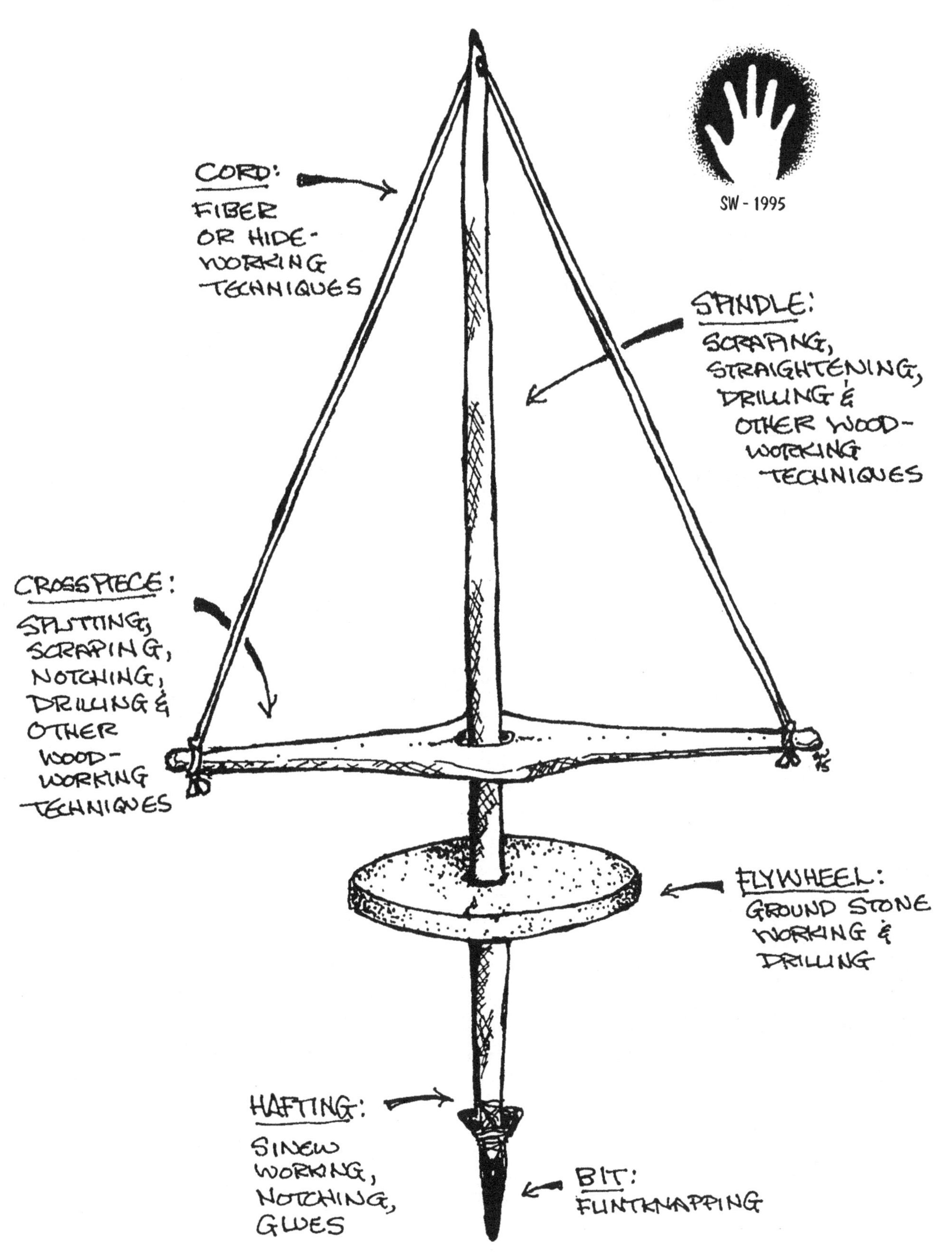

-Make of hard, medium-to-fine grained stone such as granite or quartzite

-Avoid sandstones

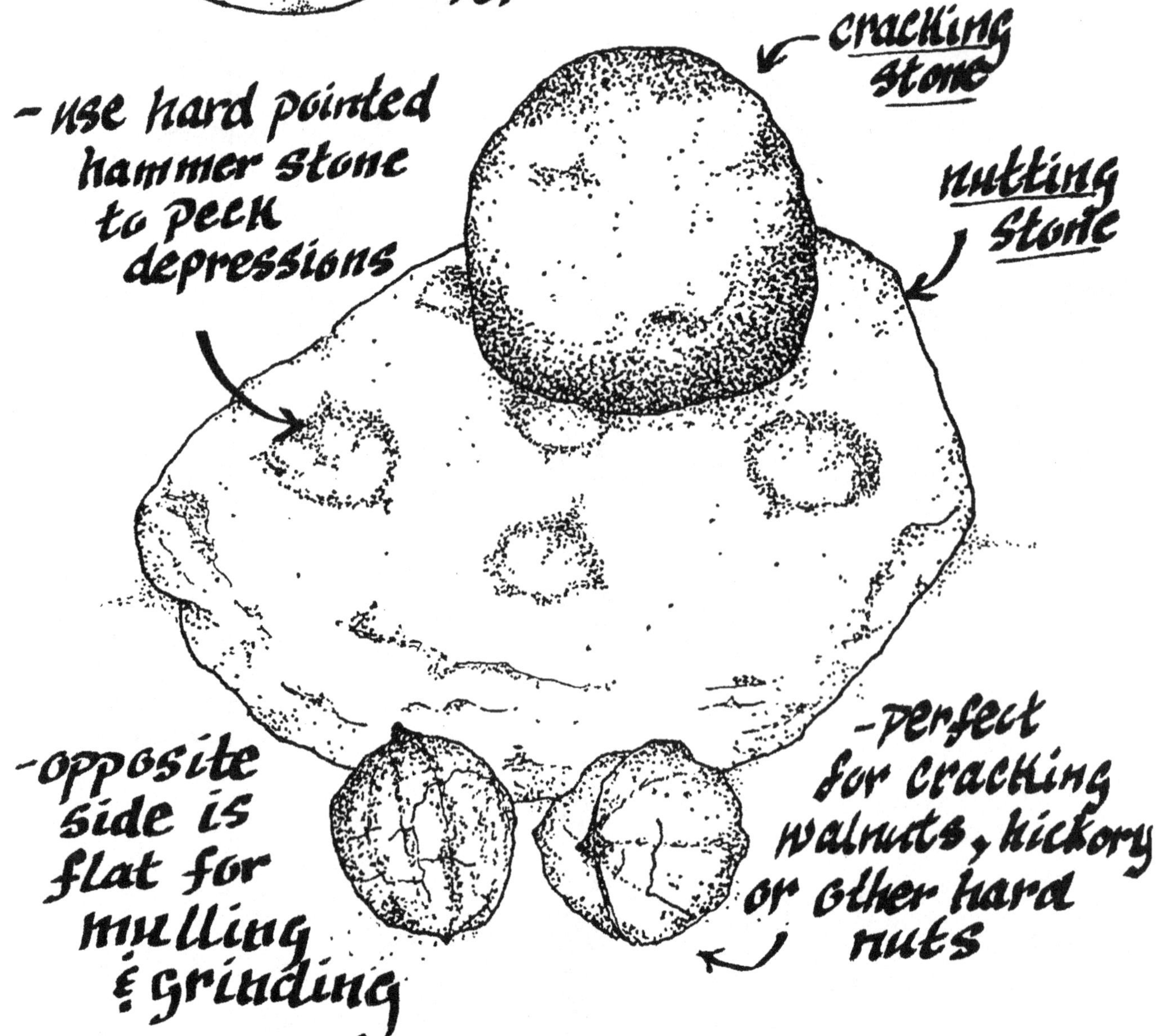

Aboriginal Uses of Bone

Tools

Awls
Needles
Chisels
Wedges
Adzes
Drill Bits
Hoe Blades
Picks/Diggers
Scoops/Shovels
Shaft Wrenches
Mauls
Knives
Handles (for knives, etc.)
Hide Fleshers
Spindle Whorls
Flintknapping Tools
Snow Goggles

Weapons/Hunting

Projectile Points (for arrows, spears, lances, etc.)
Harpoon Barbs
Fish Hooks
Fish Lures
Trap Parts (triggers & spikes)
Turkey Calls
Daggers
Composite Bow Parts
Atlatl Hooks
Rabbit Sticks
Clubs
Shell Fish Prys

Ornaments/Adornments

Ear Rings
Finger Rings
Beads
Pendants
Dangles, Baubles
Nose Pieces
Lip Pieces
Ornamental Pins
Hair Pins & Combs
Bracelets
Tattooing Tools
Fasteners: (buttons, toggles, buckles & pins)

Hearth and Home

Fuel
Bow Drill Fire Set Components
Food (marrow & bone meal)
Tent Pegs
House Framework
Sled Runners
Oil Lamps
Small Containers (vials & cups)
Spoons
Platters

Music/Art/Ceremony

Flutes
Whistles
Rasps
Drum Sticks
Chimes
Mask Components
Skull Cups
Skull Drums
Effigies/Amulets
Tubular Smoking Pipes
Paint Tubes
Click Sticks
Calender/Recording Devices
Bullroarers

Toys/Games

Tops (whorl)
Buzzers
Counters/Dice
Tally Boards

Leg-bone and scapula hoes

Bone-Working Basics

Raymond Dart, the "old man" of African prehistory, speculated (in his usual controversial way) that before any of the recognized Stone Ages, early man or early man/ape went through a formative Bone Age in which he developed an important culture. This Dart called The Osteodontokeratic . . . the bone-tooth-hoary culture.

Many critics suggested that the "tools" upon which Dart based his theory were the result of non-human "natural" forces and modification by animals other than hominids . . . and the debate continues. Whatever the case, experienced practicing primitives know the value of unmodified, or "naturally" modified bones as tools for digging, bashing, cutting etc. And, we do know that by the Upper Paleolithic our Homo Sapien forebearers were indeed "osteo-literate"- systematically exploiting bone resources for the production of tools, ornaments food, fuel and ritual objects.

"A Proposed Staging Sequence For Bone Working"

This is a possible reduction sequence for working bone . . . from the complete bone to the completed tool or ornament. This sequence was first presented in 1988 and has been used since that time both in personal replication projects and in the presentation of bone working workshops and demonstrations. It has been refined somewhat since that time and will continue to be re-evaluated as further applications are tested.

These bone working "stages" may or may not have been present in the mind and work patterns of the aboriginal craftsman, but may be helpful for replicators seeking to work with bone in a systematic way.

Stage 1- Obtaining the material

The material in this case, of course, is bone. It is: found/gathered in the environment, traded for, obtained as a by-product of butchering/cooking activities, or processed directly from the carcass for the intention of working. Fleshing, boiling, and shallow burial are common processing methods.

Stage 2 - Creating the blank

Breaking, scoring/breaking, scoring/cutting, flaking, cracking, smashing, grinding, splitting, or otherwise modifying the bone in preparation for shaping. The "blank" may be the whole bone modified, or a part or piece of the bone obtained by one or more of the above methods. In some cases "ideal" blank-forms may be required, in others a more generalized shape/size may suffice.

Stage 3 - Shaping

Grinding, carving, sawing/abrading, or otherwise modifying the blank to shape it into the final outline and cross-sectional form. Many bone implements may be completed with this stage. Others may require Stage 4 work for completion.

Stage 4 - Finishing

Polishing, notching, fine sharpening, drilling, engraving or other modifications may be applied to the shaped piece (as holes in needles, fine points on awls, etc.). Finishing procedures are most often related to specific tasks required of the tool.

The piece in hand at each stage is referred to in this way:

Stage 1. The Bone
Stage 2. The Blank
Stage 3. The Shaped Piece
Stage 4. The Finished Piece

Example: "Stages of Manufacture of a Bone Awl"

Stage 1	Stage 2	Stage 3	Stage 4
Cannon Bone (Whitetail)	The Blank	The Shaped Piece	The Finished Piece

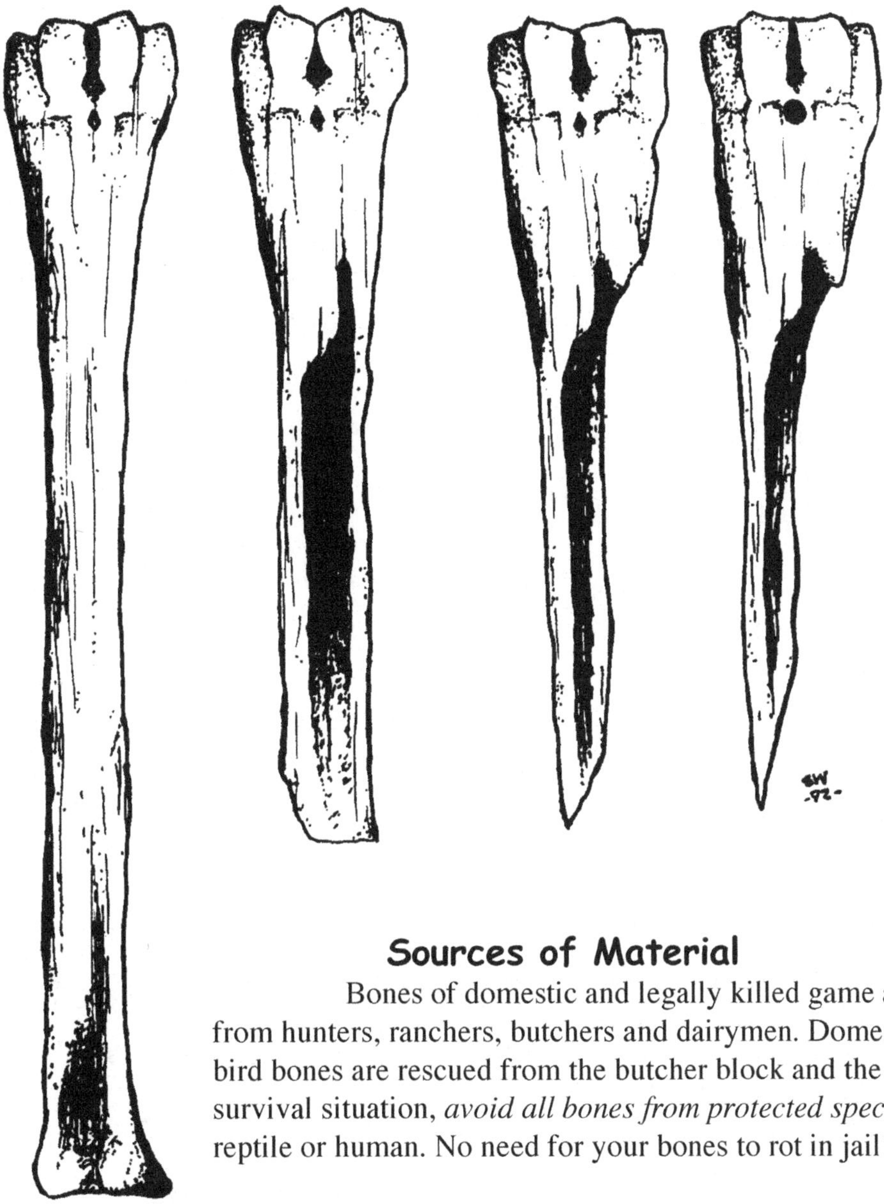

As in flint-knapping, bow making, pottery or any other aboriginal technology approached in a systematic way; stages of manufacture may often be combined. Seldom however can they be rearranged in order. Stages may be omitted completely . . . as in the case of an expedient digging/stabbing tool created by the uncontrolled smashing of a long bone with a hammerstone. In this case the bone worker moves from whole bone to the completed tool with one swift blow.

Sources of Material

Bones of domestic and legally killed game animals can be obtained from hunters, ranchers, butchers and dairymen. Domestic and legally killed bird bones are rescued from the butcher block and the stock pot. Except in a survival situation, *avoid all bones from protected species* . . . bird, mammal, reptile or human. No need for your bones to rot in jail!

Fresh or Dried?

The primitive bone worker may have little choice in his selection of raw materials in a given situation. When a choice is presented . . . which is better, fresh or dried bone?

Fresh bone seems stronger and more flexible than dried. Tools from these are less brittle and less likely to split and splinter. Yet, in manufacturing, a tendency to split can be an advantage if it can be controlled. Extremely weathered bone can deteriorate to a "spongy" state, making it the least desirable. Extremely fresh, uncooked bones can be excessively greasy, slippery and difficult to work.

As with many things, a middle ground is best. In the "ideal" situation, where time allows, the best of both worlds finds the artisan using fresher bones through Stages 1 and 2 (where cutting, smashing, splitting, etc. are most utilized), slightly drier for Stage 3, and drier still for stage 4 (final grinding, polishing and sharpening). These Stage 4 tasks are best accomplished with dry materials. Fresh bone (somewhat like green wood) never takes the finer finishing processes well. It tends to "fuzz" and "feather" on the surface, resisting polish.

Even a tool made from fresh bone will dry out over time, so completed implements should be oiled periodically to prevent weakening by checking, cracking, etc.

Raw or Cooked?

Raw bones are stronger than cooked ones, retaining their oils, structure and integrity. Baked or roasted bones may be used, but are often weakened considerably. Boiling (one of the preferred methods of processing found in Stage 1) seems to weaken bone less than other "drier" cooking methods. Boiled bones are softened slightly in the process, allowing for ease of manufacture. Firmness is regained once they are dry. And, remember, all bones can be used for a smelly fuel (highly prized by aboriginal peoples living in wood-poor environments) - fuel for cooking, heating, or processing yet more bone.

Scraps

Cut-offs, splinters, partial halves from unsuccessful splitting attempts, etc. should be saved and examined. A "waste" piece from one project may become —upon close inspection— a perfect Stage 2 blank for another. The splinter becomes an awl or a needle, the cut-off a fish hook, or almost any piece a bead or ornament. Often a "useless" scrap is just a blank waiting for a yet-to-be-thought-of project. Toss these into a gourd, basket or bag with the other discards and wait for inspiration.

Bone-Working Tools

The aboriginal bone worker's tools vary from the simple (a hammerstone) to the sophisticated (a pump drill). Tools most often utilized in the various stages of manufacture typically are:

Stage 1. Digging sticks (wood or antler) for digging up buried bones; bifaces, unmodified flakes and scrapers for butchering and fleshing fresh bones; pots for boiling; packs, baskets, skins and cordage for transporting.

Stage 2. Hammerstones with flat, rounded or edged anvils; unmodified flakes, denticulated flakes and bifaces ("saws"); mauls, large-grained grinding stones, wedges, flakers and burins.

Stage 3. Medium-grained grinding stones, "saws", unmodified flakes, drills, gravers and burins, scrapers.

Stage 4. Finer-grained grinding stones, polishing stones, buckskin and sand polishers, drills, burins/engravers, pigments, oil.

Brains, brawn, planning and perseverance are useful in all stages.

The staging sequence presented by Steve was adapted from an older reduction sequence for stone developed by Errett Callahan. It is an excellent way to approach all projects using natural materials and can be adapted to resources as diverse as shell and wood. Thinking of projects in stages gives you not only a predictable sequence of steps to a project, but also provides a blue print as to how a project may proceed in terms of processes. The Ed

Stages for Manufacture of a Fish Hook

Stage 1

Stage 2

Stage 3

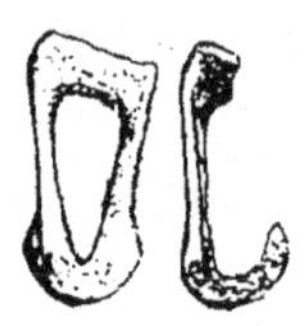

Stage 4

Scoring

For many bone-working projects (awls, needles, pins, daggers, large gorge hooks, knives, etc.) long sections of split bone are required. The nature of bone, however, does not lend itself to such splits. When unmodified and hit with a percusser, bone tends to split spirally instead of longitudinally. To overcome this the artisan carves/scrapes a groove the length of the piece (using a flake, biface or burin) before applying percussion. After scoring, the bone can be tapped with the percusser along the groove, encouraging the bone to split in this predetermined manner.

Michael Eldredge

Splitting a rib bone using the bipolar technique.

The Edged Anvil

John White (Ancient Lifeways Institute, Illinois) shared a bone splitting tip with me many years ago that I, in turn, have shared with many others since: Instead of a flat anvil, use an "edged" anvil - the edge of a core, large spall, biface etc. Partially bury this anvil in the ground or support it in some other way, placing the groove in the bone on theanvil edge, and moving the bone back and forth as you tap with the hammer stone or billet. This concentrates the energy and results in high splitting-success rates.

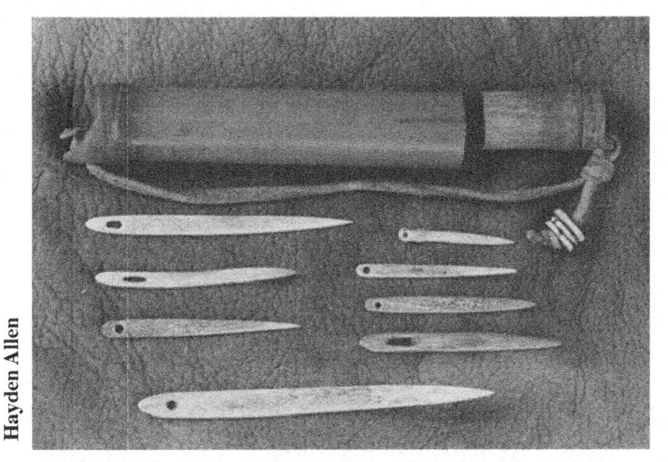

Hayden Allen

Replicas made by Steve Watts. River-cane vial and bone needles.

Bipolar Splitting

Just hitting a bone laid on an anvil with none of the above preparations will yield unpredictable results at best. (For a possible exception see "Jacketed" technique below). Yet, I've discovered that large rib bones can be successfully split without any grooving or grinding preparation using bipolar percussion. Hold the rib on edge on a slightly rounded anvil. Moving it back and forth along the anvil as you work, whack it smartly with a hardwood or antler billet. You'll most often get nice long splits (sometimes even the entire length).

The "Jacketed" Technique

During a recent (Aug. '95) deer skinning, butchering experience we "discovered" a low-tech bone splitting technique that needs further experimentation. Having skinned the legs, a participant laid the bones on an anvil and smashed them without having removed the meat, sinew, membranes/ tissues as would "normally" be done when using more formal bone splitting techniques. The object was marrow extraction, so the cleaning of the bone was neither indicated or suggested. The bones, to my surprise, split into long thin pieces producing instant needle, awl, and pin blanks. The experience was repeated with similar results. Perhaps the adhering "jacket" of tissues affected the fracture-energy in a way different from "naked" bone? Or maybe it was just a fluke. Try it.

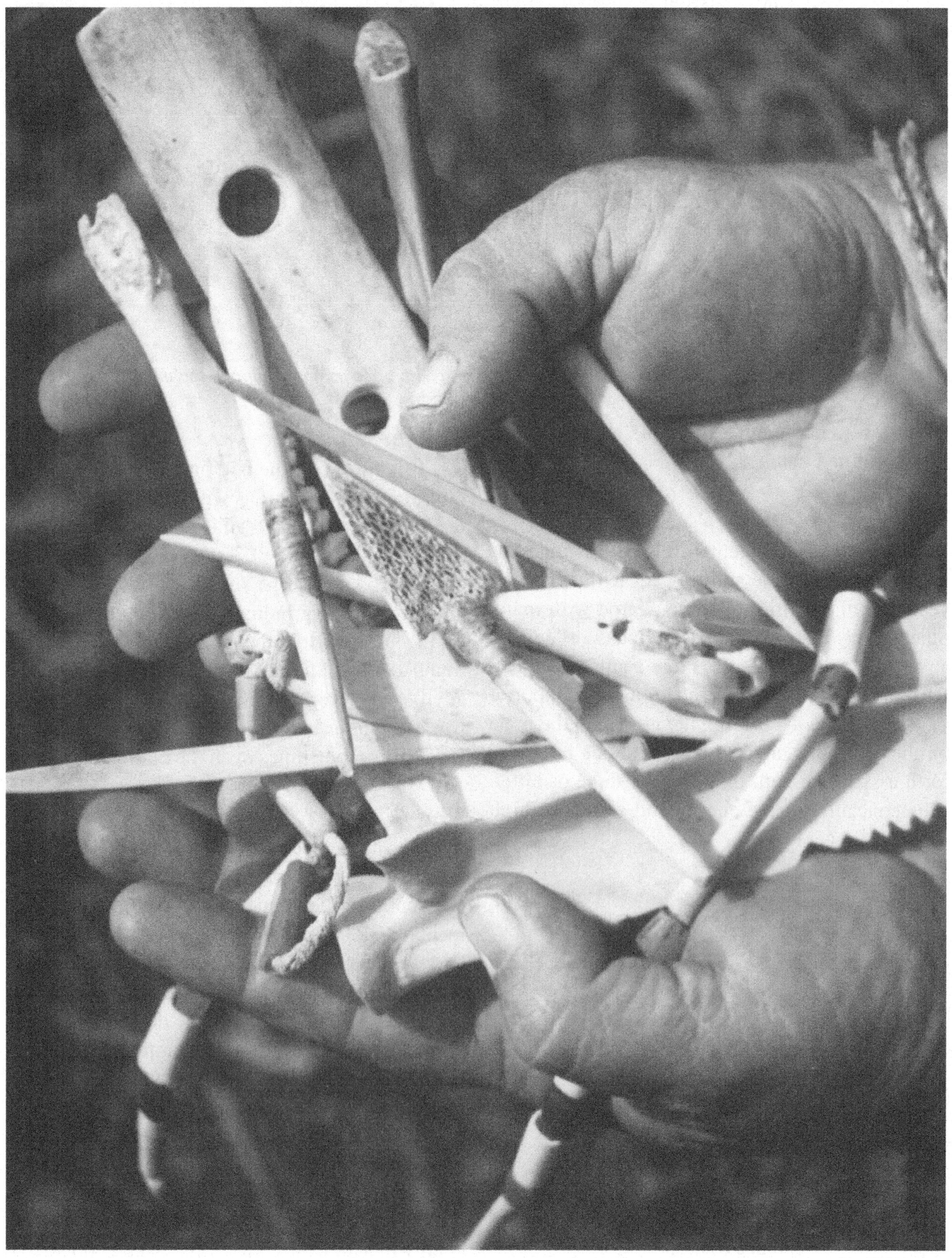

David Wescott

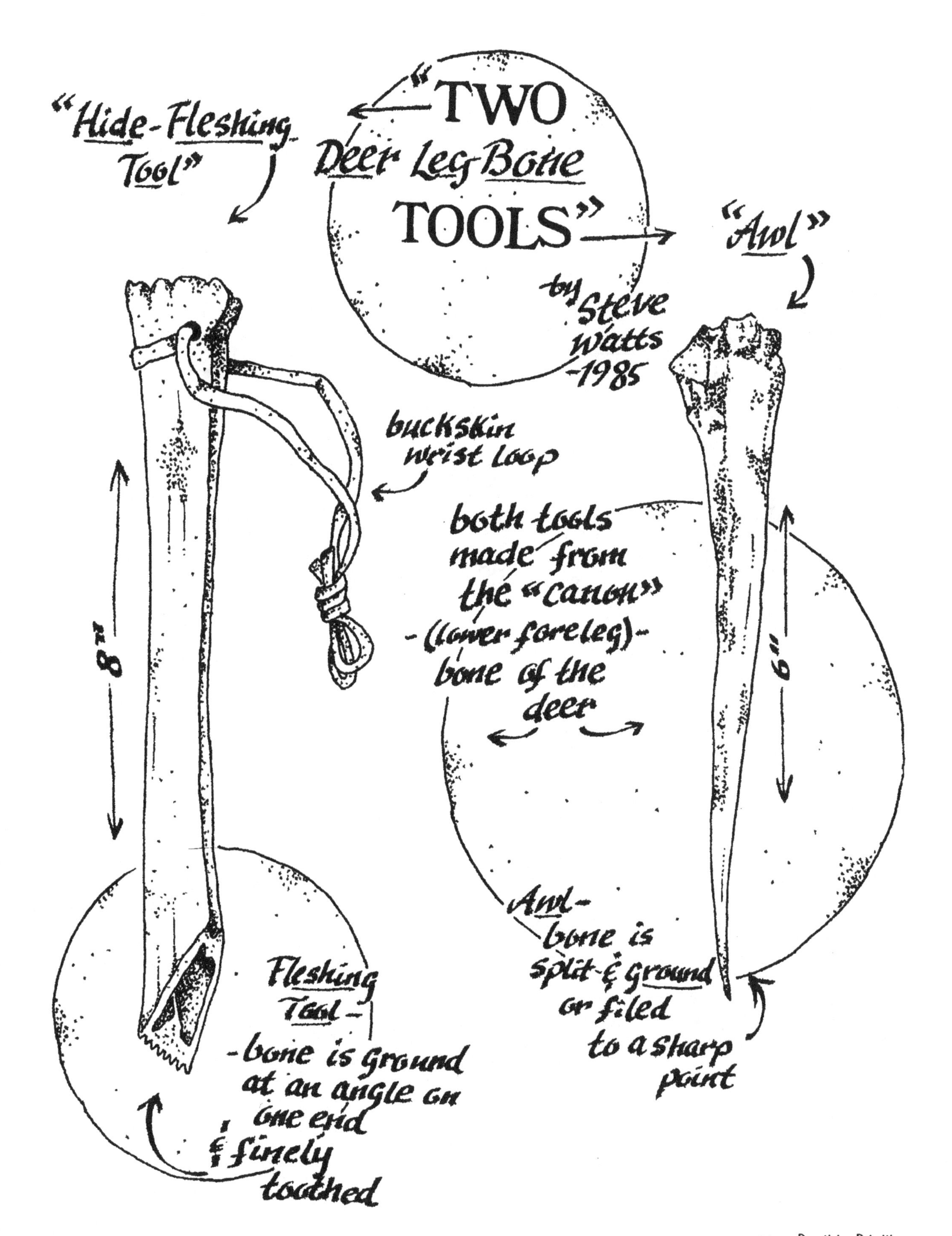
"TWO
Deer Leg Bone
TOOLS"
by Steve Watts -1985
"Hide-Fleshing Tool"
"Awl"
buckskin wrist loop
8"
6"
both tools made from the "canon" -(lower foreleg)- bone of the deer
Fleshing Tool -
-bone is ground at an angle on one end & finely toothed
Awl-
bone is split & ground or filed to a sharp point

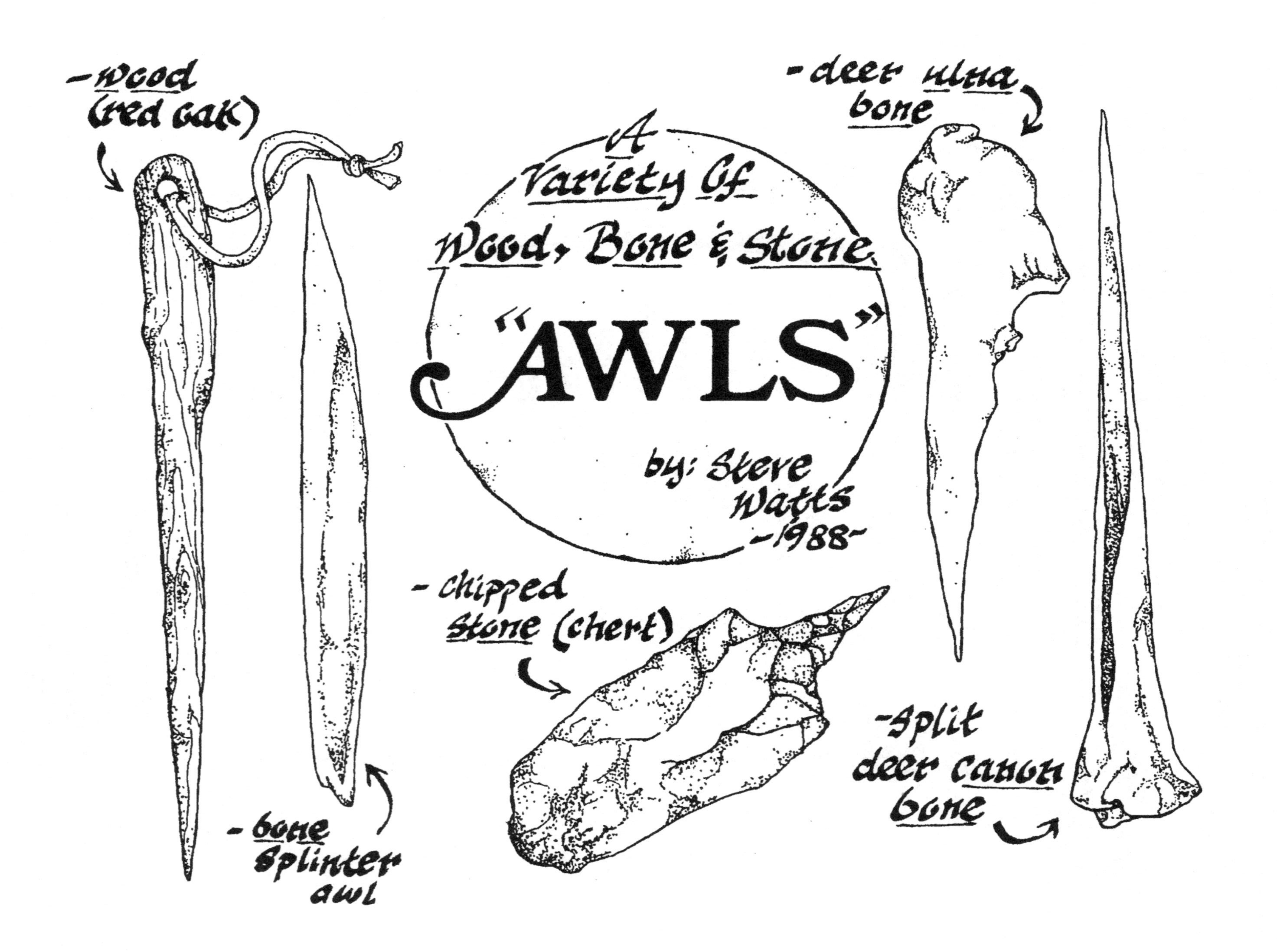
A Variety Of
Wood, Bone & Stone
"AWLS"
by: Steve Watts
-1988-
-wood (red oak)
-bone splinter awl
-chipped stone (chert)
-deer ulna bone
-split deer canon bone

Working Soapstone with Bone Chisels

Soapstone bowls can be worked from start to finish using only stone picks. hammers, scrapers and unmodified flakes (see Allison & Jones). I believe, these were the tools used most often by prehistoric bowlsmiths, and completely authentic replicas can and are created using such tools. Yet, sometimes a faint crack from ancient times leads us a bit further down the trail. Hence, this short tale.

Sometime around 1981, I decided to try to add bone and antler chisels to my soapstone working tool kit. They worked pretty well, but I discovered that they needed to be relatively narrow in the bit (1 1/2 inch or so) to be effective. Before long, I dropped their use and pretty much forgot about it.

Five or six years later I met Terry Ferguson - an archaeologist at Wofford College in Spartanburg, South Carolina. Terry has looked at more aboriginal soapstone bowls, bowl fragments and quarry sites than anyone I know or know about. His thesis work involved the location and survey of archaic soapstone quarries and soapstone bowl manufacturing sites up and down the entire eastern seaboard. He had noticed some characteristic markings on late stage bowls and bowl fragments - shallow parallel groves on both the interior and exterior. Sometimes these groves were evident even on the surfaces of completed vessels - their traces having not been completely removed by final stage finishing processes. He speculated the use of some kind of toothed implement.

With this inspiration, I returned to the bone chisel experiments. Only, this time instead of a straight bit, I created a toothed bit - much like the metal chisels used by modern-day stone sculptor (see illustration below).

These tools, when used with a wooden mallet, give the bowl maker lots of control in the final stages of work. There is less fear of breakage and the bowl walls can be thinned with regularity. The secret to the toothed arrangement lies in the spaces between the teeth. With a four toothed chisel, you essentially have four tiny chisels working together simultaneously. A broad net bit has too much to push/cut at once. Multiple passes over the same area with the toothed tool removes material at a quick rate without getting hung up on inclusions which can often stop, chip or misdirect the straight-bitted tool.

Chisel manufacture is simple. I make mine much like a bone hide flesher, but with larger, thicker teeth. Choose a strong leg bone (deer, elk, etc.) - one free from cracks - as it will take a lot of abuse. After cutting the bevel and the teeth, round off the upper end. This is the end that takes the mallet blows, and the rounding strengthens the surface and saves wear and tear on your mallet.

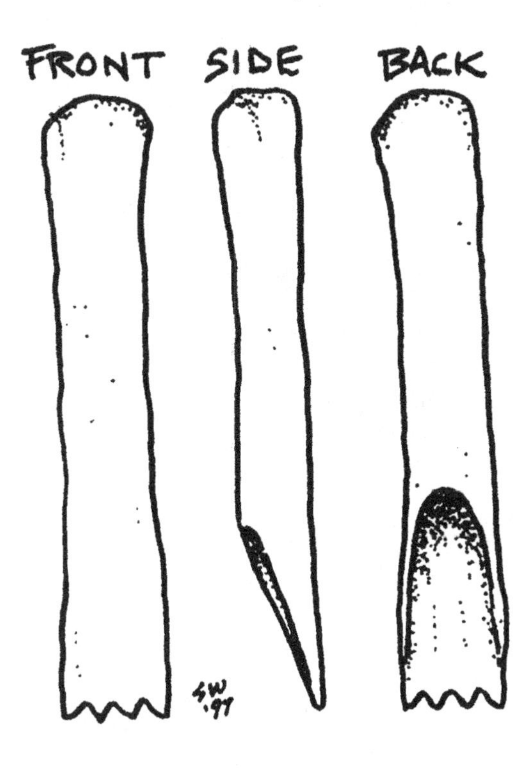

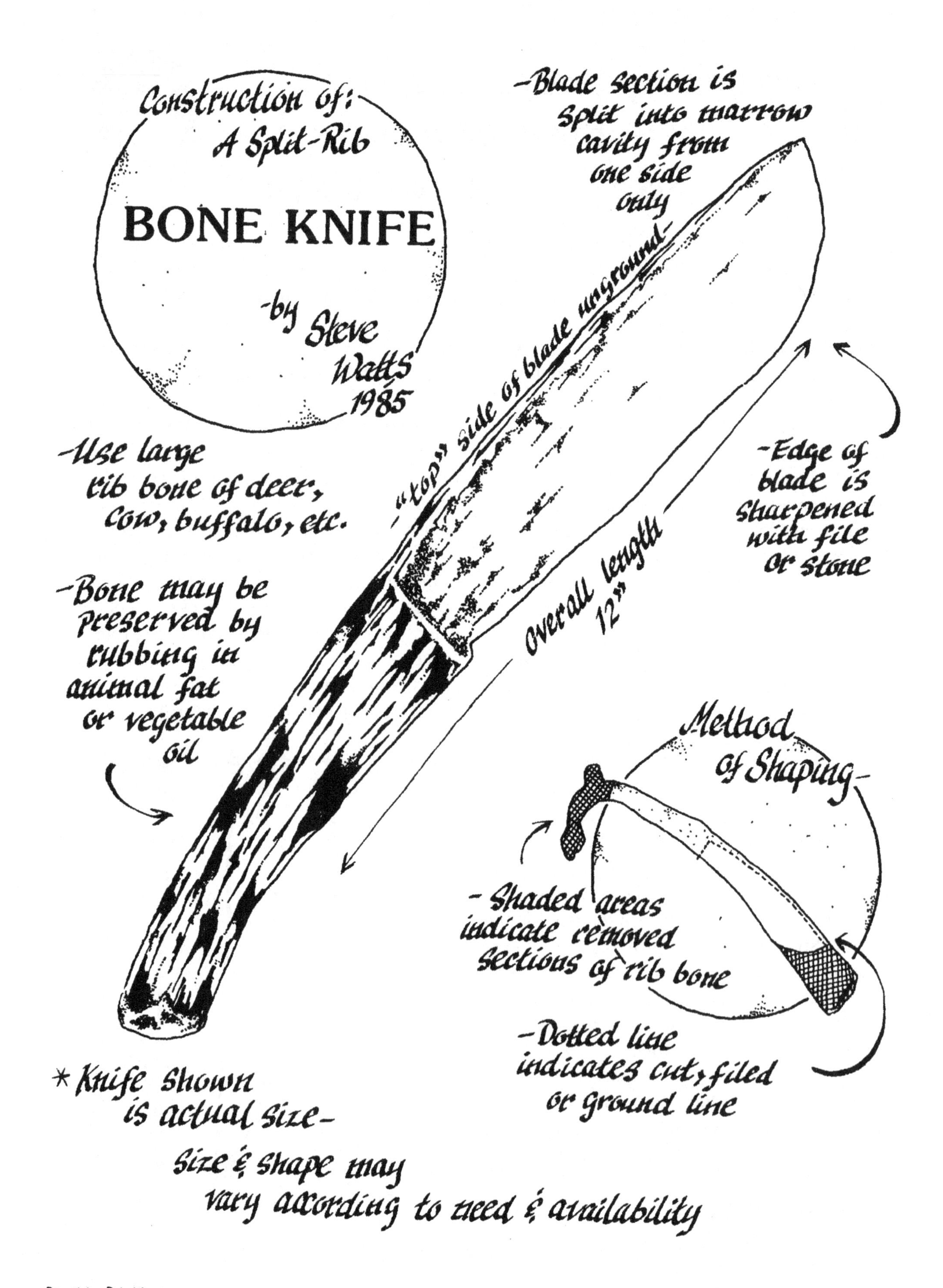
Construction of:
A Split-Rib
BONE KNIFE
-by Steve Watts 1985
-Blade section is split into marrow cavity from one side only
"top" side of blade unground
-Use large rib bone of deer, cow, buffalo, etc.
-Bone may be preserved by rubbing in animal fat or vegetable oil
Overall length 12"
-Edge of blade is sharpened with file or stone
Method of Shaping-
- Shaded areas indicate removed sections of rib bone
-Dotted line indicates cut, filed or ground line
* Knife shown is actual size-
Size & shape may vary according to need & availability

Aboriginal Uses of Antler

Weapons and Tools of the Hunt

projectile points
lances, spears & arrows
atlatl hooks and handles
knife handles
harpoons & liesters
daggers
shaft wrenches
decoys
flintknapping tools
composite bow parts
clubs & maces

Digging Tools

digging "sticks"
mattocks
picks
rakes
grubbing tools

Ornaments and Fasteners

buttons
toggles
ear spools
beads
rings
bracelets
neck & ear pendants

Hearth and Home

hooks
combs
platters
awls
needles
netting tools
vials
hide flesher
glue
celt
chisels & wedges
adzes & axe sockets

Ritual and Ceremonial

drum stick
mask & headdress components
pipe bowls
tridents
gaming pieces

Antler Digging Tools

Aboriginal-Style Antler-Working Tools

Water...for softening (more destructive alternatives are vinegar, urine & soured milk)
Burins...for cutting, carving & engraving
Flakes...for scraping, scoring, carving
Drills...for drilling, reaming & decorating (finger, hand, strap, bow & pump varieties)
Denticulate Tools...(fine toothed) for coring, sawing
Grinding Stones...(various grits) for shaping, sawing, facing, polishing & sharpening
Sand & Buckskin...for polishing
Axes & Choppers....for disarticulating racks

Antlers in the Garden

From Neolithic to historic times, Northern Hemisphere aboriginals have used deer, elk and moose antlers for the manufacture of horticultural tools. The natural shape, strength and flexibility of antlers make them the perfect raw material for such tools. With little to no modification antlers are transformed into diggers, rakes, hoes, spades, picks and other implements of the farm and field.

Photos: Mike Peters

❖❖❖❖❖❖❖❖❖❖❖❖❖❖❖❖❖❖

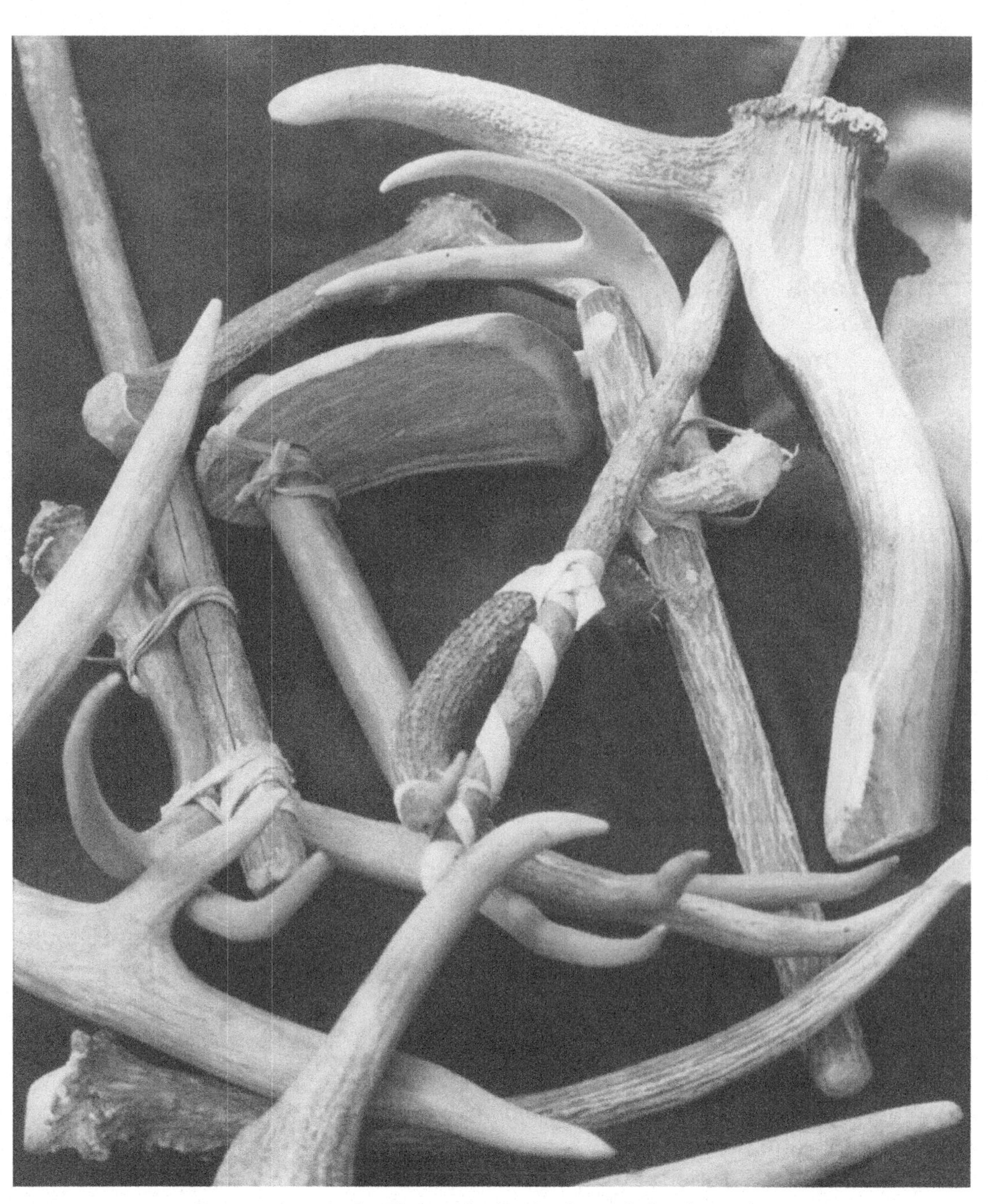

An assortment of antler gardening tools made by the author.

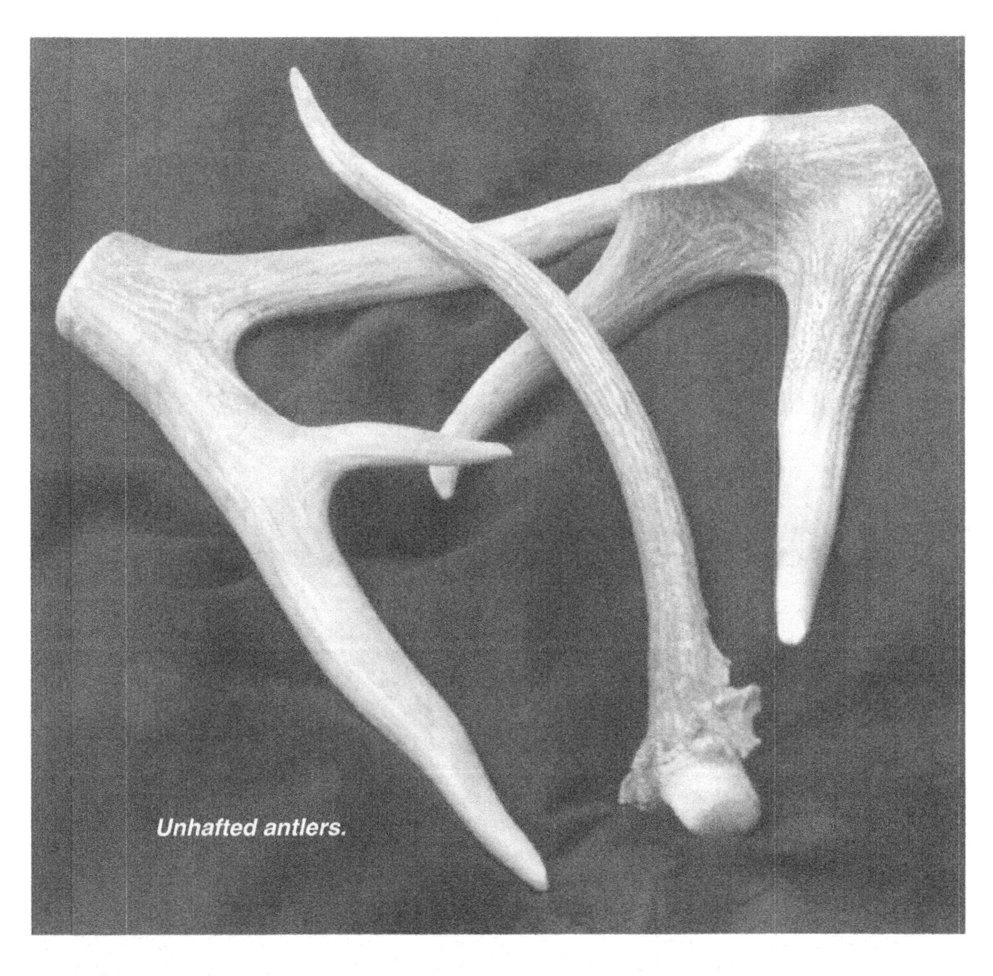
Unhafted antlers.

Unhafted Diggers

Large tines and antler sections made up of multiple tines, make perfect hand-held digging tools. Big racks are cut into manageable sections, while small ones can be used unmodified. The two multi-tined sections (Photo 2) (elk) have been used in a variety of agricultural experiments and projects over the years. The long single tine (elk) functions essentially as a digging stick. These tools are also perfect for quarrying stone, mining clay for pottery and digging for water.

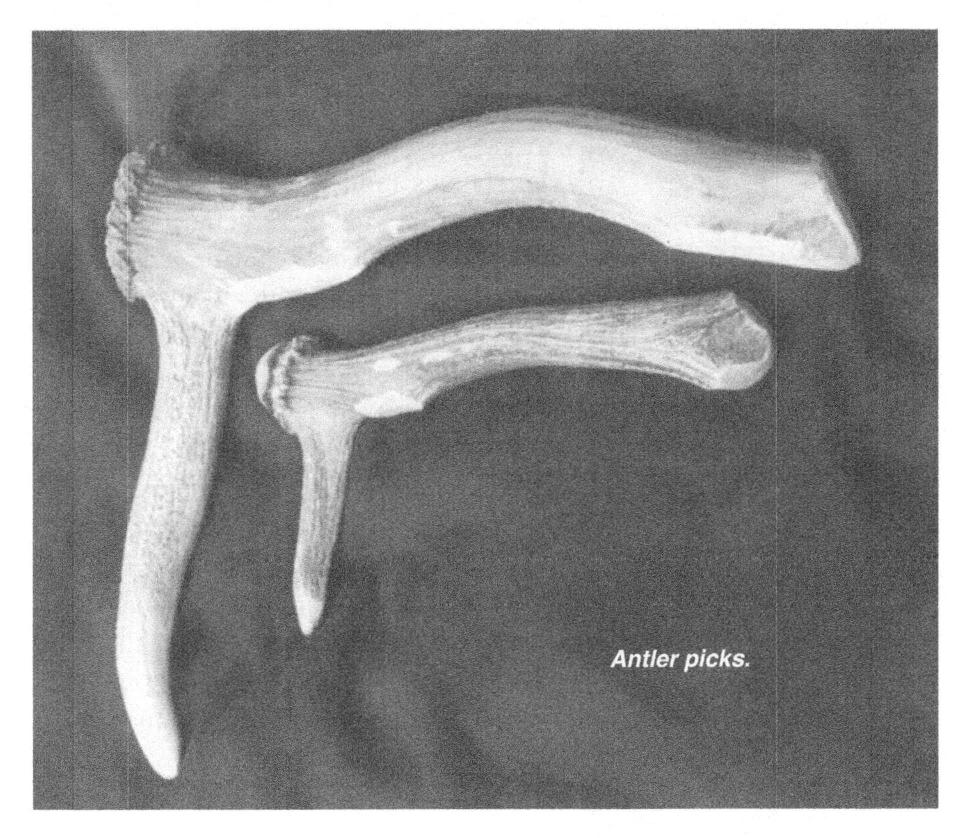
Antler picks.

Picks

The elk antler trunk and tine tools featured here (Photo 3) are modeled after Western European artifacts. There they were used both for farming and for flint mining. They are among the most common grave goods found in Late Neolithic burials in the British Isles-interred with both men and women. They are perfect for breaking up hard ground, digging trenches and gathering root crops. I've even used the 'poll" of the small one as a make-do flintknapping billet. (Just be sure to watch your back swing.)

Rakes

A half rack is a natural rake - either hand-held or hafted. Hafted examples have been recorded in both the Old and New Worlds. These examples (Photo 4) are both whitetail deer. The one on the left is bound with raw-hide and the one on the right with buckskin. Buckskin is my preference, since it may be retied and tightened easily and quickly when the tool loosens with use. Antler rakes are perfect for clearing ground, mounding hills in a garden or searching for mollusks.

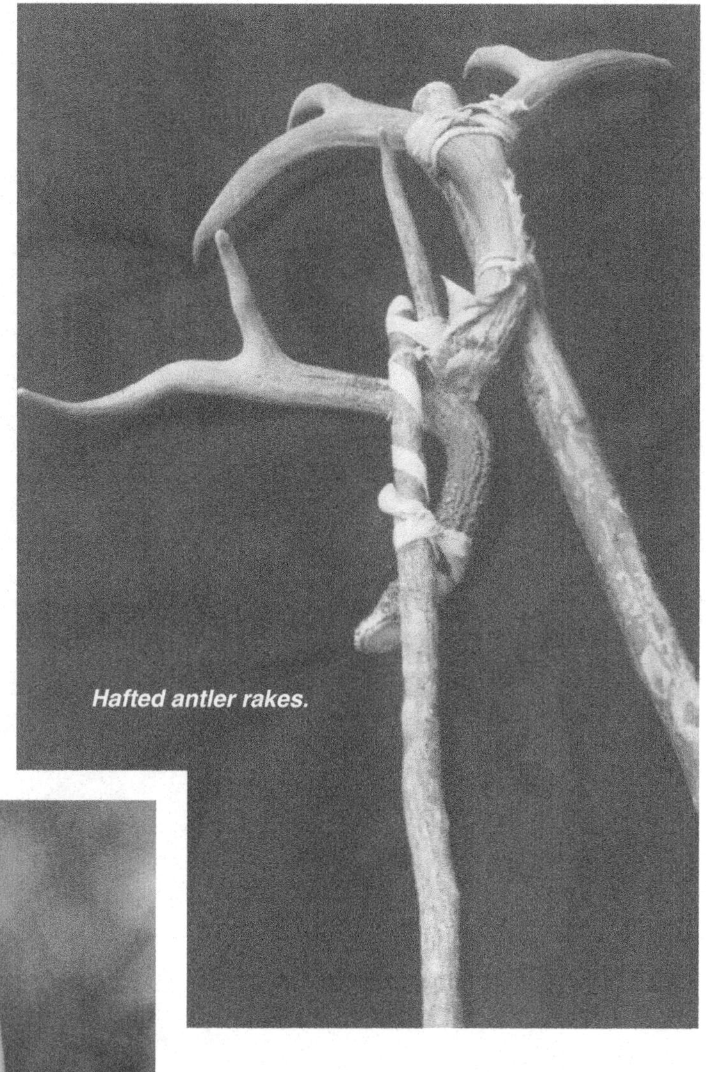

Hafted antler rakes.

Grubbers

This catch-all category includes two of my favorite antler digging tools. (Photo 5) The one on the left is a short hoe or mattock made from the palm portion of a moose antler. It was modeled after a Mesolithic tool from a site in England. The palm portion was shaped, perforated and affixed to the handle with a buckskin binding. It has seen much service over the years. The second tool is also well experienced. Made from half of a whitetail deer rack, the right angle orientation of the tines makes it the perfect "grubbing" tool. I suppose you could call it a very short rake, but I've used it mostly for digging and general rooting around. Besides seeing use as an experimental primitive tool, this little digger has found its way into my contemporary gardening toolbox more than once.

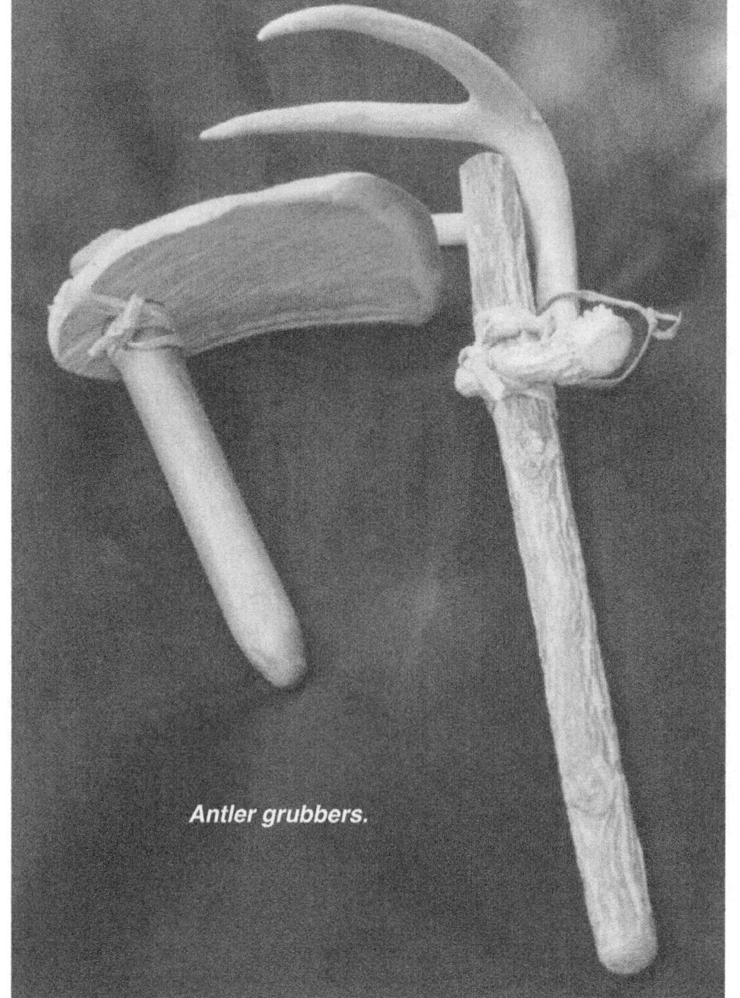

Antler grubbers.

The Domestication of the Species

For more than two million years, all of our ancestors lived as hunters, fishers, foragers and gatherers. Viewed from the comfort of the twenty-first century this way of life is seen by many to be brutish and on-the-edge. Yet, some have considered it to be the original "affluent society" - proving itself by its stability and longevity. Ethnographic studies of living hunter/gatherer cultures have convinced many that this "old way" produced much leisure time (at least in the temperate and tropical zones), leaving more time for religion, music, art, recreation, family, exploration, dance and that ever illusive "quality time". Perhaps it is the Golden Age so fondly remembered in the mythologies of cultures throughout the world. [To explore these thoughts further see: Elman R. Service's *The Hunters, Primitive Social Organization, Profiles in Ethnology*, Claude Levi-Strauss' The Savage Mind, and Lee and Devore's *Man The Hunter*.]

But, this would all change. Soon, the last great expression of the Stone Age would arrive and hunter/gathers would be pushed to the globe's margins by the technological innovations of the Neolithic. And, at the core of this New Stone Age we find the domestication of plants and animals.

This agricultural/pastoral revolution began around ten thousand years ago as the last Ice Age came to an end. In an area we call the "fertile crescent" (which stretched from the eastern shores of the Mediterranean to north of the Persian gulf) our ancestors began an experiment that would shape all of history to follow. They began to settle in permanent villages in places where edible wild grains like wheat and barley grew in abundance. This new, wetter, warmer world allowed them to gather, store and sow these grains to increase their harvest. New technologies arose. Grinding, mulling and milling stones allowed the nutrition locked within these grains to be released. Ovens transformed the meal into bread. Pottery provided a means of boiling these hard seeds, and a way to store them, protected from the rodents now drawn to these settled communities. Hoes and plows replaced digging sticks. Large tracts of land could be tilled with the aid of newly domesticated cattle. Now tamed and controlled, pigs, sheep, and goats more easily gave up their skin, flesh and milk. Stone axes with finely polished bits were made to clear the land of trees and make room for fields and villages.

These villages and towns, supported an ever-increasing population. Larger families provided a larger workforce for planting, herding, tending, harvesting and processing. Specialists developed—potters, toolmakers, jewelers, bakers, shopkeepers and priests. Permanent housing replaced the mobile hunter's shelter, and storehouses were built to cache the excess goods. Talley systems developed to keep up with the surplus and its distribution. Writing and bookkeeping were born. Roads replaced trails, and soon they would be worn as much by the wheel as by the foot.

As this new way of living spread throughout the Middle East, western Europe, and northern Africa, new social systems evolved. Large populations required more complicated governmental structures. Societies became stratified and pyramidal. A large work force kept the goods coming while a smaller group of "higher ups" stored and distributed wealth, provided services, and insured the social order. The old animism gives way to new religions modeled after the agricultural way of life with its dynamic interchange between earth and the heavens.

These new ideas and technologies arose independently (and varied) a few thousand years later in Asia. There the Neolithic innovators based their new economies on the domestication of millet and rice. A little later still in the Americas, these same techniques gave the world corn, beans, potatoes, tomatoes, chilies and squash.

A door was opened and a door was closed. There would be no turning back. Even though the ground stone axes and finely flaked stone knives of this New Stone Age would soon be replaced by tools of copper, bronze and iron -the technological innovations and societal changes created during the Neolithic would live on.

This is our inheritance. Though few of us are farmers or herders, our society still rests on that broad base laid down by the Agricultural Revolution thousands of years ago. We are richer and poorer for it. The specialization which developed from it gives us great abundance, yet separates us from the source of that abundance. Our large populations allow us to accomplish great things, yet threaten the very environment in which we live.

Everything is a trade-off. The domestication of plants and animals has meant the domestication of humans as well. Once domesticated you can never be wild again—only feral.

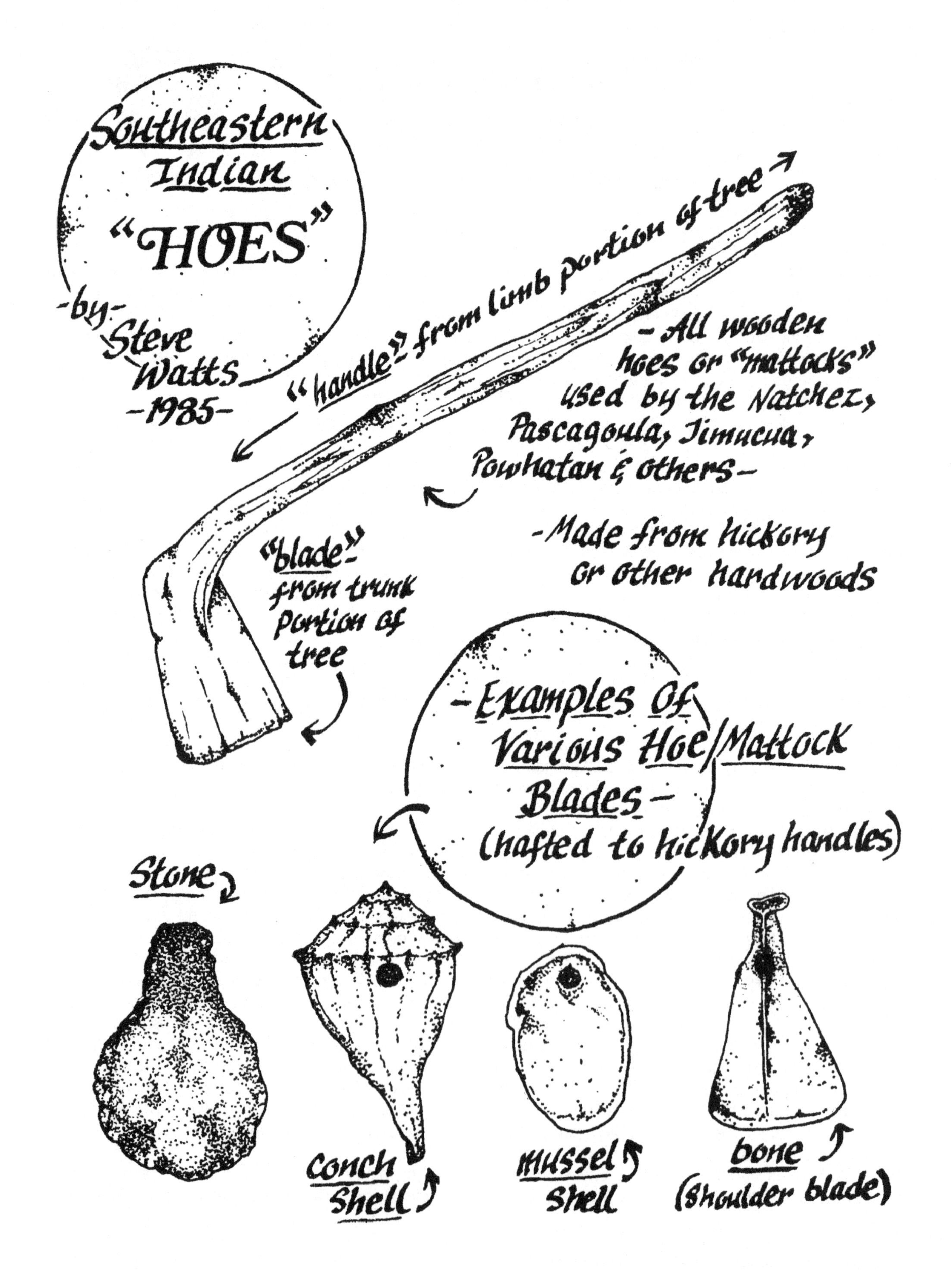
Southeastern Indian "HOES"
-by- Steve Watts -1985-
"handle" from limb portion of tree
- All wooden hoes or "mattocks" used by the Natchez, Pascagoula, Timucua, Powhatan & others -
"blade" - from trunk portion of tree
- Made from hickory or other hardwoods
- Examples Of Various Hoe/Mattock Blades -
(hafted to hickory handles)
Stone
Conch Shell
mussel Shell
bone (shoulder blade)

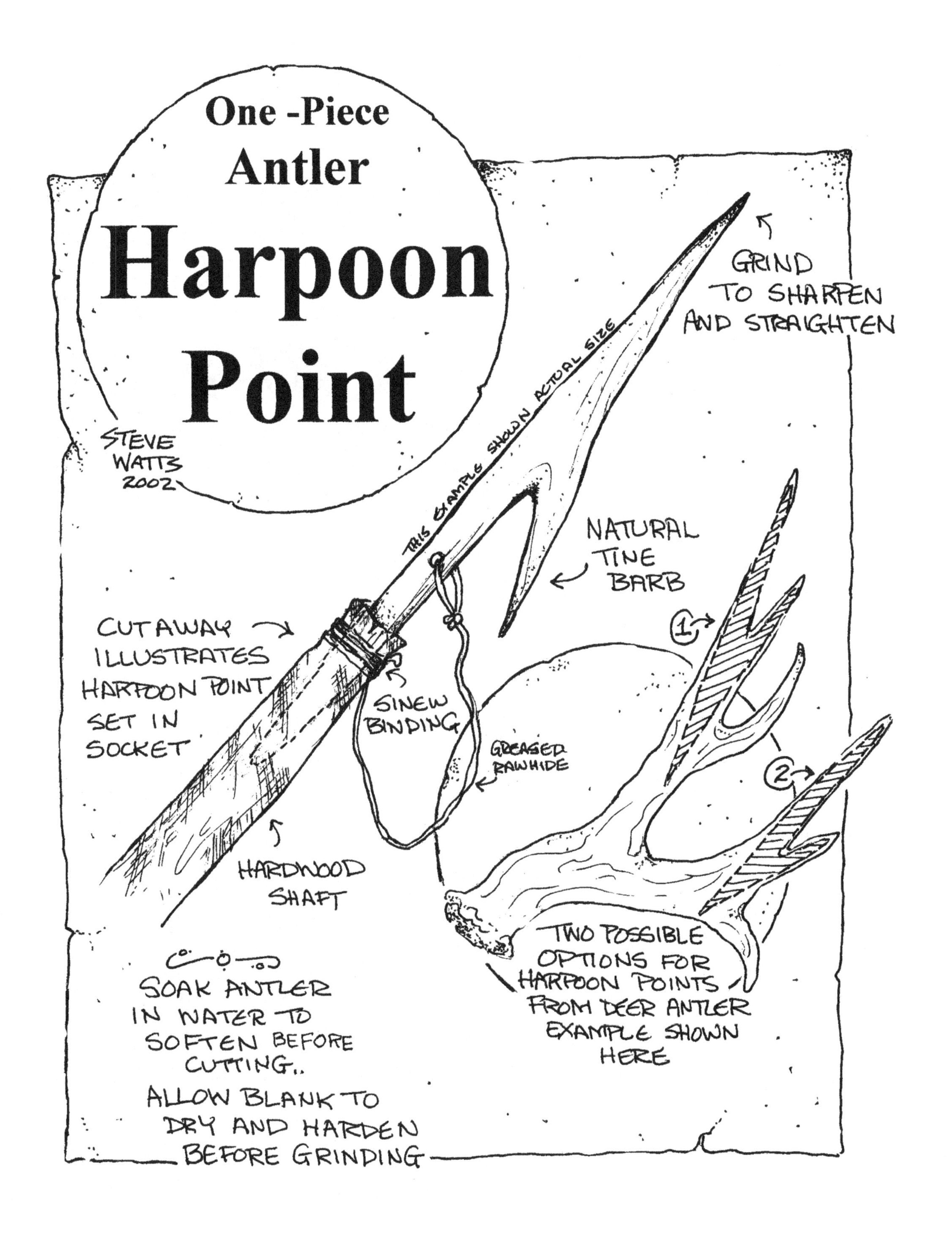
One -Piece
Antler
Harpoon
Point
STEVE
WATTS
2002
THIS EXAMPLE SHOWN ACTUAL SIZE
GRIND
TO SHARPEN
AND STRAIGHTEN
NATURAL
TINE
BARB
CUTAWAY
ILLUSTRATES
HARPOON POINT
SET IN
SOCKET
SINEW
BINDING
GREASED
RAWHIDE
1
2
HARDWOOD
SHAFT
SOAK ANTLER
IN WATER TO
SOFTEN BEFORE
CUTTING..
ALLOW BLANK TO
DRY AND HARDEN
BEFORE GRINDING
TWO POSSIBLE
OPTIONS FOR
HARPOON POINTS
FROM DEER ANTLER
EXAMPLE SHOWN
HERE

Aboriginal Uses of Shell

Tools
Hoes/Grubbers/Picks
Axes/Adzes
Chisels/Planers
Knives—Ground & Serrated
Scrapers
Hammers
Anvils
Fiber Strippers
Needles/Awls
Tweezers
Food Processer

Mike Peters

Welk-shell cup

Utensils
Bowls/Cups
Spoons
"Dishes"

Ornaments
Pendants/Gorgets
Beads
Rings/Bracelets
Ear Pins/Ear Spools
Fetishes
Overlays

Music
Trumpets
Rattles

Hunting/Fishing
Projectile Points
Fish Hooks/Lures
Net Weights
Netting Gauges
Sinkers/Plummets
Harpoon Blades

Misc
Pottery Temper
Agricultural "Lime"
Paint "Pots"

Illumination
Oil/Grease Lamps
Reflectors

Steve Watts

Shell ornaments.

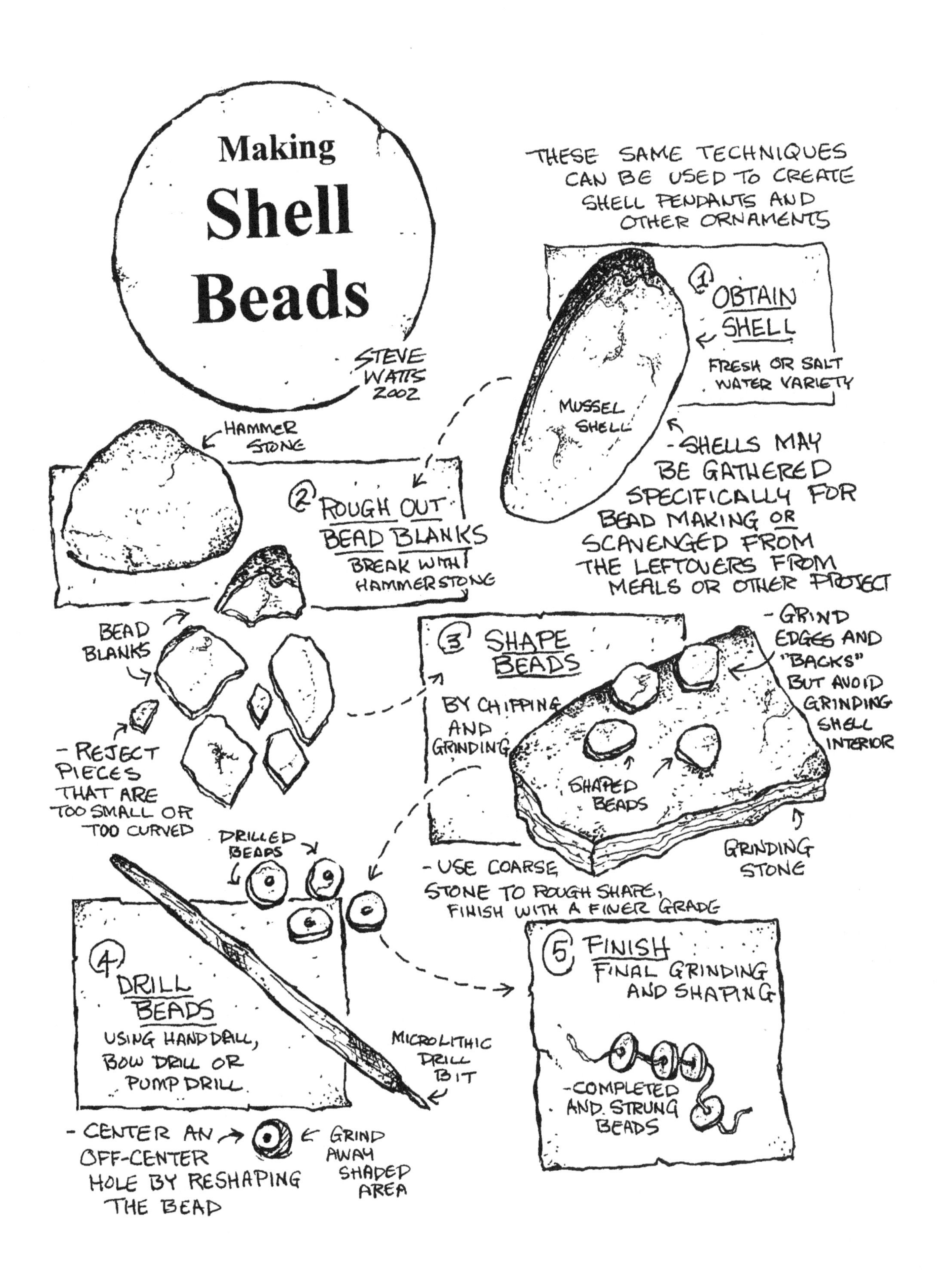
Making
Shell
Beads
STEVE
WATTS
2002
THESE SAME TECHNIQUES
CAN BE USED TO CREATE
SHELL PENDANTS AND
OTHER ORNAMENTS
① OBTAIN
SHELL
FRESH OR SALT
WATER VARIETY
MUSSEL
SHELL
- SHELLS MAY
BE GATHERED
SPECIFICALLY FOR
BEAD MAKING OR
SCAVENGED FROM
THE LEFTOVERS FROM
MEALS OR OTHER PROJECT
HAMMER
STONE
② ROUGH OUT
BEAD BLANKS
BREAK WITH
HAMMERSTONE
BEAD
BLANKS
- REJECT
PIECES
THAT ARE
TOO SMALL OR
TOO CURVED
③ SHAPE
BEADS
BY CHIPPING
AND
GRINDING
- GRIND
EDGES AND
"BACKS"
BUT AVOID
GRINDING
SHELL
INTERIOR
SHAPED
BEADS
GRINDING
STONE
- USE COARSE
STONE TO ROUGH SHAPE,
FINISH WITH A FINER GRADE
DRILLED
BEADS
④ DRILL
BEADS
USING HAND DRILL,
BOW DRILL OR
PUMP DRILL
MICROLITHIC
DRILL
BIT
- CENTER AN
OFF-CENTER
HOLE BY RESHAPING
THE BEAD
GRIND
AWAY
SHADED
AREA
⑤ FINISH
FINAL GRINDING
AND SHAPING
- COMPLETED
AND STRUNG
BEADS

3
Sheltered in Prehistory

Michael Eldredge

The peaks of the conical skin tents
of Lapps and Lakotas
The thatching of wattled and daubed
homes from Guatemala, to Africa, to
Korea . . .
The domed roofs of barks, mats and
ice arching over Iroquois, Kickapoo
and Inuit . . .
The layers of leaves shingled and
sloped to shed rains blown in from
the Pacific and Carribean . . .
And the painted ceilings—dancing
in the flickering light deep in
caves from California to the
Mediterranean . . .

All these and more have sheltered the Family of Man through millenia of dark nights and through generations of times good and bad. All these and more we see now as we look up, back, and within to that ancient architectural heritage which covers us all.

From the expedient use of an existing rock shelter for an overnight bivouac, to the scientific reconstruction of an entire Neolithic village - primitive technologists explore the wide variety of solutions to the age-old problem of protection from the elements. Aboriginal responses to the need for shelter are as different as the cultures and environments from which they come. The exercise of recreating these hearths and homes may thereby open new doors of perception into those peoples and places of the then and there, and ultimately, into we of the here and now.

Primitive house building projects may be undertaken for the sake of research, educational interpretation, sheer utility, or the pleasurable satisfaction of curiosity. All of these motives are valid in their own sphere and all require that many aspects of aboriginal technology be brought to application. Tools, techniques, use and availability of natural resources, seasonal considerations, and group/family/social structure all figure into the mix when planning, building and maintaining such reconstructions. It is an area of primitive technology which often calls for monumental effort and a drive to persevere against odds and the unknown.

The Catawba Indian Village mat-and-hide-covered house was made with stone-age tools.

Evolution of an Idea

"House reconstruction - the physical realization of one possible interpretation."
Peter Reynolds, Buster Ancient Farm Research Project, England

"They have other sorts of Cabins . . . that are covered overhead; the rest left open for the Air. These . . . serve for pleasant Banqueting-Houses in the hot Season of the Year." **John Lawson, 1701**

"Any particular reconstruction may be almost right, or totally wrong, or any degree inbetween. This applies to the reconstruction of a structure, a tool, or a process. It may be proven right or wrong to a greater or lesser extent by evidence from the past, or functionally so or not-so by experimental use. In all cases it must be constantly re-evaluated."
Steve Watts, 1988

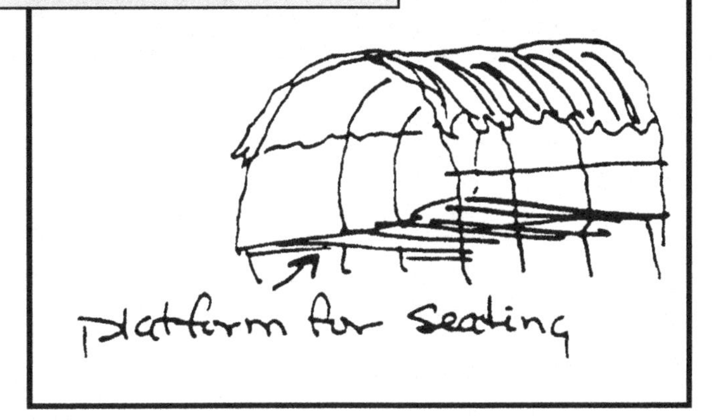

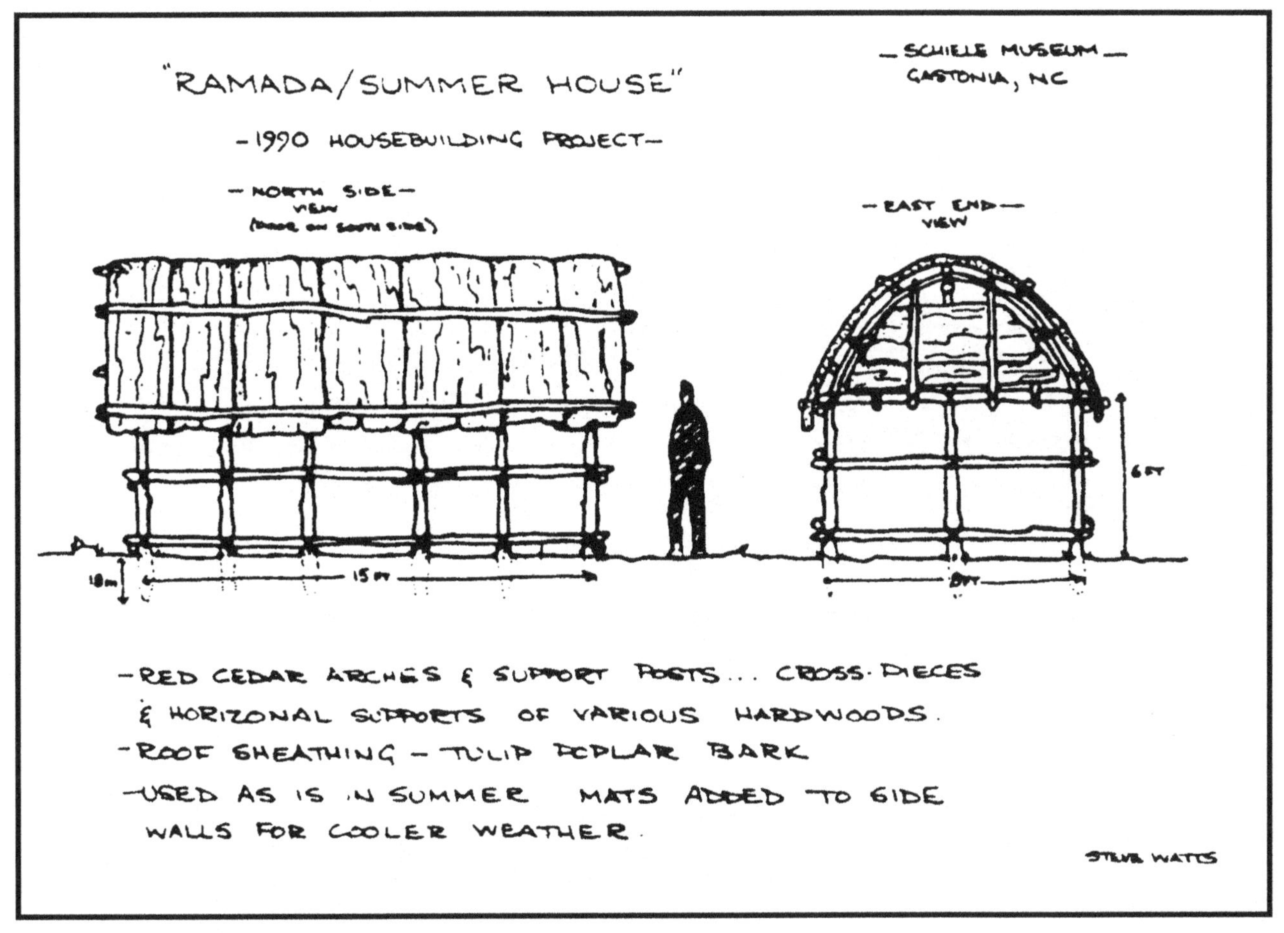

Drawings on page 57 from
The Watts Notebook, page 21, June 28, 1988.

Michael Eldredge photos

Bark-covered ramada, 1989.

Mat-Covered Wickiup
(1991)

Michael Eldredge

Cattail-Thatched Wickiup
(1998)

Steve Watts

Mat-Covered Ramada
(1991)

Michael Eldredge

Palmetto Leaf House
Pritchard's Island, S.C. (1994)

Steve Watts

The Cast Away Shelter
Punta Chueca, Sonora, Mexico (1995)

David Wescott photos

SW - 1995

Steve trains William K. Broyles, screenwriter for the Tom Hanks movie *Cast Away.*

Reconstructing a Lower Catawba River Aboriginal House: Considerations of Form and the Application of Method

Photos by Michael Eldredge, Jim Green and Steve Watts

Form

What are the options for Late Prehistoric/Early Historic house forms in the Lower Catawba River Valley? The important archaeological work now being done in this area at sites like *31GS30* in Gaston County, North Carolina may in time produce one or more sets of posthole patterns from which we may reconstruct house forms specifically, yet until that time we must look to the early historic record for clues.

Simply stated, aboriginal house forms in the eastern United States may be divided into two broad categories - *Northern* and *Southern*. *Northern* house forms are perhaps best typified by the Algonkian *wigwam*: a bent-pole structure, round or oval in plan, covered with bark and/or mats, and used by Algonkians from Maine to North Carolina. The Iroquois in New York and Pennsylvania built the *longhouse* variation of this form. *Southern* forms find their expression in the wattle-and-daub houses of the historic Creek, Cherokee, Natchez, and others from Georgia and Louisiana: round, square or rectangular floor plans formed by walls of upright posts interlaced with saplings or cane and covered over with clay. Roofs are covered with thatch or bark slabs (Swanson 1946:386-421).

To which of these forms do the early historic records point? Unfortunately, the journals of the Spanish expeditions of Juan Pardo into the area in 1566 and 1567 do not deal in any detail with the house forms encountered. It is not until 1701 and the writings of John Lawson that we get our first real picture. Lawson traveled up the Santee/Wateree/Catawba River in that year, spent time with Siouan groups living there (including the Catawba and Waxhaw), and gives us the best early historic record of housing for this area. Swanton (1946:410) calls Lawson's account *"our only good description of the Siouan . . . house used by individual families."* Lawson (1714:187) recounts:

> *These savages live in wigwams, or cabins, built of bark, which are made round like an oven, to prevent any damage by hard gales Of wind . . . . In building these fabrics, they get very long poles of pine, cedar, hickory, or any other wood that will bend; these are the thickness of the small of a man's leg, at the thickest end, which they generally strip of bark and warm well in the fire, which makes them tough and fit to bend. Afterwards they stick the thickest ends of them in the ground, about two yards asunder in a circular form, the distance they design the cabin to be (which is not always round, but sometimes oval), then they bend the tops and bring then together, and bind their ends with bark of trees that is proper for that use . . . then they brace them with other poles to make them strong; afterwards cover them all over with bark, so that they are very warm and right, and will keep firm against all the weathers that blow.*

This house form seems to be typical in Lawson's account. He makes reference to no other house form for individual family dwellings in the area. The Algonkian word *wigwam* (or *wingwam*) is already a part of his vocabulary. And, in his journal (referring to the Waxhaws) he says, *"all their Dwelling-Houses are covered with Bark"* (Lawson 1714:33). He also notes, however, a more

Debarking cedar poles with stone flakes. Meg Benko and Robert Likas.

typically *Southern* house (or building) form among the Waxhaws. His description seems to distinguish it both in form and function from the bark houses already described (Lawson 1714:33):

> *These revels carried on in a House made for that purpose . . . This Edifice resembles a large Hay-Rack, its top being pyramidal, and much bigger than their other Dwellings, and the building whereof, every one assists till it is finished. All their Dwelling-Houses are covered with Bark, but this differs very much; for it is very artificially thatched with sedge and rushes.*

So, what are we to make of Lower Catawba River Valley house forms during Lawson's time? And, do these house forms reflect those of several hundred years earlier? The answer to the first question (based on Lawson's meager but fairly detailed account) seems to point to an area in which both *Northern* and *Southern* forms existed side by side, with wigwams serving as dwelling places and round or square thatched buildings serving as special structures for civic and religious activities. Swanton (1946:413) states.

> *The eastern Siouan territory and that of thc southernmost Algonkians along the coast constitute a transition area between thc characteristically Gulf house patterns and typical Algonkian Wigwams The resemblances between the town house of the Waxhaw and corresponding structures among the nations to the west has been noted and also the use of wattle walls by some of the tribes. However, Lawson's description of the common Siouan house suggests a pattern closely like the wigwam. One distinction between southern and northern houses consists in the fact that in the former the roof and walls are usually created as distinct elements, while in the true wigwam they are not. In this transitional region, however, we shall find the two types overlapping . . .*

Date 7-3-87

Celt #	User's Initials		Type of Wood Cut R. Cedar	Hickory	Other	Time Spent Cutting (min.) Large End	Small End	Limbs	Comments
3	SMW				maple	(1½") 2'00"	1 hit 0' 03"	1'04"	
3	LTG				Maple	(1¾") 1:38	1 hit 0:02	0:53"	
3	MAB				Maple	(1½") 1:17	0:03	0:48	
3	LTG				Maple	(2") 2:39	0:12	0.21	
3	SMW				Maple	(1¾") 1:18	0:03	0:43	
3	LTG			✓		(1¾") 1:22	0:04	:14	
2	MPE				Maple	(1¼") 0:24	0:02	6:54	
2	SMW				Maple	(1") 0:43	0:03	0:29	
4	LTG			✓		(2") 1:51	0:08	0:57	
3	WHS			✓		(1½") 1:14	0:01	0:29	
3	RWL				Dog wood	2:18 (1½")	0:10	—	
3	RWL				Maple	(1½") 1:44	:26	:30	
3	MPE			✓		(2") 2:00	:06	:58	
3	MPE				Dog wood	1½" :36	:04	:08	
Totals				4	10	21:04			

The Lower Catawba River Valley area has been cited by others as "transitional" as well - placing it on the dividing line between the Middle Atlantic and the Southeast subareas of the Eastern Woodlands culture area (Willey 1966:247-248).

While it can be argued that the southernmost Piedmont Siouan groups and perhaps those in the southern Coastal Plain were somewhat acculturated to the Southeastern cultural patterns in the Late Woodland and Protohistoric periods, the degree of acculturation appears to have been no greater than that of the Carolina and Virginia Algonkians who are assigned to the Northeastern area (Phelps 1983:15-16).

Lacking further ethnographic evidence from the period, we can best assume that the typical family house form of the Catawbas in the very first

Cutting latching poles and recording data. Meg Benko, Steve Watts, and Scott Jones.

days of the eighteenth century was the Northern wigwam form.

The second question - namely, what were the sixteenth and seventeenth century forms? - is less easily answered. Were the house forms which Lawson observed representative of an old Lower Catawba River form or some recent intrusive form? Only archaeology can answer the question for sure. Yet, we can speculate based on information available to us now.

The seventeenth century accounts of Virginia Algonkian and Siouan house forms point to a Northern bent-pole structure. And, of course, the drawings of John White and the journals of Thomas Hariot from sixteenth century coastal North Carolina depict in great detail Algonkian examples of the same house forms (Callahan 1981:61-65). Archaeologically, we have evidence for such a form as well from the Chesapeake region - the Algonkian Great Neck site (Egloff and Turner 1984:36-39) and, a post hole pattern from the Mitchem site in the North Carolina Piedmont (Dickens et al. 1987:57) which suggest an oval, bent-pole structure of the typical wigwam form. More Virginia evidence points to the ancient lineage of the wigwam form. If the interpretation of the post hole pattern at the Thunderbird site in the Shenandoah Valley is correct, we have a *Paleo* wigwam example (Bombard 1986)!

Whether or not any of this has anything at all to do with pre-1701 house forms as far south as the Lower Catawba River Valley is hard to say. But, if the cultural relationships to more northern Siouans and/or Algonkians existed prehistorically, then perhaps the architectural traditions were in place as well. Could this influence from the north have occurred just prior to Lawson's time? Certainly it could have. But, it can be argued just as well that it was the Southern influence (as demonstrated by the Waxhaw/Catawba townhouse form) that was the late arrival. If we accept the premise that traditional societies are by nature conservative and exhibit a great deal of continuity, then there seems little reason to believe that this wigwam form is

Cutting rawhide lashing with flake tools. Mark Butler and Hugh Sherrill.

representative of a "new" tradition in house building. Until evidence to the contrary is presented, the bent-pole form seems to be our best educated guess.

Lastly, in consideration of form, it seems important that we explore what the Catawba people themselves believe to be their aboriginal house style. Margaret Brown (born around 1835) was in Gastonia, North Carolina in 1905 selling pottery on the street with her family. When an interviewer from the local paper asked her about Catawba traditions she offered that when she was young *"the Catawbas lived in wigwams and talked the native language"* (Rock Hill Herald 1905). Gilbert Billie Blue, present Chief of the Catawba Nation, reports that when he was a young boy, his grandfather Chief Samuel Blue taught him how to build a *"traditional Catawba house."* Live saplings were bent over, fastened together at the top, forming a circular enclosure that was then covered with canvas. Old Chief Blue told Gilbert that in the old days the covering was of bark (Gilbert Billie Blue, personal communication 1985). Without exception, all of the modern day Catawbas with whom I have talked concerning the question of house form opt for the bent-pole, bark covered option - *suk yanapis* ("house" "bark") in their language. This of course proves nothing about house forms in the distant past. Yet, it is what the Catawbas have been taught. It is a part of their tribal-history and identity, and so it is honored here.

Method

With these considerations of form in hand, the Southeastern Native American Studies Program at the Schiele Museum of Natural History in Gastonia sought to undertake a one-year/three-phase project in experiential house building. The desire was to build a bent-pole, bark covered house reconstruction using stone tools and a set of techniques which combined information from the ethnographic record of the area, historic and living methods of the wigwam-building native peoples of the Eastern United States, the important insights gained by Dr. Errett Callahan during his house building experiments at the Pamunkey Project in tidewater Virginia (Callahan 1981) in the 1970s, and the hands-on approach to Woodland-style Algonkian house building of John White of the Ancient Lifeways Institute (John White, personal communication 1985, 1987) with some insights and methods of our own gained through several years of experimentation and research.

We also sought to apply this method to the best of our ability within the framework of the high standards that have been set by two pioneers in the field of experimental archaeology: John Coles and Errett Callahan.

Coles, in his book *Experimental Archaeology* (1979), defines "the rules of the game." Referring to the "rules," Coles states that:

> *some of which must be observed for all experiments; and all of them must be observed for some experiments. The acceptance of these, or versions of them, are essential for uniformity of procedures, reliability of observations, and acceptability of results (1979:46).*

Finishing touches on Phase I.

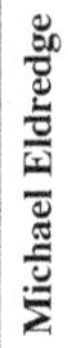

Phase I in the snow.

Briefly stated, his standards are:

> *1. The materials employed in the experiment should be those considered to be originally available to the society under examination . . . 2. The methods used in the work should be appropriate to the society and should not exceed its presumed competence . . . 3. Modern techniques and analytical studies should be carried out before, during and after the experiments . . . 4. The scale of the work must be assessed and fairly stated . . . 5. Repetition of the experiment is important to avoid a freak result . . . 6. During each experiment certain experiments will be examined in the hope of gaining answers. But improvision should also be considered . . . 7. Experimental results should not be taken as proof of ancient structural or technological detail . . . 8. A final test, at least as important as the others, can best be described as 'honesty' . . . (Coles 1979:4648).*

Likewise, Callahan has devised a set of standards based on his extensive experience in the building of more than fifty aboriginal-style houses around the world. In addition, Callahan (1985:1819, 33-43) has recently introduced a system of classification for the building of house replicas. Callahan uses the designations "Level I, Level II and Level III" to identify the levels of investment or integrity in reproductions. Level III (the highest designation) projects are defined as "authentic and scientific, the true experimental archaeology level":

> *This class of reconstruction also offers reproductions which are successful, functional units undertaken with the correct period tools, materials and procedures which are scientifically monitored. While authentic tools may not be employed for the acquisition of all materials, they are indeed used for all processing of same. Extensive data is kept and research reports, either in the form of lectures or publications, result. Ongoing studies are sometimes structured into the projects, with data monitored for years. It should not be forgotten that resolution includes not simply the building of a dwelling . . . but the monitoring and the analysis of the associated data as well as the presentation of a report. Unless the results of a test are made available so that the experiment may be repeated by others, that test was a Level II experiment and not a Level III experiment. (Callahan 1985:40).*

One additional aspect of our vision of the project was the attempt to involve the public in the construction of the house. The site chosen for the house building was the Catawba Village on the grounds of the Schiele Museum. This site ensures that it will be seen by and interpreted to thousands of school students and other visitors in the years to come. The construction took place during three weekend workshops, one in June, 1987, one in June, 1988, and the third in July, 1988. Participants in these workshops included several museum professionals, public school teachers, factory workers, machinists, an industrial engineer, a retired chef, a graphic artist, an aboriginal skills instructor and an archaeologist. None of the participants had been involved in house reconstruction prior to this time. Some had experience in the use of stone tools gained through participation in previous workshops conducted as a part of an on-going education program at the Schiele.

Phase I

The goal of Phase I of the project was to determine how much of a house frame could be completed by a small group of workers in a three-day period using only replicated tools of stone, bone and wood. The first task was the cutting of 82 trees to be used in the house frame construction. Without a doubt, the most important tools used in the experience proved to be the replicated celts. These were made of Virginia and Tennessee greenstone, hafted into hickory handles.

As the trees were cut, data was collected. Information captured included celt being used, person

Above - Phase II - Completing the frame by replacing temporary year-old jute lashings with buckskin and rawhide lashings. L-R Roger McDaniel, Scott Jones, Meg Benko, Hugh Sherrill, Arlene Meer, and Robert Likas.
Below - Sheathing going on the east face. Greg Smith, Hugh Sherrill, Tom Ogburn, Meg Benko, Michael Eldredge.

Michael Eldredge

using celt, type of tree being cut, diameter of tree at base, and time spent felling, sizing and trimming tree. Red cedar was chosen to serve as the in-the-ground support poles. This choice was based not only on Lawson's account, but on the tree's well-deserved local reputation as a species resistant to decay. Twenty-eight cedars were cut. Cedars used for support posts ranged in basal diameter from 2 to 4.5 in. Average felling time for 3 inch diameter cedar poles was 2 minutes, 45 seconds. Fifty-four smaller trees were cut to be used as horizontal reinforcement poles. This group included a variety of hardwoods - maple, dogwood, sourwood, ironwood, white oak and hickory. Average basal diameter for this group was 1.75 in. Actual chopping time spent in the felling of the combined 82 trees was 2 hours, 45 minutes, 1 second. Time data was recorded for the trimming of trees after felling, as noted above, but averages for this task seem too variable to be meaningful in and of themselves. Because the number of limbs present from tree to tree varied so greatly, the cutting time for the trimming of these trees fluctuated in one direction or another to the extreme. This may or may not have been a consideration aboriginally. But, it was noted that participants in this experiment began to consciously choose trees with fewer limbs.

After all trees were felled, the bark was removed to retard insect infestation. Several methods were used, including hand pulling, scraping/peeling with unmodified rhyolite flakes, and a "spokeshave" scraping method using split rivercane knives. Large amounts of bark were collected to be used later for tinder and cordage materials.

After two clays of work, all trees had been felled, sized and trimmed. Most had been debarked. Thc basal ends of the cedar support posts were then charred in an open fire. It has been suggested that charring might retard decay in the ground (Callahan 1981, 1985). Several support posts were left uncharred to test this theory on a limited basis in the future. After charring, the poles were scraped with a rib bone tool bringing them to a blunt taper to facilitate easy entry into prepared post holes.

Day three began with the actual assembly of the frame. Ten sets of arches were prefabricated on

Mid-Phase III - Bark sheathing in place on east face and south end.

the ground (Callahan 1981:449). These consisted of two cedar support posts bent and tied together, with a hardwood crossbeam lashed between them approximately eight feet from the basal end. These arches, which form the main support system for the frame, were then carried to the site. Two holes were created for each set of support poles using sweet gum stakes driven to a depth of 18 inches with locust and hickory mauls. These stakes were then worked back and forth in the ground and removed leaving a prepared post hole. This method seemed preferable to attempting to dig a small diameter hole to the required depth using shell, bone or stone hand-held tools. The arches were then set into these holes and worked down until seated. As the arches were put into place, a series of horizontal reinforcement poles was lashed to the arches, connecting them and adding strength to the structure laterally. At the beginning of the construction phase, an oval floor plan of approximately 10x20 feet had been laid out on the site using small sticks and stones found at hand. The actual floor dimensions measured nearer to 11x25 feet when completed.

Approximately 800 foot of commercial two-ply jute cord was used for all lashings. This was meant to serve as a substitute for milkweed or dogbane cordage, materials perhaps used aboriginally. Time and time again we have seen through various outdoor situations that the natural fiber, hand-twisted cordage is both stronger and more decay-resistant than the commercial jute. It is estimated that the making of 800+ feet of milkweed or dogbane cordage would take several hundred hours to complete. It was decided that the jute would be replaced in the final stages of construction with either rawhide binding or bark lashing as described by Lawson.

During the final three hours of the construction day the site was opened to the public so that they might observe the work in progress and interact with the participants. Eleven people had succeeded in completing Phase I within the three day period (Watts 1987:4).

First firing.

Phase II

During the fall and winter of 1987-88 five additional trees were cut, sized, trimmed and debarked. Phase II, construction of interior bench supports and frames, was also completed. This was accomplished in small bits and pieces of museum staff time and with the help of students participating in the 1987 University of North Carolina at Charlotte (IJNCC) Archaeology Field School and high school students from the "Ventures in Science and Mathematics - UNCC." Dr. Alan May, Director of the Carolina Piedmont Archaeological Project and Dr. Janet Levy of UNCC coordinated the participation of these students. The trees cut during this phase brought the total to 87. Once again data were kept and the pattern of two to three minutes required for felling appropriately sized trees continued.

Phase III

Two weekend workshops during the summer of 1988 were required to complete Phase III of the project - the covering of the house frame with bark sheathing. Twelve participants took part in the workshop. Once again the public was invited in to view the work in progress.

Celts were used to cut an additional 41 trees for added frame supports and for use as latching poles to compress the bark sheathing from the outside. Species used included red cedar, maple, dogwood and white oak. Data were recorded, and once again conformed to average times recorded in Phase I. It was our desire to keep complete tree cutting data throughout the project. These data, from three tree chopping episodes over a year's time, confirms what Callahan has proposed, namely, that wood cutting times are predictable to some extent based on past data (Callahan 1981). While no attempt is made to say that our average chopping times relate directly to times required in the distant past, we can at least make educated judgements about our own levels of investment for future projects. This brought the total number of trees cut for this project to 128.

All of the commercial jute lashings from the previous year were then replaced with rawhide or buckskin lashings. These were 1/4 to 3/8 inch wide strips cut using modified flakes of chert or rhyolite. One full raw cow hide, one raw deer hide, and two commercially tanned deer hides were used from which to cut the lashings. This is much stronger than the fiber cordage and based on our experience with a previous simulated bark house, much longer lasting.

Once the lashings were replaced, the frame was covered with bark sheathing. Tulip poplar bark was chosen because of its abundance in the area and its availability as a by-product of local lumbering. Both commercial and private lumbering operations donated the bark to the project. We traveled to the tree cutting site and peeled bark from downed trees. Aboriginal bark was perhaps removed from standing trees. Bark was removed in 8 to 14 foot lengths. Tree diameters ranged from 8 to 24 inches. This yielded slabs of bark of various widths up to 50+ inches. Most were considerably narrower. The bark peeled in June slipped from the tree more readily than that peeled in July. After the middle of July it was impossible to remove the bark in large pieces without much splitting. A May-June schedule would seem preferable to a June-July schedule of bark gathering. Celts easily scored the bark and wooden sticks were preferable to the experimental rib bone tools used for bark removal.

Bark was applied first to the side walls and lastly to the roof. Deer antler and wooden awls were used to create holes through the bark through which the lashings were passed, connecting the interior frame to the exterior latching poles. Sometimes

Jim Green

Completed Bark House Project 1987-88; workshop participants with the completed house, July, 1988.

these awls could be simply pushed through. At other times (as when going through several layers of bark at a time) they were driven with wooden mauls. The tendency of the bark to split and curl when drying was anticipated, so as much overlapping as possible was done. Several months after completion of Phase III further cracking occurred. Roof cracks were patched with left over pieces of bark. A double layer of bark on the roof would have eliminated much of the problem.

Conclusions

Based on the above applied method, it is estimated that a group of a dozen or so workers could construct a house of this size within a six to ten day period. This is, of course, in reference to the present, not the prehistoric past. Some of this uncertainty about time has to do with our lack of experience removing large amounts of bark from standing trees. That awaits further testing.

Initially, it was felt that the amount of tree chopping and processing required for this reconstruction might prove to be a monumental task. That was shown not to be the case. The stone celts, flakes, and other bone and wooden tools utilized in this project worked well and seemed more than adequate for the required tasks. The anticipated desire to substitute modern-tools for the Late Woodland-style ones we were using did not arise. In retrospect, our use of replicated tools throughout the frame building process resulted not only in the less "contaminated" final product, but a more personally satisfying one as well. Participants took great pride in their work and the "stone tools only" approach to the project.

The public response has been a positive one as well. Visitors to the site seem truly interested in the tools, research, and processes involved in the construction of such a structure. With this modest project we hope to add understanding and appreciation to that curiosity, and help to open new windows of insight into the technological past.

Further house building projects seem in order for the future, and additional work will continue on this project. Plans for the coming year include the construction of interior wall mats and some limited living experiments involving overnight occupations during the winter to experience sleeping, cooking and other activities in the structure.

References

Bombard, Carole
1986 The Flint Run Paleoindian House Reconstruction. ***Mammoth Trumpet*** *2(3):1, 56.*

Callahan. Errett H.
1981 ***Pamunkey House Building: An Experimental Study of Late Woodland Construction Technology in the Powhatan Confederacy.*** *Ph.D. Dissertation, Catholic University. University Microfilms, Ann Arbor.*
1985 ***The Cahokia Pit House: A Case Study in Reconstructive Archaeology.*** *Manuscript in possession of the author.*

Coles, John
1979 ***Experimental Archaeology.*** *Academic Press, New York.*

Dickens, Roy S., H. Trawick Ward & R. P. Stephen Davis
1987 ***The Siouan Project: Seasons I and 11. Monograph Series 1,*** *Research Laboratories of Anthropology, University of North Carolina, Chapel Hill.*

Egloff, Keith T. and E. Randolph Turner
1984 ***The Chesapeake Indians and Their Predecessors: Recent Excavations at the Great Neck.*** *Notes on Virginia 24:36-39.*

Lawson, John
1714 ***The History of Carolina.*** *North Carolina Division of Archives and History, Raleigh.*

Mathis, Mark and Jeffery J. Crow (editors)
1983 ***The Prehistory of North Carolina.*** *An Archaeological Symposium. North Carolina Division of Archives and History, Raleigh.*

Phelps, Davis S.
1983 ***Archaeology of the North Carolina Coast and Coastal Plain: Problems and Hypotheses. In The Prehistory of North Carolina.*** *An Archaeological Symposium, edited by M. Mathis and J.J. Crow, pp. 1-51. North Carolina Division of Archives and History, Raleigh.*

Rock Hill Herald
1905 *August 15, 1905. Rock Hill, South Carolina.*

Swanton, John R.
1946 ***The Indians of the Southeastern United States.*** *Bulletin 137, Smithsonian Institution, Bureau of American Ethnology, Washington D.C.*

Watts, Steven M.
1987 Experimental Housebuilding Project 87/88. ***Keeping Track,*** *Fall 1987 Schiele Museum of Natural History, Gastonia, North Carolina.*

Willey, Gordon R.
1966 ***An Introduction to American Archaeology,*** *Vol. 1. Prentice-Hall, Englewood Cliffs, New Jersey.*

Michael Eldredge

Bark House III
(1993)

Michael Eldredge

Cattail House I
(1996)

Cattail-Leaf Thatch/Mat House Construction Sequence

Aboriginal Studies Program
Schiele Museum, Gastonia, North Carolina

Phase I: Planning/Preparation

A. Research/References

Survival Arts of the Primitive Paiutes, Margaret M. Wheat, 1967
Tule Technology: Northern Paiute Uses of Marsh Resources in Western Nevada, Catherine S. Fowler, 1990
Native American Architecture, Peter Nabokov & Robert Easton, 1989
Bulletin of Primitive Technology, Vol. 1, No. 3, Spring, 1992

B. Tool Preparation

For cutting/sizing framework elements (uprights and cross members) and cutting/sizing thatch/mat ribs.

- Celts
- Handaxes
- Hafted flakes
- Hafted bifaces
- Serrated shell, slate & bone knives
- Composite sickles

For cutting yucca leaf lashings

- Unmodified flakes

For cutting cattail leaves

- Unmodified flakes
- Bifaces
- Handaxes
- Deer jaw saws

For excavation

- Stake & maul
- Digging sticks
- Antler picks

Phase II: Material Procurement

A. Harvesting saplings and limbs

For framework elements
For thatch/mat ribs

B. Harvesting yucca lashing

C. Harvesting cattail leaves

Unmodified blade-flakes (for cutting cattail and yucca leaves)

Michael Eldredge

Phase III: Frame Construction

A. Selecting site and laying out ground plan

B. Excavation of holes and erection of frame uprights

C. Lashing cross members, bracing, and shaping of framework

Phase IV: Sheathing

A. Constructing thatch/mats
B. Applying thatch/mats to framework
C. Attaching door-frame bundle

Mike Peters

Phase V: Finish Work and Optionals

A. Construction

Door
Awning
Hearth
Run-off ditch

B. Dedication

Cattail House I (1996)

Cattail House II (2001)

Steve Watts

Neolithic House (2003)
Stone Age Heritage Site - Aboriginal Studies Program
Schiele Museum, Gastonia, North Carolina.

4
By the Hearth

Our ancestors used fire to cook their food, heat their homes, give light to the darkness,
and keep the scary things away at night.
It was "tended" and "fed" - like the other precious things of life - the children and the gods.
Today, we still use fire for all the same purposes. Today, that fire most often runs through copper wires.
Though no longer the open fire of the past, it continues to feed us, light us and keep our fears at bay.
Humans and fire - still we live and travel together on a shared path.

Tried-and-True Bow-Drill Fire-Making Materials
of the North American Southeast

WOODS
(For Hearths and/or Spindles)

Willow
Box Elder
Cottonwood
Tulip Poplar
Basswood
Yucca
Red Cedar
Trumpet Vine
Cattail
River Birch
Mullein
Sycamore
Sassafras
Clemantis Vine

BOWS
Large Rib Bone
Strong Bowed Limb
(dried is best . . . not too flexible)

BOW STRINGS
Buckskin
Rawhide
Twisted Fiber Cordage
(strong . . . like dogbane, milkweed, etc.)

SOCKETS
Stone
(soapstone, slate, etc.)
Hardwood
(dogwood, locusts, oak, hickory, etc.)
Pine Knot
Bone
Antler
Shell

LUBRICATION
Facial or Scalp Oil
Ear Wax
Animal Fat
Pine Pitch

EMBER PLATES
Bark
Wood Slivers
Broad Leaves
Buckskin
Mat Fragment
Pottery Cherd

TINDER
Barics (inner,'shredded)
Red Cedar. Willow, etc.
Cattail Down
Thistle Fibers
Dried Grasses
Pine Needles
Fine Wood Shavings
Mouse & Bird Nests

CONTAINERS
Buckskin Bags
Rawhide Pouches
Bladder Bags
Bark Tubes
Gourds and Horns
(for tinder)
Woven Bark Bags
Twined Rush Bags

Bow-Drill Fire-Making Equipment

Steve Watts, 1998

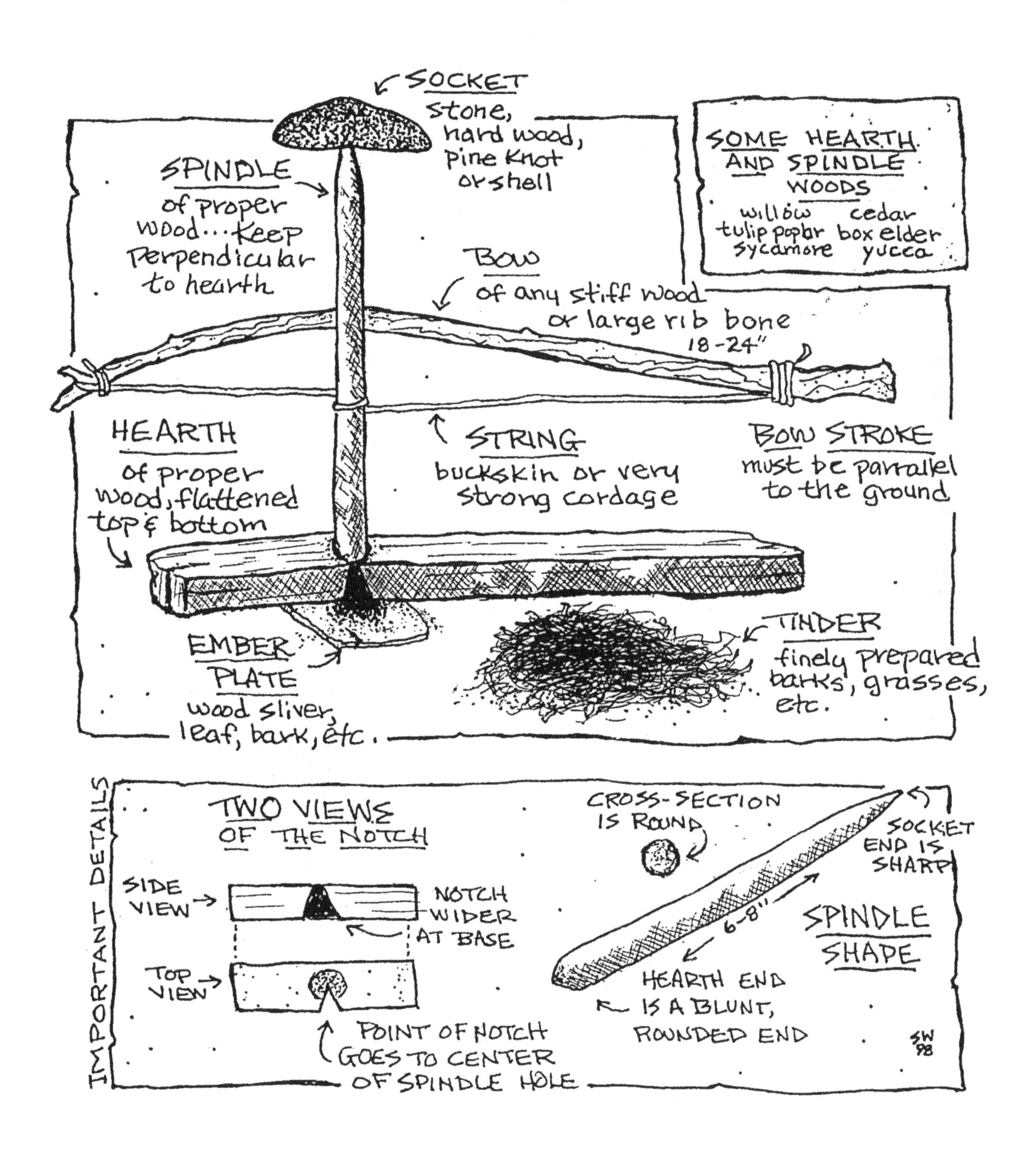

Some Documented Aboriginal Uses of Fire

Heating/Warming: *bodies and shelters, drying firewood*

Cooking/Food Preparation: *boiling, baking, roasting, frying, smoking, drying, singeing hair from animals, pre-firing/firing/ cleaning (re-firing) cooking pots*

Light: *hearth, lamps, torches, candles*

Insect Control: *repellent /fumigation*

Adhesives: *preparing hide or pitch glues*

Wood Working: *felling trees, hardening, hollowing (from bowls to canoes), socketing (as with tool hefts), decorating (pyro-engraving), sizing/cutting/shaping, loosening bark and wood fibers*

Hide Working: *smoking tanned or untanned hides*

Flintknapping: *quarrying, thermally altering stone*

Art: *altering mineral pigments, charcoal for black pigment*

Music: *lightening drum heads*

Agriculture: *clearing land/undergrowth, altering soil chemistry*

Hunting: *driving animals, killing animals, "spotlighting" fish (as with torches)*

Protection/Security: *repelling animals (hearths/torches), signaling*

Destruction/Warfare: *shelter demolition, torture*

Water: *purification (by boiling), melting snow or ice for drinking water*

Personal Care: *trimming hair, perfuming, cauterizing wounds*

Social/Ceremonial: *ritual, entertainment, incense, cremation*

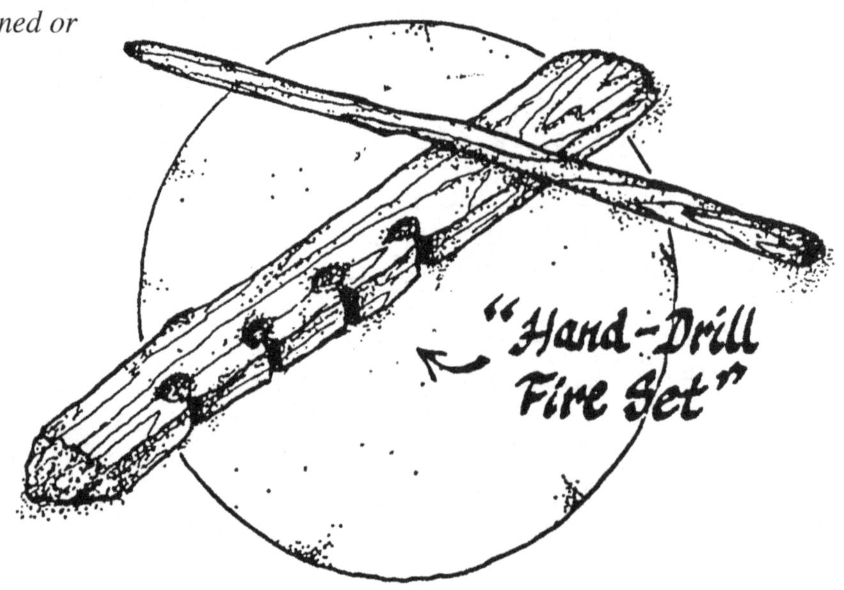

A Southeastern Indian Gourd "Rib"
(pottery shaping tool)

Primitive Pottery Class (1996)

Steve demonstrates the use of a "rib" to shape and thin the sides of a new clay pot.

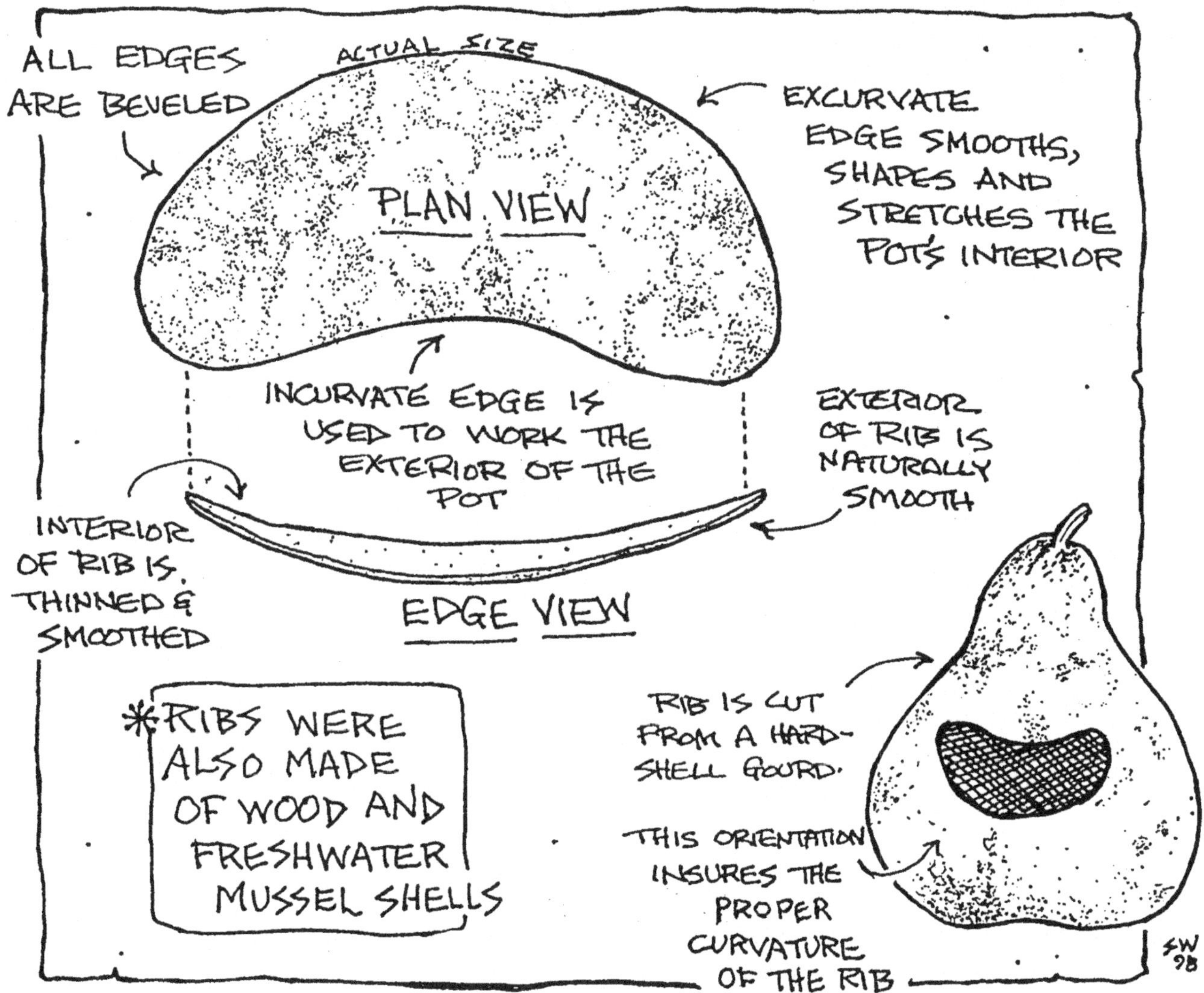

A Small-Scale, Primitive Pottery Firing Strategy

Pots cooling in the ashes of the campfire. Pots by Joe Herbert and Steve Watts. (photo: Ann Tippitt, Schiele Museum.)

Ethnographic studies done among pottery using aboriginal peoples in South America and the Philippines may serve as a window into our own prehistoric pasts. They reveal that families lost cooking vessels to breakage at an average of six to twelve pots per year. The number one reason for breakage was dogs (foraging in the pots for leftover food), followed by children (running/playing), followed by non-potter adults (carelessness) followed by adult potters (the least likely to break a pot). Yet all primitive pottery eventually fails if used long enough - if not by accident or intent - by use and thermal stress.

So it seems that a family only needed to replace a dozen or so pots over the course of a year. And, not all of these pots needed replacing at the same time (barring some catastrophic event such as fire, flood, storm or attack). This replacement strategy is quite different from the mass pottery manufacture/firing industry most familiar to us today. With the development of villages, towns and cities in the Neolithic, craft specialization becomes the norm. In this situation, potters are no longer just family members, but rather they become members of a cottage industry or a larger guild of potters providing wares to the non-potting members of the society. Thus pottery firing takes on its massive characteristics - large numbers of vessels being manufactured and fired simultaneously for sale or trade to others.

This commercial model, so commonplace to us today, is not necessarily reflected in the pottery firing traditions of small family groups in the prehistoric past or the ethnographic examples of the recent past.

Fire was a constant in the life of aboriginal

peoples. This constant is the key to understanding pottery firing in the family/non-commercial setting. The scenario: A pot is broken and needs replacing. The potter of the family manufactures a replacement piece - or two or three pieces - in anticipation of the predicted failure of an old pot in the inventory, or as "insurance" in case of failure in the firing. An extra pot or two is no great burden even to a seasonally mobile family. Old pots can be left behind if there are new ones on hand. The pot is then allowed to dry (or force dried by the fire). Remember, a fire is going all the time anyway. It is needed daily for cooking, warmth, insect control, etc. When dry, the pot is pre-fired around the hearth during the evening meal. When the pre-fired temperature is reached, the vessels are transferred to a bed of coals, the fire is built up to firing temperatures, and tended for an hour or so. As the fire dies down, precautions are made to protect the pot from the wind (banked with ashes, screened, etc). All go to bed and awake the next morning to a newly fired pot. The firing sequence is standard. It is the context which differs from the large-scale commercial approach.

Over the years, so many of my personal firing episodes have been a part of a larger firing. In a workshop situation, with a dozen or so participants, all having made multiple pieces, it's easy to wind up with 30 to 60 vessels around the pre-fire. It's usually then that I stick in a piece or two. I no longer practice such a method-preferring the quieter, more casual feeling of firing my pottery in the setting of a small camp or cooking fire. Gone are the massive flames (and the massive amounts of wood needed to produce them). Gone is the tension of multiple "products" being subjected to unevenly prefired neighbors, or a fire site so large as to be almost uncontrollable. In its place are the ashes of a small family-sized fire-easy to monitor, pleasant to tend, and leaving behind no more archaeological evidence than that produced by an overnight campsite.

Primitive Pottery Construction Sequence

SW - 1989

Obtain Clay ••••••
(creek or river bank, "bottom", deposit, etc.)

Fresh Clay - ***Process*** ***Remove large rocks and organics. Add water if needed. Wedge, knead, remove lumps.***

Dried Clay - ***Process*** ***Pound (with mortar). reconstitute, let settle, let dry if too wet. Wedge, knead, remove lumps.***

Add Temper
Sand, grit, shell, grog, etc.
1/5 - 1/3
Knead/wedge

Vessel Construction
Moulding Welding
Modeling Stretching/Thinning
Slabbing Smoothing
Coiling Malleting, etc.

Surface Treatments
Smoothing
Stamping Cob Impressing
Burnishing Punctating
Cord Marking Incising, etc.

Interior Treatments
Smoothing
Burnishing
Painting

Drying
3-10 days (depending on conditions)

Prefiring
Expedient or Formal

Firing
Using formal firing setup or expediently in cooking/heating fire.

Use
Cooking, storage, transportation, burial, processing, eating, etc.

Primitive Pottery Use Notes

• To me the pottery trip is divided into three parts:

1/3 is making it	(Good clay-well prepared, proper temper, and good construction techniques)
1/3 is firing it	(Proper prefiring, and a thorough high firing with adequate cool down time)
1/3 is using it	(proper care and use for storage, cooking, etc.)

After all, using pottery is the main purpose for making it. For a pot to be functional, it must be well made. In other obvious words - the better a pot is constructed and fired, the better it will operate as a cooking vessel.

• On a microscopic level, pottery starts to break down as soon as you start to use it. But a well made pot will last thru many cookings if taken care of and treated properly.

• Pots should be stored in a secure spot, properly supported and protected from running children, dogs, etc.

• An under-fired pot (in whole or in part) will fall apart when first used - literally dissolve. Many pots made for display only fall into this under-fired category.

• Of course shock must be avoided - putting cold water into a hot pot or vice versa.

• Some folks suggest filling the pot with water prior to use and letting it stand in the pot long enough to thoroughly saturate the walls before using. Others have suggested preheating and oiling the pot to season it-ala cast iron.

• Both of the procedures are probably useful, but my experience is that with a well made pot one simply adds "room temperature" water plus the food to be cooked to the unheated pot and sits it on the fire. Stoke up the flames and cook away.

Schiele Museum

Steve Watts cooks grits in a ceramic pot (1989). Grits, that southern delicacy, is a gift from the Native Americans of the American southeast. Wood ashes added to coarsely ground corn produces lye. Lye helps to "unlock" the nutriments in corn. This technique, along with parching, helps humans digest what is otherwise an almost undigestable seed crop.

Recycling a Broken Pot

Steve Watts, 1998

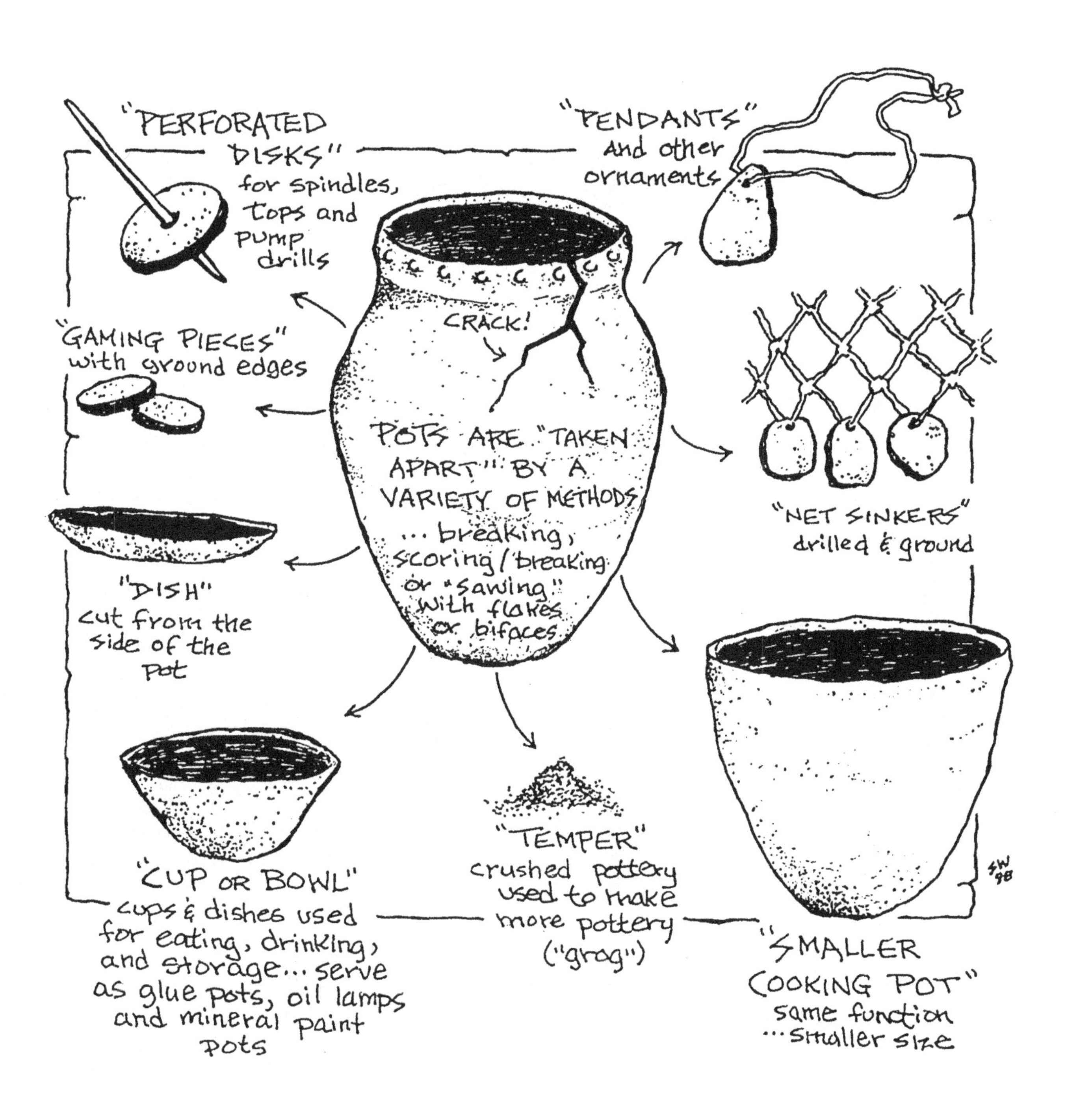

Five Salvage Strategies for Cracked Pot Rims

Steve Watts, 1998

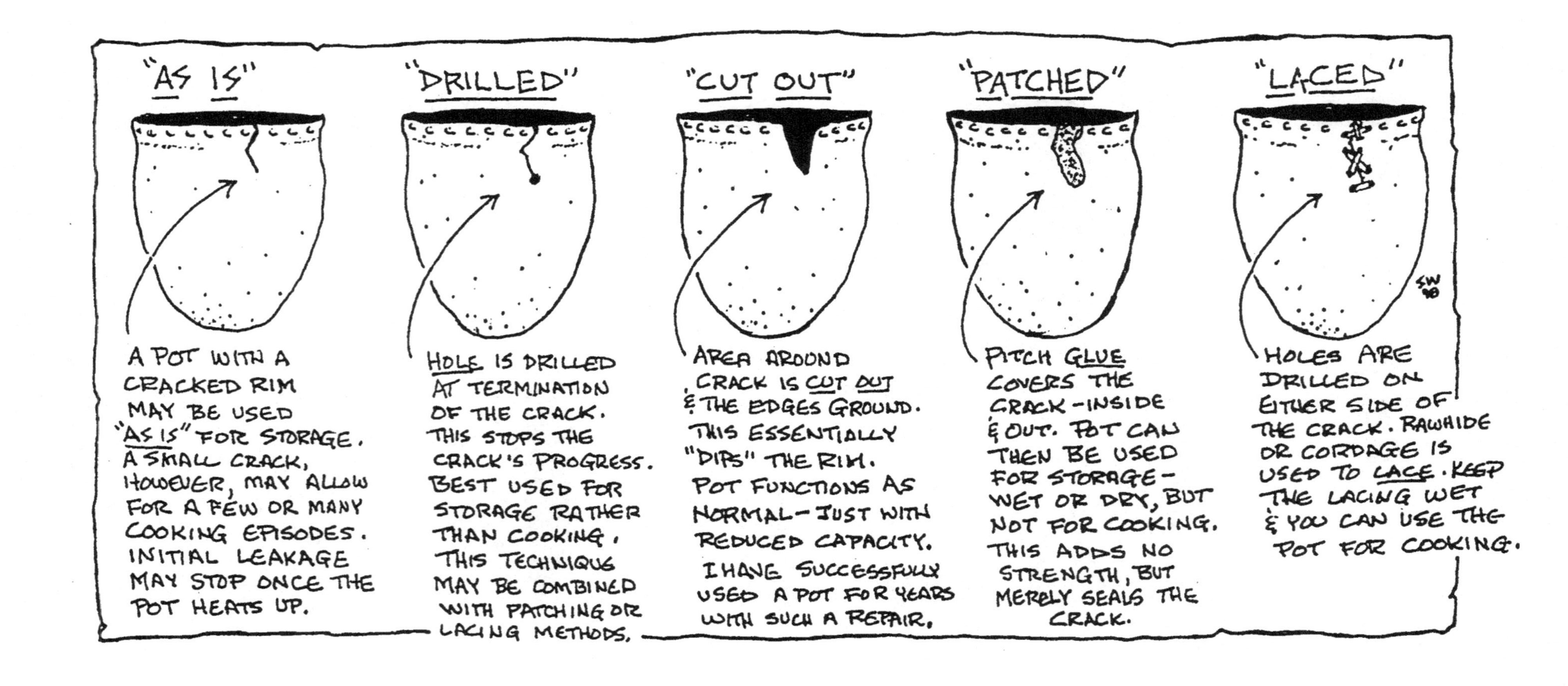

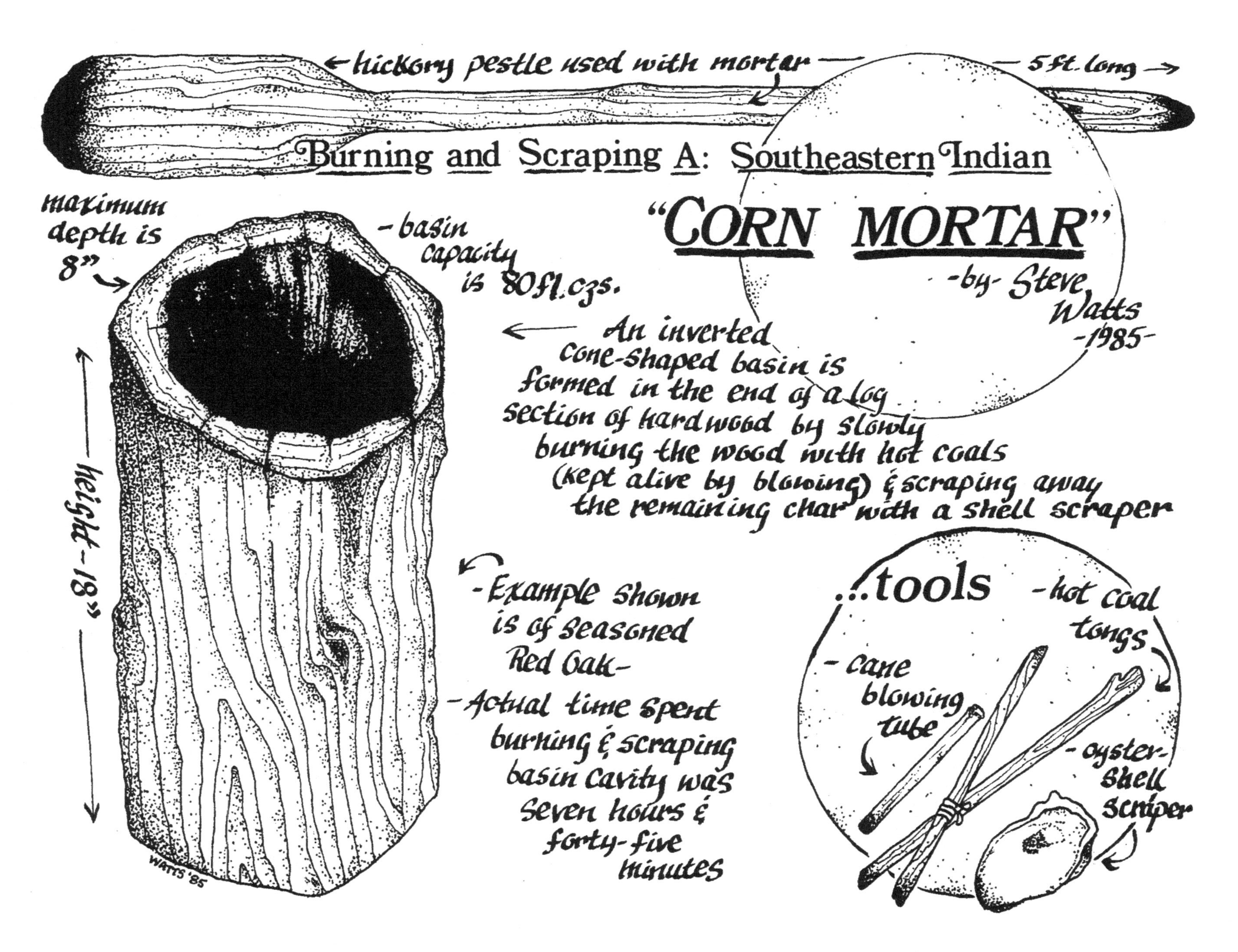

←hickory pestle used with mortar — — 5 ft. long →
Burning and Scraping A: Southeastern Indian
"CORN MORTAR"
-by- Steve Watts -1985-
maximum depth is 8"
-basin capacity is 80 fl. ozs.
An inverted cone-shaped basin is formed in the end of a log section of hardwood by slowly burning the wood with hot coals (kept alive by blowing) & scraping away the remaining char with a shell scraper
height - 18"
-Example shown is of seasoned Red Oak-
-Actual time spent burning & scraping basin cavity was seven hours & forty-five minutes
WATTS '85
...tools
-hot coal tongs
-cane blowing tube
-oyster-shell scraper

5
Woven Through Time

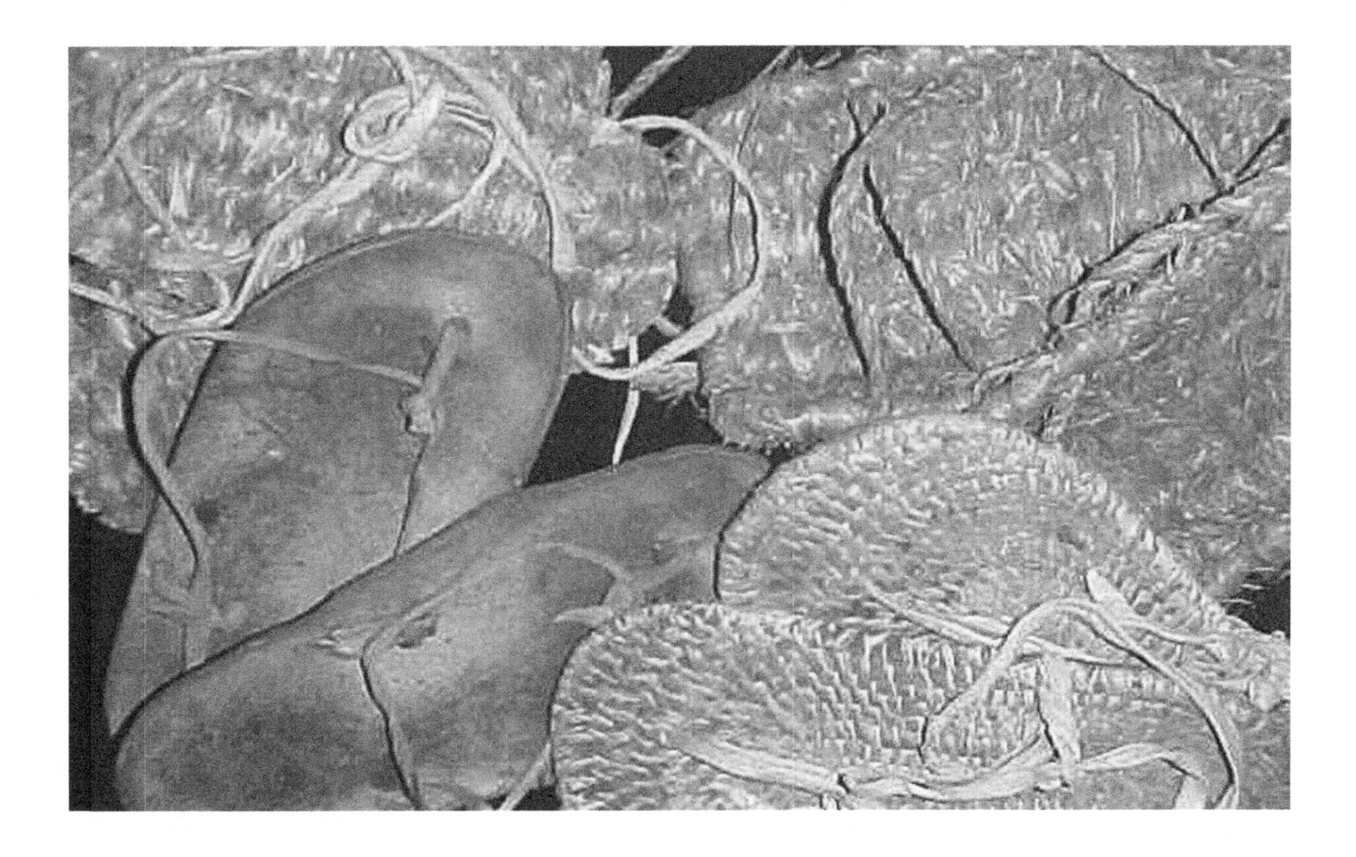

The world of our Stone Age ancestors was literally tied together. And, we are tied to that world.

In the days before nails, screws, nuts, bolts and space-age adhesives - our forebears used the fibers of plants and the hides and sinews of animals to knot, lash, splice, net, loop and weave together the necessities of life.

Tools and weapons were bound to handles . . . the frames of homes were lashed together . . . nets for fish, game and storage were tied . . . baskets were fashioned from a vast array of plant leaves, stems and roots . . . clothing was woven, sewn and laced . . . rivers and oceans were crossed in rafts and boats and propelled by woven sails . . . strings powered toys, entertained children and made the music that accompanied an incalculable number of camp and home fires throughout millennia.

Our heritage is woven through time . . .
across its collective warp we weave our individual wefts . . .
and through it we are as connected as knots on a string.

SW - 1990

Good Cordage-Making Materials from the Southern Woodlands

"If it'll make string . . . then make string"

Weeds

Dogbane (Indian Hemp)
Stinging Nettle
Milkweed
Thistle

These are abundant plants, with long and strong fibers. They are best gathered after they reach full maturity (after the first frost). Fibers can also be obtained by resting.

Inner Barks

Most Hardwood Trees
(Locust, Tulip Poplar, Mulberry, etc.)
Red Cedar
(short, but soft fibers)

These are best rested by soaking in water for two or more weeks - then shredding the layers into bundles of fibers. Often these fibers are "naturally rested" by flooding, extended contact with moisture, etc. Look for trees down in creeks or boggy areas.

Miscellaneous

Grasses (strongest when green)
Yucca Leaves (green or dry)
Spanish Moss (rested)

Deer (and other animal) Parts

Rawhide
Tanned Hide (pre-stretch hide before cording)
Sinew
Human (or other animal) Hair

There are many, many options . . . Experiment . . . Fibers are what you 're after.

Opposite Page - Fibrous Stuff
Poplar inner bark skirt (Watts) - Loom-woven sash (England) - Tule visor (Kidder) - Looped string bags (Guatemala & New Guinea) - Gourd carry-all in net bag (Watts) - Coiled poplar bark sandals (Watts) - Twined poplar bark bag (Watts) - Willow & rawhide burden basket (Watts) - Gourd canteen in buckskin net bag (Simmons) - Ceramic water jug (Watts) in knotted bag (Herrington) - Coconut water carrier in knotted palm-leaf carrier (Watts) - Weighted fish net with gourd floats (Watts)

Mike Peters

Photos 1 and 2 - Two photos of students and teachers tying knotted string bags - Hammond School, Columbia, North Carolina, 1998. Steve Watts photos.

Photo 3 - Steve taught participants to make finger-woven slings and tumplines at Rabbitstick, 1990.

Steve Watts photos

Photo 3

Suzanne Simmons

Twined, Shredded-Bark Bag Workshop

Schiele Museum in Gastonia, North Carolina, 1990.

Steve Watts photos.

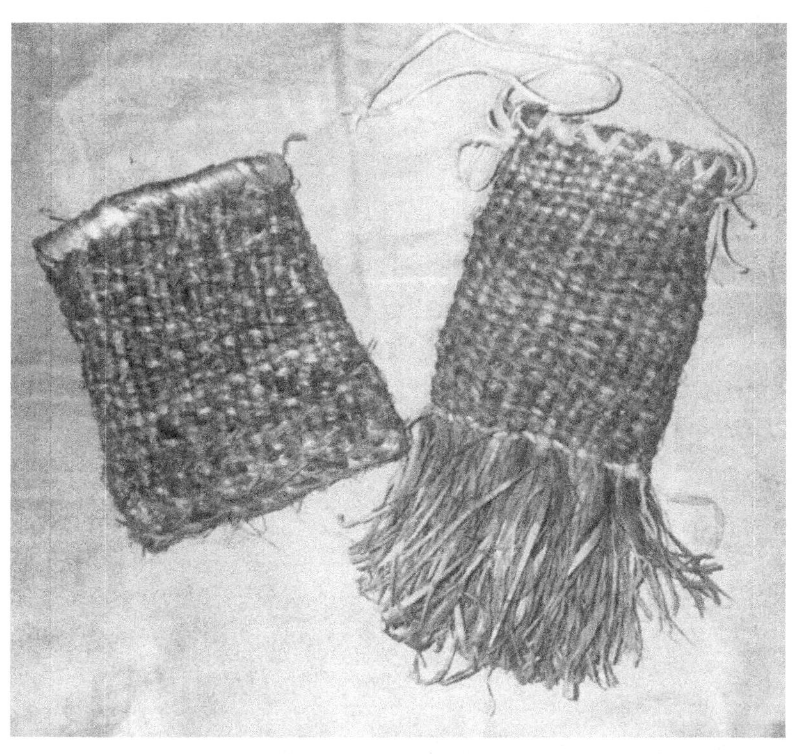

Two styles of twined-bark bags.

Testing retted tulip bark to see if it's ready to work.

Retted tulip poplar inner bark, shredded and drying.

Workshop participants display partially completed twined bags.

Yucca-Leaf Lashing

SW - 1999

"Men made this sort of tough rope by tearing in two the sword-like leaves of the bear grass or the yucca and tying the two halves together. No one could start to build a house until he had a pile of such tying material . . ."

Ruth Underhill, The Papago Indians of Arizona and Their Relatives The Pima, United States Bureau of Indian Affairs, 1941

David Wescott Photos

The construction of aboriginal-style houses may require hundreds or even thousands of feet of lashing material. Plant fiber cordage, hardwood inner barks and rawhide are all serviceable but "expensive" (read: labor intensive). Yucca leaf lashing is an economical (read: low-tech) alternative. Tremendous amounts can be produced in a very short time. It is completely adequate for small shelter projects, and when combined with other stronger materials, has a place in the most serious of house building projects.

In the reconstruction of Eastern Woodland Indian bark houses in recent years, I have used rawhide for lashing ridge poles and main structural supports, and bark strip and Yucca filamentosa leaf lashings for everything else. It's the "everything else" that eats up lashing yardage-cross members, arches, interior supports, etc. I have also come to rely on it for many other expedient uses: lashing tripods, tying up bundles, binding rafts, and even rough hafting jobs (hoes and flaked axes).

Removing the thick leaf base with a stone blade.

Wide leaves are split lengthwise to desired size.

Split leaves are tied together with a sheet-bend.

The author with nearly twenty feet of lashing materials prepared in a five minute demonstration.

Lashing can be manufactured from freshly cut leaves. This lack of processing is part of the appeal. If time allows however, leaves can be cut and allowed to "leather up". Cut yucca leaves (at least here in the southeast) can remain pliable for days or even weeks. Split the leaf lengthwise into two, three or four sections - depending on the width of the leaf and the width/strength requirements for the task at hand. Cut off the needle-like points and an inch or so at the base if it is excessively thick and fleshy. The base sections can also be pounded to loosen them up and thin them down. Tie strips together end to end (thick, thin, thick, thin, etc.) using a sheet bend or fisherman's knot. One leaf can thus produce several feet of lashing. In just a short period of time, you are lashing material rich.

Mike Peters

Workshop participants assemble Bark House IV frame using yucca strip lashing for most cross members. Corner posts, ridge pole and other crucial points were lashed with rawhide. Schiele Museum - Summer, 1998.

Dr. Fred Hoerr (Auburn, AL) lashes bent-pole roof supports with yucca strip lashings.

Cutting Cattails

Steve Watts, 1998

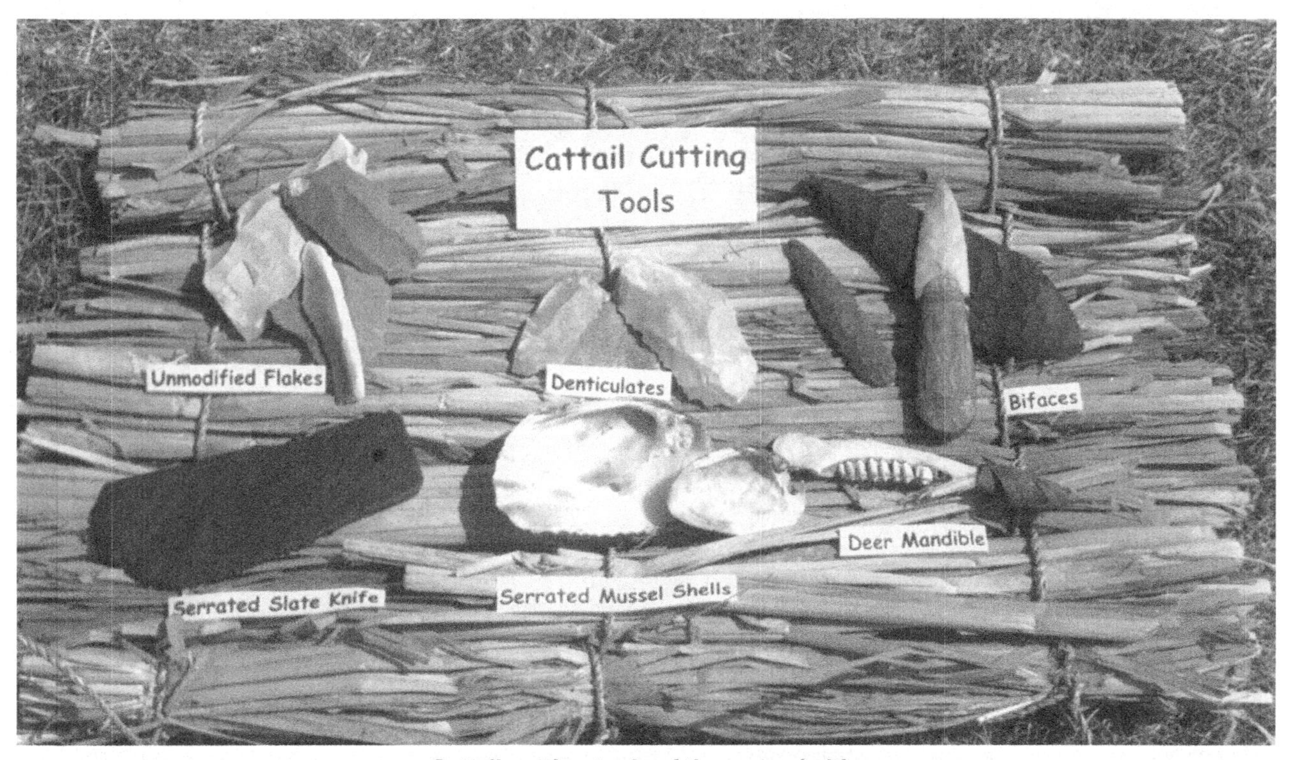

Cattail-cutting tools of the neo-primitive.

Cattail-cutting tool kit packed for the field: hair-on rawhide sheath with large bifaces and deer-jaw saw inside . . . large, serrated mussel-shell knife/saw is lashed to the outside.

Serrated mussel-shell tool . . . and results.

The deer-mandible saw in action.

This man may not appear happy but he is! Watts with a biface in a mature stand of cattails.

A big biface (or better yet, a hafted one) is an efficient cutting tool.

Jim Green photos

Detailed view of serrated edge on slate knife.

Proper, efficient cutting technique (almost too simple and natural to describe) . . . one hand holds and the other whacks away. Hundreds of plants can be gathered by a few people in a very short time.

Six to eight leaves are quickly twisted into single-ply cordage for tying up cattail bundles.

Michael Eldredge

Cattail leaves cut, bundled and dried, ready for a variety of uses (cordage, basketry, thatching, matting, etc.).

Cattail Thatched House

Schiele Museum, Gastonia, North Carolina, 1996.

All the framework was cut with stone axes and about half of the cattail leaves were cut with stone, bone or shell tools.

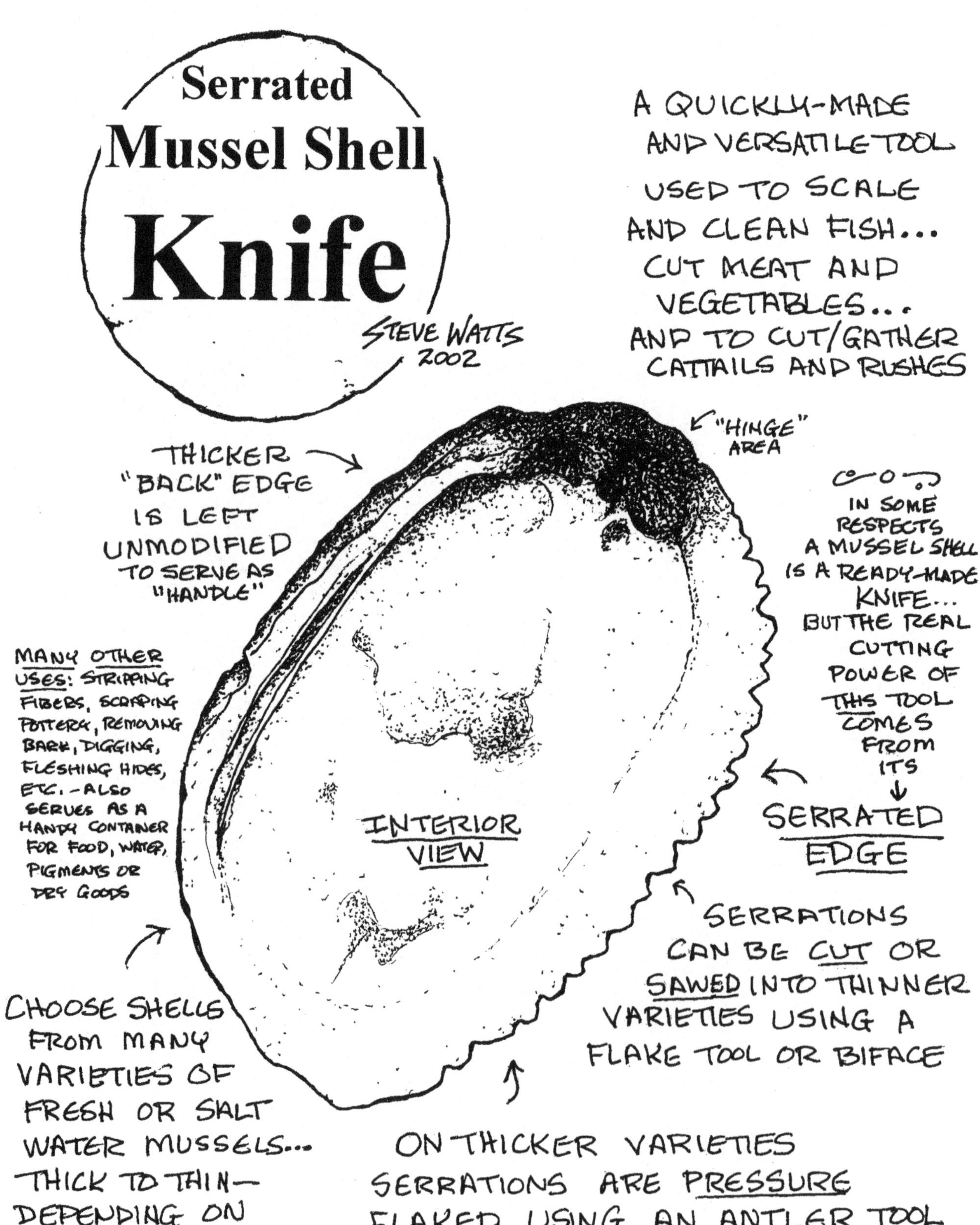
Serrated
Mussel Shell
Knife
STEVE WATTS
2002
A QUICKLY-MADE AND VERSATILE TOOL
USED TO SCALE AND CLEAN FISH... CUT MEAT AND VEGETABLES... AND TO CUT/GATHER CATTAILS AND RUSHES
"HINGE" AREA
THICKER "BACK" EDGE IS LEFT UNMODIFIED TO SERVE AS "HANDLE"
IN SOME RESPECTS A MUSSEL SHELL IS A READY-MADE KNIFE... BUT THE REAL CUTTING POWER OF THIS TOOL COMES FROM ITS
SERRATED EDGE
MANY OTHER USES: STRIPPING FIBERS, SCRAPING POTTERY, REMOVING BARK, DIGGING, FLESHING HIDES, ETC. - ALSO SERVES AS A HANDY CONTAINER FOR FOOD, WATER, PIGMENTS OR DRY GOODS
INTERIOR VIEW
SERRATIONS CAN BE CUT OR SAWED INTO THINNER VARIETIES USING A FLAKE TOOL OR BIFACE
CHOOSE SHELLS FROM MANY VARIETIES OF FRESH OR SALT WATER MUSSELS... THICK TO THIN— DEPENDING ON THE NEED AND AVAILABILITY
ON THICKER VARIETIES SERRATIONS ARE PRESSURE FLAKED USING AN ANTLER TOOL
FLAKE FROM INSIDE-OUT AFTER ABRADING THE EDGE TO ELIMINATE ANY WEAK SECTIONS

Mrs. Kompost's Extraordinary Cattail-Leaf Visor

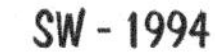

Begin with 20 leaves folded in half.

These initial weavers form the base for the brim of the visor. Note how the weavers start out being split and woven as "singles" at the outset, and alternate starting on the upper or lower leg (Figures 1 & 2). This alternating split or single weaver method is required to maintain the checkerboard pattern along the brim. Once all ten weavers are put into place as singles, each weaver (with its two halves) may now be used as a single unit or double weaver for the remainder of the checkerboard pattern (Fiure 3).

Figure 1. Start corner like this.

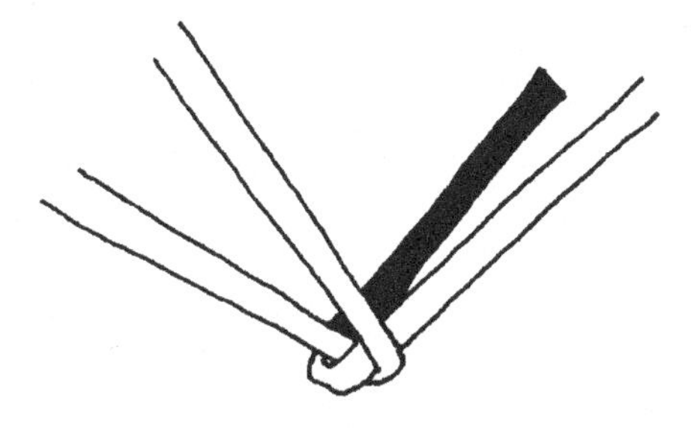

Figure 2. Initial setup - every other weaver is a single both ways.

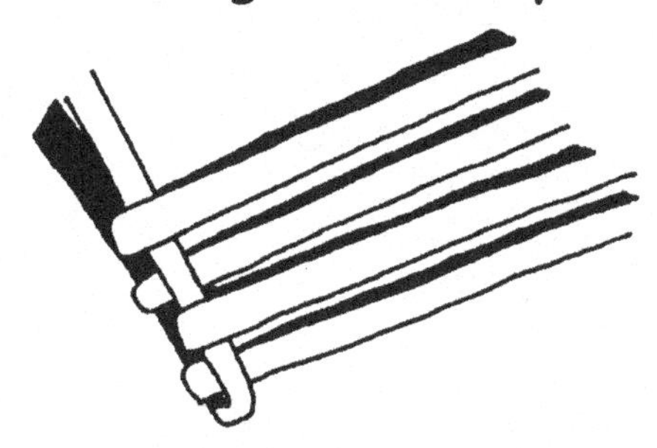

Turning the inside weaver back creates a 45 degree fold in the weaver. Weave over and under with the double weaver until you reach the brim (Figre 4). Bend the weaver around the brim and weave back. Pick up a new double weaver and begin weaving back toward the brim with both weavers until the original one runs out. Continue until they're all used up (Figure 5).

3. Checker-weave 10 weavers in each direction (using both "halves).

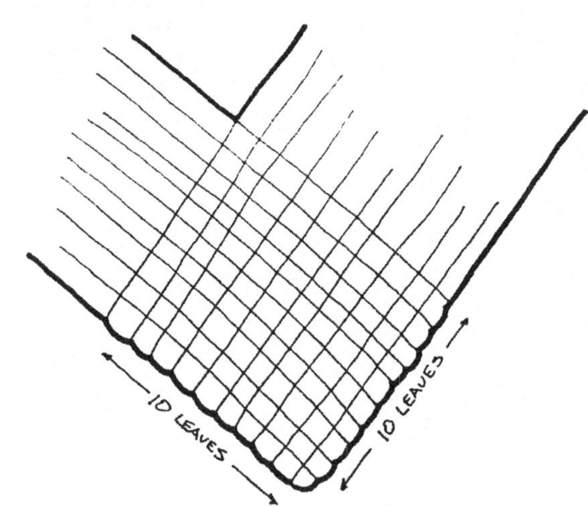

4. Fold inside double-weaver back, weaving over and under to front and back. Pick up a new weaver each trip back.

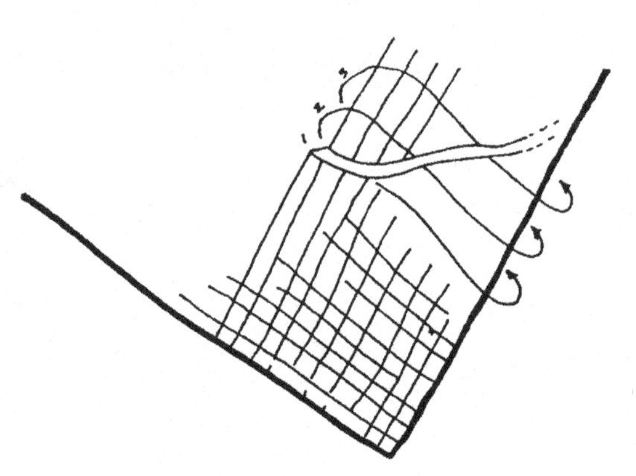

5. Continue this reduction to the ends and tie.

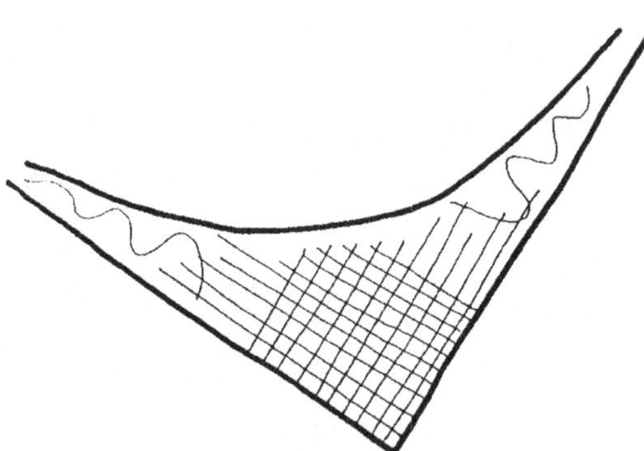

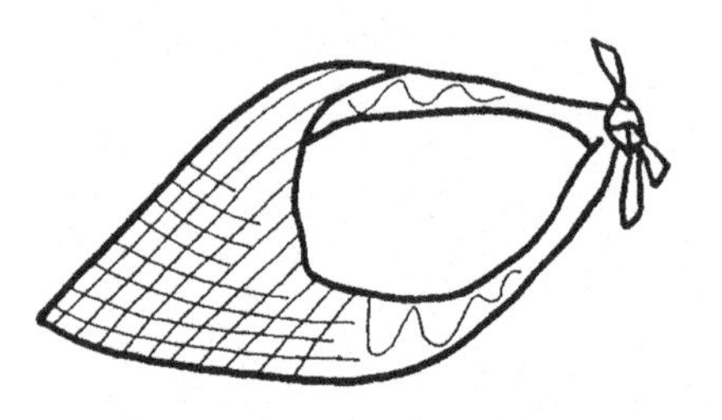

David Wescott photos

Tie the ends together, tattoo your belly and play the flute.

Netting Notes

SW - 1992

***net**- n [ME nett, fr. OK; akin to OHG nezzi net, L nodus knot] 1. a. an open-meshed fabric twisted, knotted, or woven together at regular intervals b. something made of net as (1): a device for catching fish, birds, mammals or insects.*

No one knows when, where and how our prehistoric relatives first brought their fiber skills together to form the Ancestral Net. Perhaps it was a child's string figure gone a wry . . . or the sartorial pause in which order was discovered in the chaos of tangled cordage on the shelter floor . . . or the creative combination of knots necessary to secure the previous bundles of food, medicine and tools for the treacherous crossing of a river approaching flood stage . . . or the attempt to recreate the symmetry of the orb web weaving spiders' traps hung by the water's edge highlighted by the dew, sunlight or an early frost.

Net tying, like all traditional skills, is best learned firsthand.

Yet, sometime, somehow-in all places where our human antecedents dwelled - patterns expressed themselves with fingers, shuttles and string . . . and, the Net became a part of our common technological heritage.

It has brought food to our hearths, born our burdens, bound our hair and when stretched between trees and house posts lulled us to sleep and dreams. The rhythm of mesh upon mesh survives - a symbol of our connectedness - "networked" . . . we are joined.

Although loose weaving and string looping methods are sometimes referred to as "netting" (generically as in Webster) what we are focused on here (more specifically) is a technique most commonly labeled "knotted netting". These true nets are created by the repeated tying of knots in a measured pattern resulting in a series of square or diamond shaped spaces called "meshes". In this respect nets are "tied" - not woven.

Knotted netting can be accomplished by freehand techniques alone, without the use of specialized tools (See the next article in this issue). The first nets were most likely constructed in this way. But, at some point, net makers throughout the world developed two simple devices designed to control the string delivery and the mesh size and thereby increase the speed and uniformity of their work. These tools were and are - the netting needle and the mesh stick.

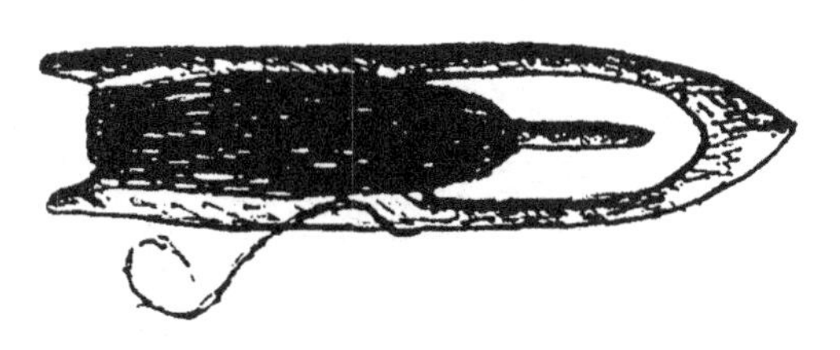

Mesh- and Tool-Size Considerations

The size of net's mesh is determined by the net's use. In fishing this is related to both the size of the fish and net type (dip, trap, gill, drag, etc.). Mammal and bird nets (as in Great Basin and Australian Aborigine examples) exhibit mesh size appropriate to specific species. Burden nets (bags, gear slings, etc.) have meshes related to the size and weight of the anticipated articles to be contained. And, so on.

A mesh stick's width reflects the length of one of the four sides of the mesh it produces. Is it too obvious to say that the mesh stick determines the size of the finished mesh, and/or the size of the mesh is determined by the mesh stick width? Maybe so, but I said it anyway.

A netting needle's width should be narrower than the mesh stick being used.

The String

The most time consuming aspect of net making in the aboriginal style is not the net tying (which goes steadily and smoothly once mastered), but rather the making of the string itself. Materials must be gathered, processed and then spun or laid into thread or cordage of the correct dimensions - in adequate quantity for the size and style of net desired. Several yards to several miles may be required (from a small bag to a gill net which spans the river's width). A net maker working on a major project may pass the work of many others through

NETTING NEEDLES

Netting needles (also called "shuttles" and "bobbins") come in both "open" and "closed" styles. Variations in design and ornamentation occur, yet remarkably similar models are found worldwide. This has led many to present complicated and convoluted diffusion scenarios designed to explain this uniformity. But, finding common solutions to common problems seems to be a more likely and straightforward answer.

The needle's purpose is to transport stored (yet easily released) lengths of cordage throughout the knotting series smoothly, with speed and control. Well made needles therefore tend to be strong, yet light in weight and in possession of a certain undefinable "grace" which allows them to turn, slide, glide (or swim?) through the tight spaces they must. Hardwoods, bone, antler, horn and ivory are the materials of choice when making netting needles. These media allow the craftsman to create thin, springy tools capable of taking a smooth finish. A fine polish develops with use, further eliminating snag and drag problems. The patina of a well worn needle attests to the net maker's skills and commitment.

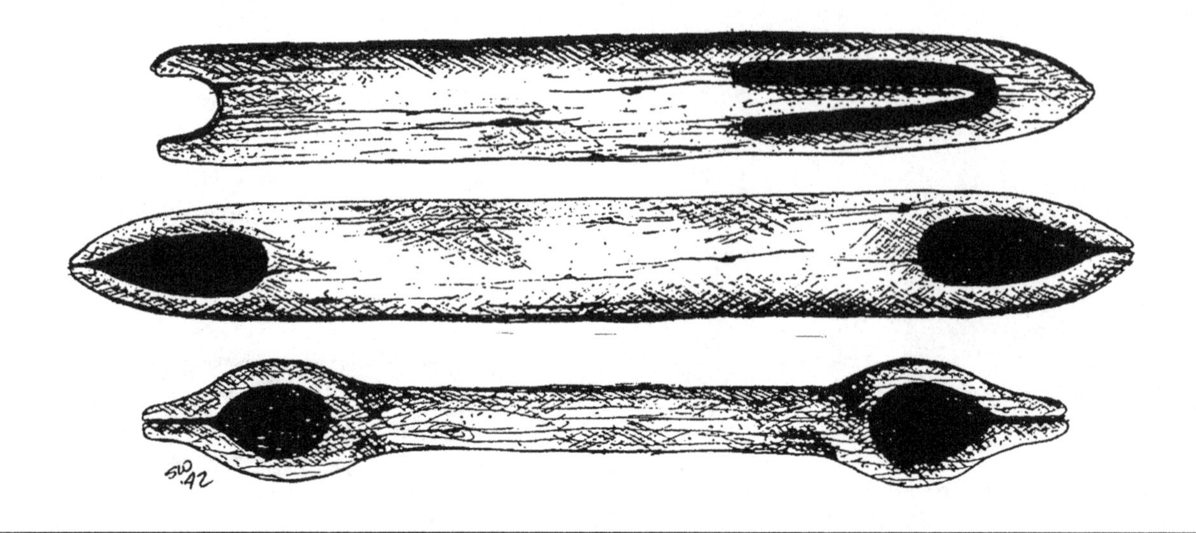

his fingers - the needles loaded with the efforts of an entire community.

Rawhide, sinew, flax, dogbane, cedar, milkweed, cotton, wool . . . the list goes on. Throughout man's history nets have probably been tied from almost every fiber capable of being made into string. There are cultural preferences, of course. The Paiutes insist on dogbane for their rabbit nets, while Northwest Coast peoples look to stinging nettle fibers for their large deep-water nets.

Once again the importance of string becomes paramount when considering the aboriginal lifestyle. If a net means food, then indeed the string is the "thread of life" itself.

Overhands, figure eights, square knots and others are often found in traditionally tied nets. But, it is the sheet bend (also called the "mesh knot") that is pandemically the net maker's knot of choice.

An excellent knot for joining two lengths of rope, the sheet bend serves in netting to link the meshes. When properly tied it will not flip or slip as will a square knot, and it is better suited to use with a mesh stick than are overhands or figure eights.

What may seem difficult at first, soon becomes a familiar task. With each tying of the sheet bend the pattern is reinforced.

The Knot

MESH STICKS

Mesh sticks (also called "gauges" and "sizers") are used to control the distance between knots. This insures that the mesh size meets the requirements for the net's function (not too small or too large). It also results in a finished product which exhibits symmetry. The net makers familiarity with his variously sized mesh sticks allows him to predict the amount of cordage and the number of meshes required to produce a net of given size for a given purpose.

The mesh stick's width and thickness determine the mesh size. Length is a matter of personal choice. Some traditional net makers prefer a stick only long enough to sit in the single mesh being tied. Others opt for a longer tool which rests in several previously formed meshes at once.

Smoothness of finish is important here as well; so hardwood, bone, horn, antler and ivory once again prove to be the chosen materials for mesh stick production.

Flat, oval, lenticular and teardrop cross sections have all been observed in aboriginal models. This may reflect personal or cultural preferences. Some mesh sticks are simplicity itself, while others (the Inuit types come to mind) exhibit various sized sections, handles and awl or marlin spike type points for knot separation. While some veteran net makers can, by their experience, tie a very uniform net using fingers and eyesight alone to gauge mesh size, a mesh stick is used by most and could be considered a must for the novice.

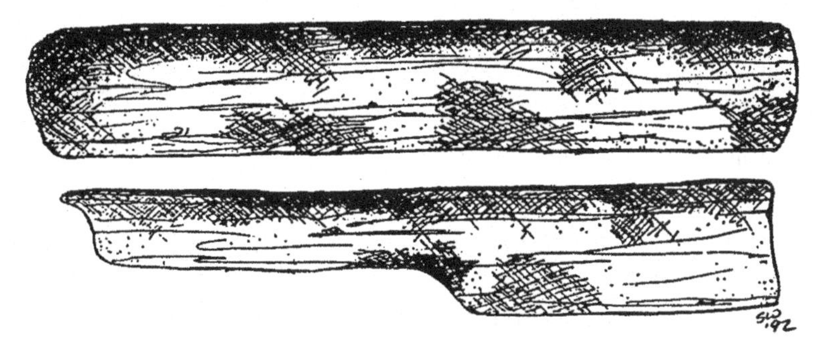

Two styles and sizes of netting needles.

Net tying, like all traditional skills, is best learned firsthand.

These are "netting notes" - not step-by-step instructions. Net tying, like all traditional skills, is best learned firsthand.

My thanks goes to John White for teaching me and to Pegg Mathewson for inspiring me They are my connections to the ancient world of net tying - the most recent knots in a series of meshes reaching back . . . back to the first net and beyond.

The Knot

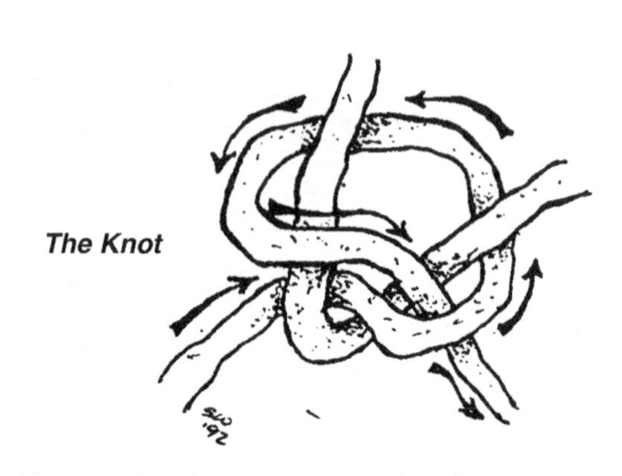

A Rawhide-and-Willow Burden Basket

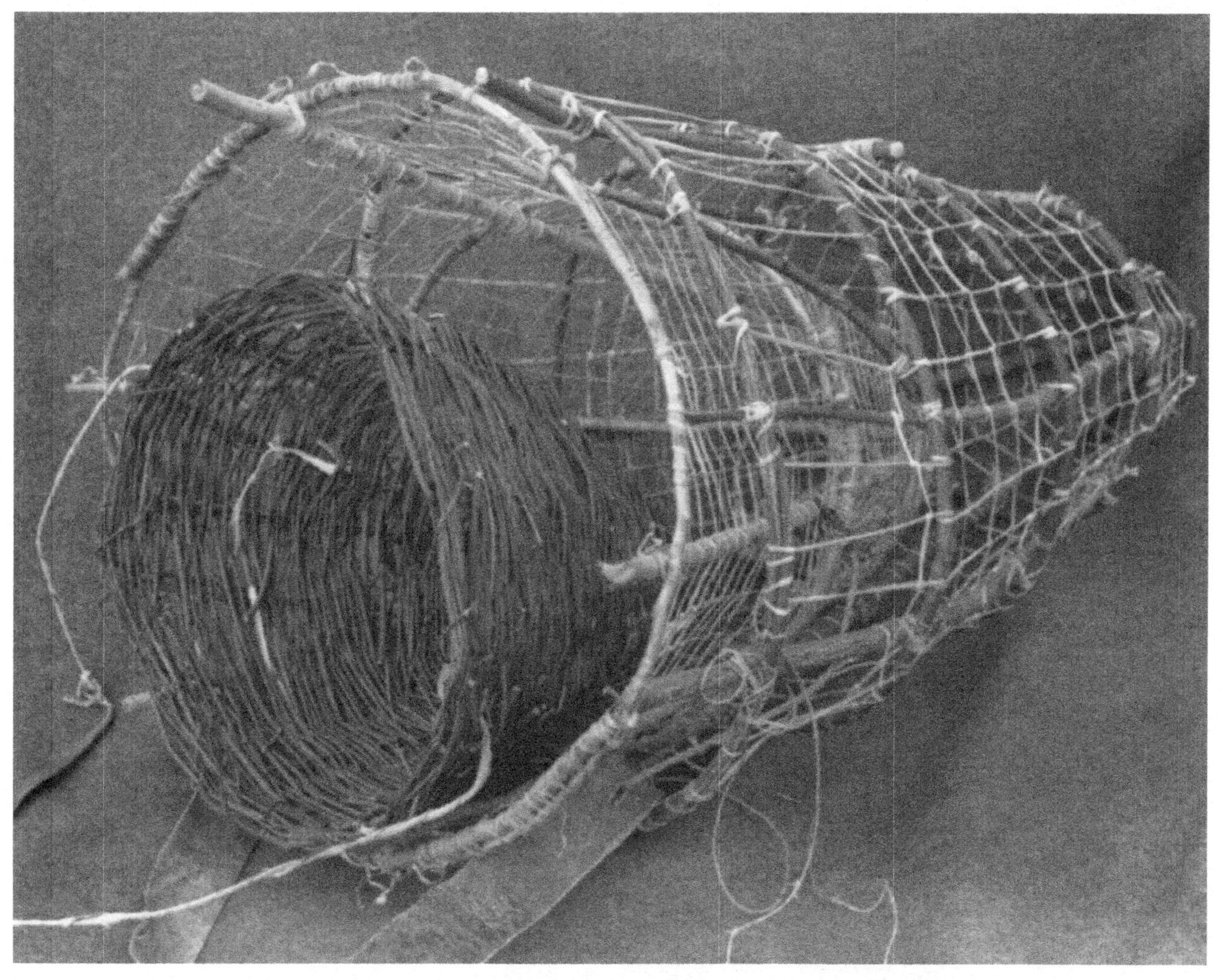

Three conical burden baskets. Left to right: willow (Starwalker Watts), willow/rawhide (Geri McPherson), willow/rawhide (Suzanne Simmons).

For more than ninety-five percent of our history, our ancestors traveled afoot or afloat. They peopled six continents long before the Neolithic Revolution introduced domesticated beasts of burden - a mere ten thousand years ago or less. Long before the wheel, these ancient travelers traversed the globe from burning deserts, to high mountain passes, to unknown seas. And somewhere in the distant past, the burden basket was born.

Conical-shaped burden baskets are found in use among aboriginal peoples throughout the world. Their shape allows one to carry heavy loads up high (much in the manner of the modern pack frame). The strength of the cone design allows them to be constructed of lightweight materials, resulting in a somewhat flexible vehicle capable of containing items of many different shapes and weights.

Conical burden baskets may be woven from a wide variety of materials using varied techniques. They may be coiled, plaited, twined, or wicker-woven, depending on the tradition of a particular time and place. The model presented here is based on a combination of ethnographic examples from Africa, Mexico, the Andaman Islands, the North

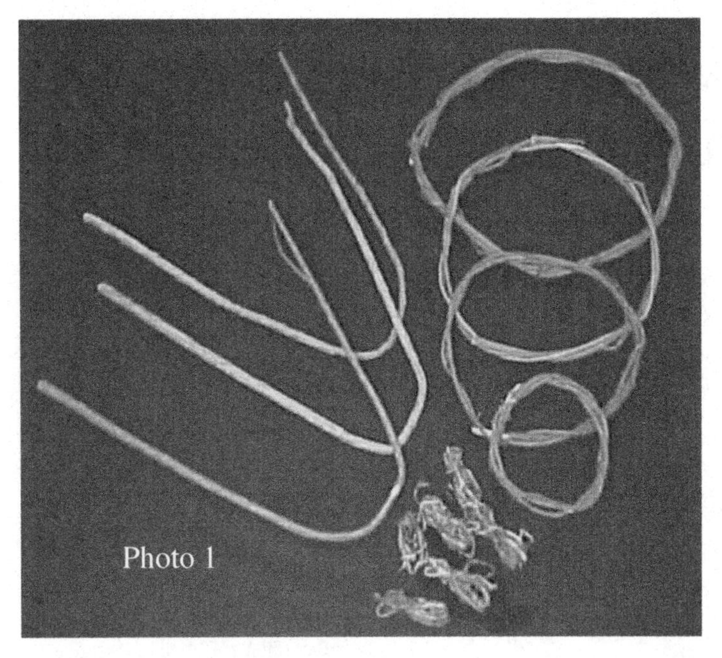

American Southwest, the Great Basin and a field tested gift specimen made by Geri McPherson in the early 1990's. It combines a rigid wooden framework of lightweight willow with a rawhide webbing constructed by a method that Mason labeled "wrapped work" (Otis Tufton Mason, *American Indian Basketry*, 1904) According to Mason, "wrapped basketry consists of flexible or rigid warp and flexible weft". In the model herein presented, we have both flexible (rawhide) and rigid (willow) warps wrapped with a flexible (rawhide) weft.

This design creates a strong yet lightweight pack for the trail. Fitted with shoulder or forehead tumplines, these baskets have been put to the test during applied primitive skills courses and a variety of field conditions - from gathering firewood, to hauling food, supplies and camping gear.

Photo 1: Components — Ready for Assembly.

Left: Three willow vertical supports (each about 4 1/2 ft. long in this example) - bent and dried in a "v"-to-"u" shape.

Right: Four willow hoops - in graduated sizes.

Center: Bundles of deer rawhide lacing - cut 1/2" wide, soaked and stretched out.

(In a Mohave example described by Mason, agave cordage was used instead of rawhide.

The modern practicing primitive might substitute all manner of cordage materials in place of the rawhide.)

Wooden components can be cut and dried previous to assembly, or cut green and used on the spot. If used green, your basket will loosen up slightly in a day or two, but it matters little. The framework is totally interlocked by the rawhide lacing.

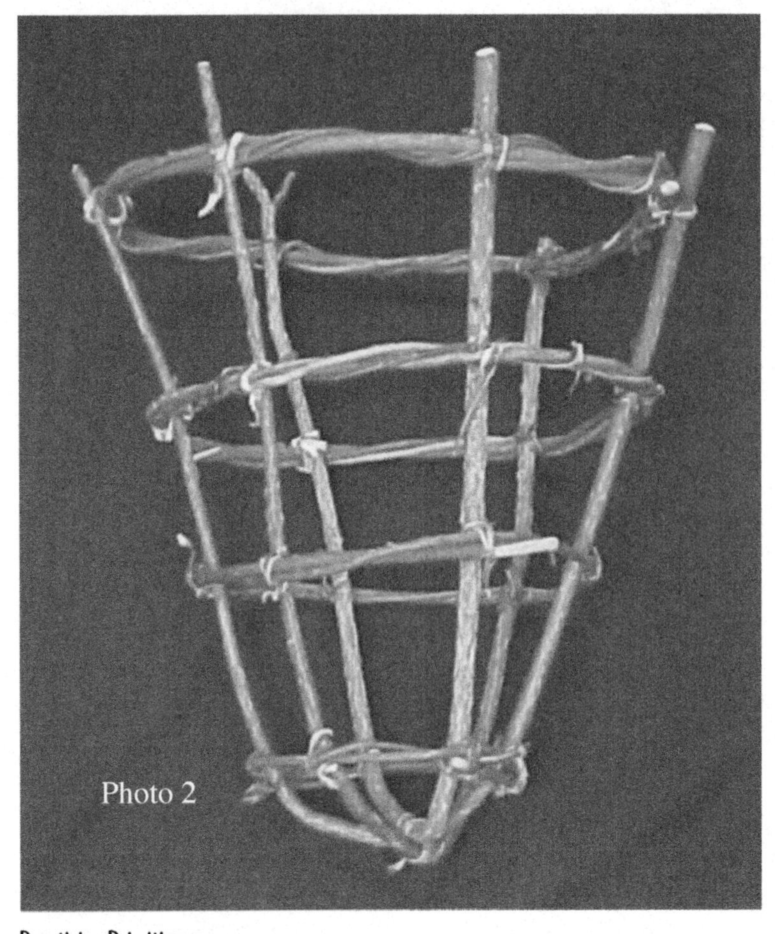

Photo 2: Frame Construction

The three vertical supports are lashed together at their centers in the bends. This creates six vertical ribs. Attach the largest (top) hoop first, spreading the ribs evenly as you go. Lash the other hoops in place using rawhide lacing and square lashings.

The ribs can be lashed to either the inside or outside of the hoops. Placing them inside increases the basket's strength.

Photo 3: Rawhide Webbing (the warp)

Tie on rawhide lacing to the bottom hoop - close to a rib. Move up to the next hoop and wrap around a full 360 degree turn. Keeping the rawhide taught, move from hoop to hoop, wrapping as you go. When you reach the top hoop, spiral the lacing around the hoop the distance you want your mesh width to be. Now move downward hoop to hoop- wrapping as you go (see detail-Photo 6).

You continue in this manner, up and down around the framework until you have completed the vertical (warp) portion of your webbing. When a length of lacing runs out, you can tie off to a hoop and begin with anew piece at that point. Or, you can simply tie a new lace length on to the old with

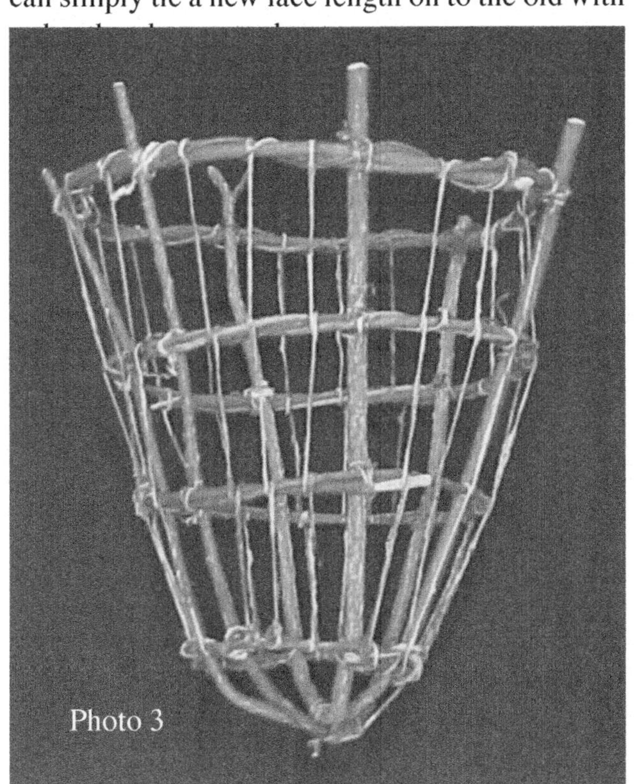
Photo 3

Photos By Michael Eldredge

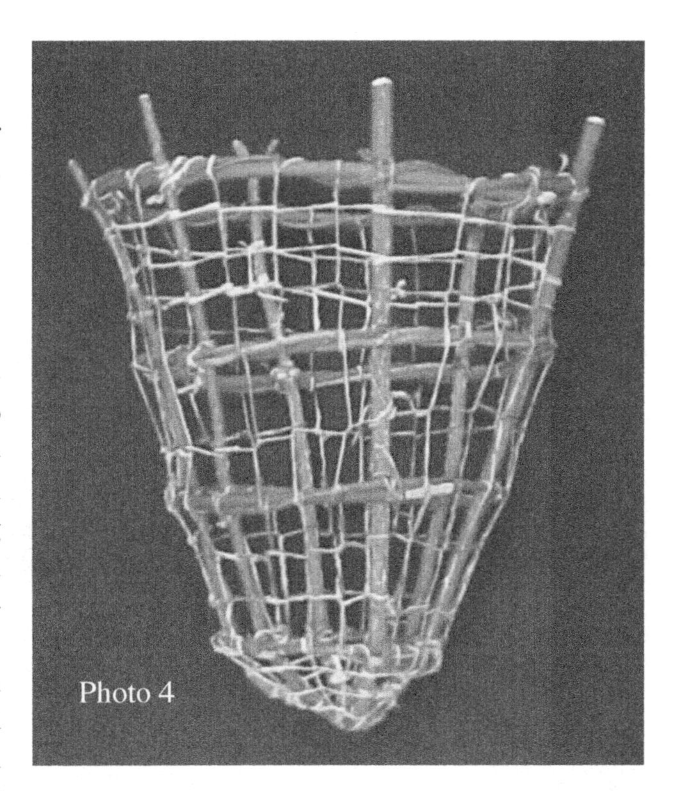
Photo 4

Photo 4: Rawhide Webbing (the weft)

Beginning a few inches from the top, tie on rawhide lacing to a vertical rib. Work your way around and down the basket, wrapping around the vertical rawhide warp elements and the vertical

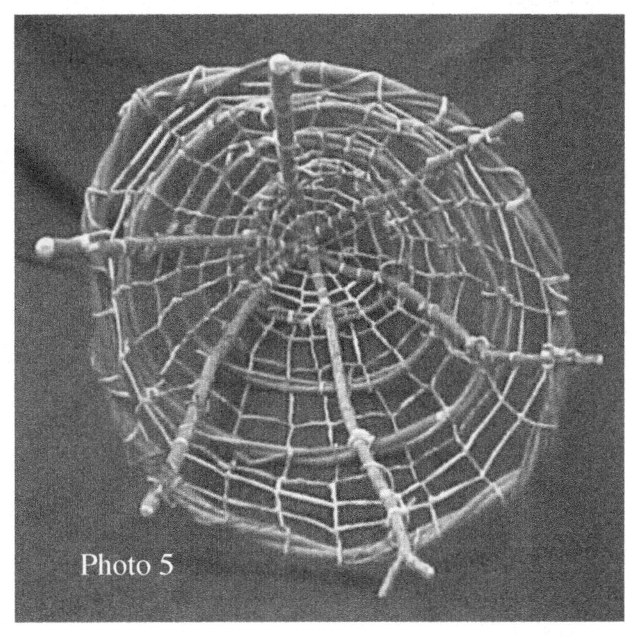
Photo 5

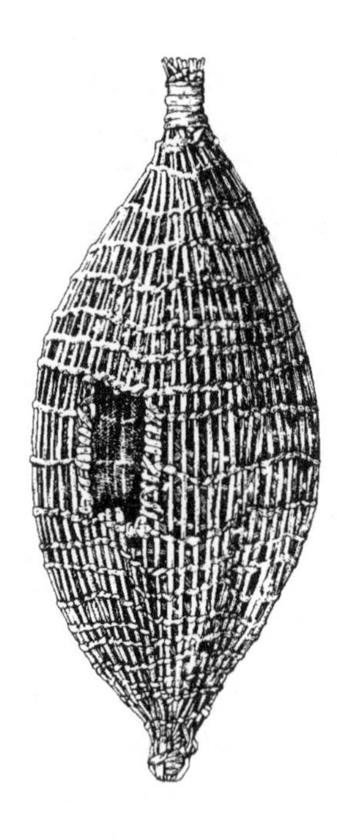

wooden ribs as you go. Space the rows to match your desired mesh size. Keep lacing pulled taught.

When you reach the smallest hoop, the webbing is complete except for the very bottom where the bent vertical ribs cross. Fill in this space with rawhide warp and weft.

The basket is now complete and ready for the attachment of a chest or forehead tumpline. This example is approximately 25" high and 18" wide at the top.

Photo 5: Interior View

Photo 6: Detail

Shows completed webbing with wraps around vertical ribs and hoops. Note spiral wraps on top hoop which moves lacing to next position (left to right in this example).

Photo 7: Detail

Shows close up of wrapping method. Rawhide weft wraps 360° around both wooden ribs and

Primitive Fiber-Bundle Watercraft:
A Materials Primer

From the Nile and Indus river valleys, to the lakes of the Andes, to the shores of the Mediterranean, to the backwaters of northern Australia, to the marshes of the Great Basin, to the coasts of California and Mexico . . . Native Peoples have used bundles of rushes, reeds and barks to construct a variety of watercraft. The tropical and temperate zones of the globe yield up an abundance of raw materials suitable for the manufacture of such vessels.

Sedges and Rushes

These pithy-centered wetland plants with round, square or triangular cross-sections represent perhaps the most widely utilized category of fibers for bundle boat construction. "Bulrushes" (*Scirpis sp.*) of many varieties can be and have been used throughout the world, with the giant "Tule" (*Scirpis californicus & Scirpis acutus*) serving as the raw material for a wide range of raft/boats: from small egg and tool carrying "marsh buggies", to one man boats (as reconstructed by Jamison, Baugh, Kidder, Riggs and many others) to large sea-worthy craft (as reconstructed by Kidder).

Rush boats are also found in South America, with the *Uru* and *Aymara* canoes of Lake Titicaca being the most well known. Africa, still supports surviving bundle boat traditions in the areas of Okavanga Swamp, Lake Chad and Lake Turkana. In France, Hungry and eastward into India, Korea and Japan the interplay of bulrush and humans continues with fiber bundle watercraft technologies appropriate to local conditions.

North Africa yields the famous papyrus sedge (*Cyperus papyrus*) of the Nile valley - most often associated with Egyptian paper making but equally useful as the raw material for the construction of both ancient rivercraft and the modern experimental sea-going vessels of Thor Heyerdahl (the *"Ra"*, *"Ra II"* and the *"Tigris"*).

A note on two confusing terms often encountered in the study of fiber bundle watercraft:

*The word **"reed"** is used to refer to a multitude of plant stems and fibers used in bundle boat construction. It may refer to rushes, sedges, canes ore other grasses. Likewise, "reed boat" may refer to vessels made from a variety of materials.*

*The word **"balsa"** is used (as in Richard W.Cunningham's California Indian Watercraft, 1989) to refer to "a canoe constructed of multiple bundles of wands, canes, reeds, sedges or bark rolls lashed together and arranged in such a fashion as to create a cavity or hold". "Balsa" used in this way refers to a type of watercraft - not to be confused with the tropical "balsa tree" (Ochroma logopus) found in South America. (This wood, by the way, has its own place in the world of primitive watercraft - Heyerdahl's "Kon Tiki", which sailed in 1947, was an ocean-worthy raft constructed of balsa logs.)*

Grasses

Certain hard-shelled, hollow-stemmed, segmented plants of the grass family lend themselves especially well to the construction of fiber bundle rafts and boats. While not as flexible or as easily harvested and manipulated as rushes and sedges, these large grasses offer excellent floatation due to their isolated hollow chambers. Being hard shelled, they also resist water absorption and decay much better.

Throughout the Orient and in Pacifica the giant of all grasses, "bamboo" (*Bambusa sp.*) is used for an almost countless number of tasks including the

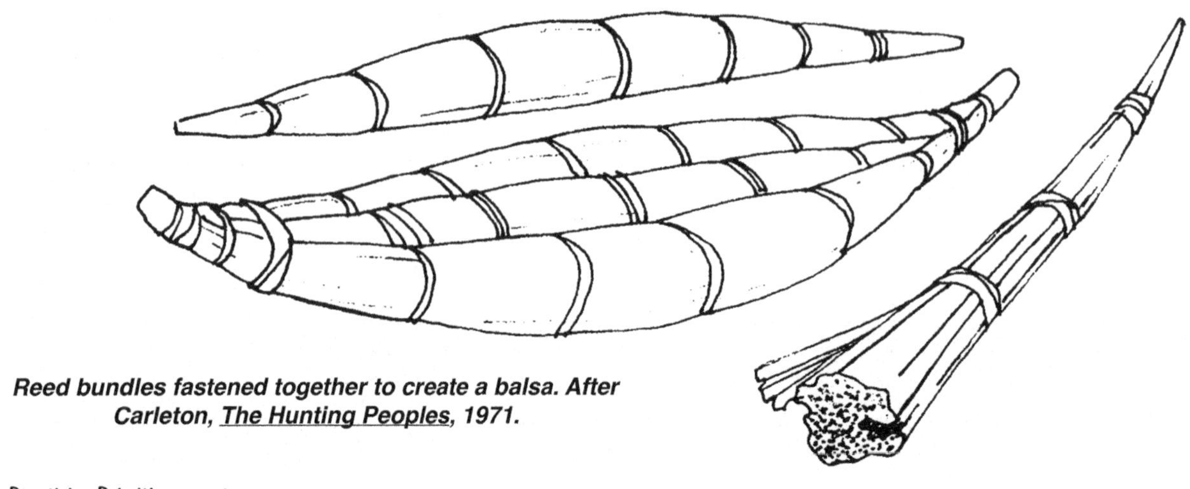

Reed bundles fastened together to create a balsa. After Carleton, The Hunting Peoples, 1971.

construction of bundled rafts and boats. The large size and strength of some bamboo species allow for vessels capable of transporting great amounts of weight. The spread of bamboo around the globe in historic times makes it an available boat building resource for the modern-day *neoaboriginal* living within its expanded range.

For a bamboo cousin that is native to North America we look to the southeastern United States. Here along the creeks and in the river bottoms we

Steve Watts

Using a windless to tighten cane bundles. A cane balsa containing 646 pieces is replicated at the Schiele Museum, 1993.

find "rivercane" (*Arundinaria sp.*). Although no contemporary Native Americans in the area have living traditions related to bundle boat construction (the typical aboriginal vessel being the dugout canoe) there are early historic references to the construction of rivercane rafts among Indians of the Gulf region (an experimental model has been reconstructed by Watts). In fact, the Spanish invaders who entered the southeast in the 16th century were impressed enough by these rafts to adopt them

Steve Watts

Adding a cattail-and-cane gunwale.

Jim Green

The finished rivercane balsa.

for their own use. Other *Arundinaria* species are found in South America.

Another widely distributed grass useful for boat building is "phragmites" or "reed grass" (*Phragmites australis*). The most famous examples of phragmites boats are those constructed by the Seri Indians of western Mexico. These are long and sleek and have been called by Richard W. Cunningham "one of the most graceful watercraft built by primitive man". *Phragmites* does not attain the strength or size of either bamboo or rivercane, yet still possesses more rigidity than any of the sedges or rushes.

Palms

The stalks of fronds from plants of the *Palmae* family (palms and palmettos) are lightweight, pithy, buoyant and strong. Bundled boats made from these stalks have been documented in the Gulf of Oman and other Mid Eastern locations. On at least one occasion, Heyerdahl used palm frond stalks to reinforce the bottom of one of his ocean-going papyrus craft.

Bark

The mention of bark in relation to boats typically brings to mind birchbark canoes or other bark-clad vessels. Yet, in Australia and Tasmania aboriginals used bark in a totally different way. Using the thin peeled bark of Melaleuca or other "stringy" barked trees, several bundles were bound separately then secured together forming a raft/boat with pointed bow and stern (An excellent example is illustrated in *Discovery*, March 1993, *Ten Thousand Years of Solitude*).

Steve Watts

Rivercane Balsa

Some Aboriginal Uses of Bamboo

Food, Food Preparation, Cooking and Eating

Shoots
chop sticks, cups/bowls/platters
steamers, canteens
canisters/vials
cook pots
buckets
whisks
strainers
spoons/forks
ladles/dippers
knives
baskets

Fire

Tinder, fuel, firesaw components, torches

Music

Drums, shakers, clappers
Thumpers, click sticks
flutes, didgeridoos, bells
wind chimes, rainsticks
whistles, trumpets,
anklungs
resonators for stringed instruments - various

Tools and Weapons

Bows/cross bows,
arrows/spears, projectile points, blowguns/darts,
fish traps/fishing poles
sheaths/handles
poison sticks, quivers,
daggers, knives
lacing & latching needles
netting & weaving shuttles
pens, pins

Shelter/Furnishing

House/shelter frames, mats, lashing, flooring, "planks," "shingles," fencing, gates, furniture, gutters

Transportation

Boats, rafts, litters, packs, packframes, bridges, trail and road beds

Toys

Game pieces, pop guns, woven balls, toy animals, kite frames, stilts, quoits, model boats/rafts, hoops

Ornaments

Pendants, beads, bracelets, combs, hairpins

Bamboo Raft Project

"The bamboo raft is no mere novelty. Its importance should not be underestimated. Humankind's first great ocean-going migration (from Indonesia to Australia 40-60,000 years ago) was more than likely accomplished by the use of bamboo rafts.

The routes to New Guinea and the rest of the Indo-Pacific were opened by these rafts of giant grass. Even today, large decked cargo vessels made of bamboo transport people and supplies throughout China and Southeast Asia."

Steve Watts, 2000

A. Lashing dried tulip poplar cross-braces.

B. 14 bamboo pieces - 12 feet long, 4-6 inches in diameter.

Schiele Museum Aboriginal Studies Program, 1999

Photos by Jeannie Alleva

C. "Z" bracing insures rigidity.

D. Capable of floating two with ease.

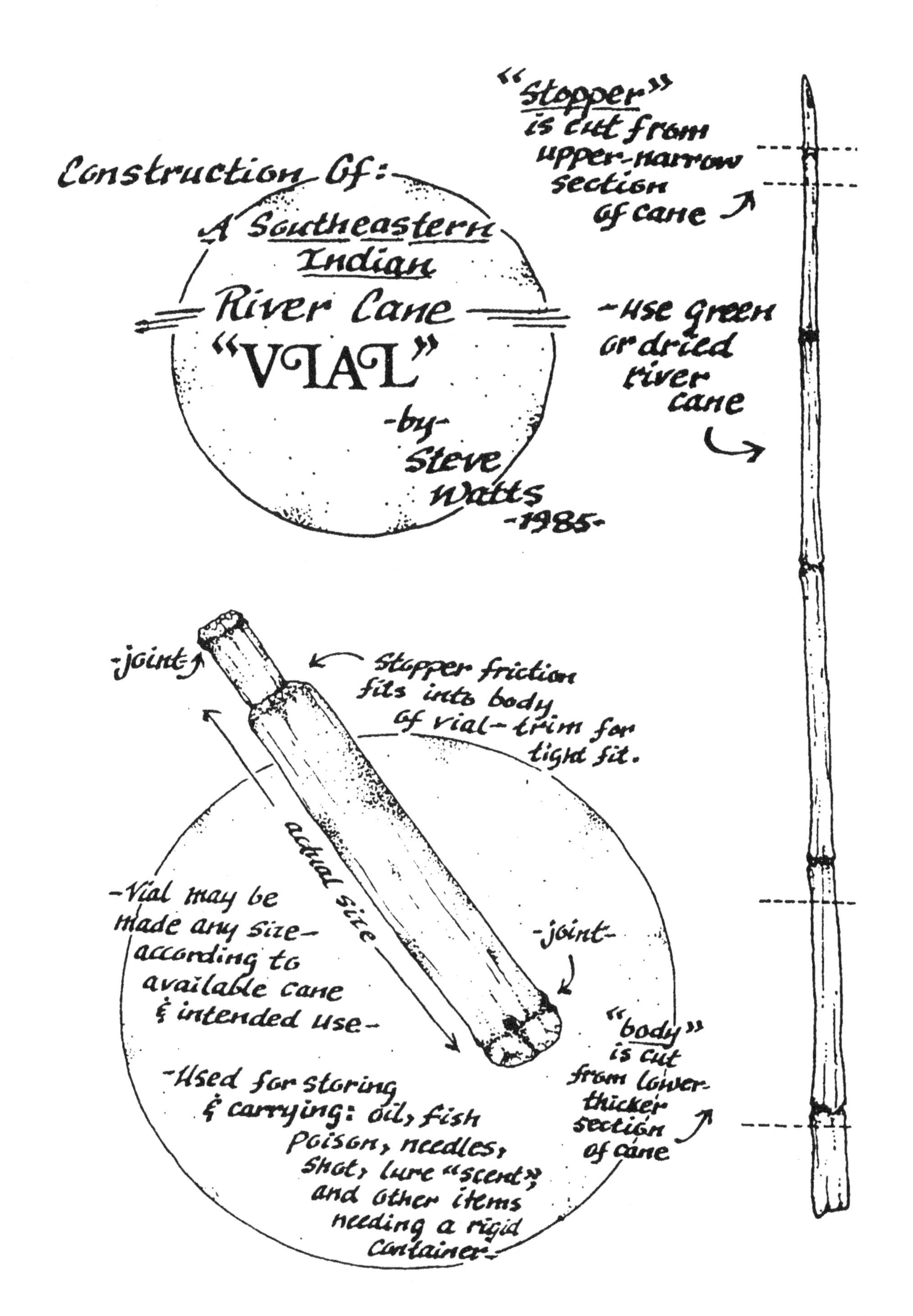

Construction Of:
A Southeastern Indian
River Cane
"VIAL"
-by-
Steve Watts
-1985-
"Stopper" is cut from upper-narrow section of cane
-use green or dried river cane
-joint-
Stopper friction fits into body of vial-trim for tight fit.
actual size
-Vial may be made any size-according to available cane & intended use-
-joint-
"body" is cut from lower-thicker section of cane
-Used for storing & carrying: oil, fish poison, needles, shot, lure "scent", and other items needing a rigid container-

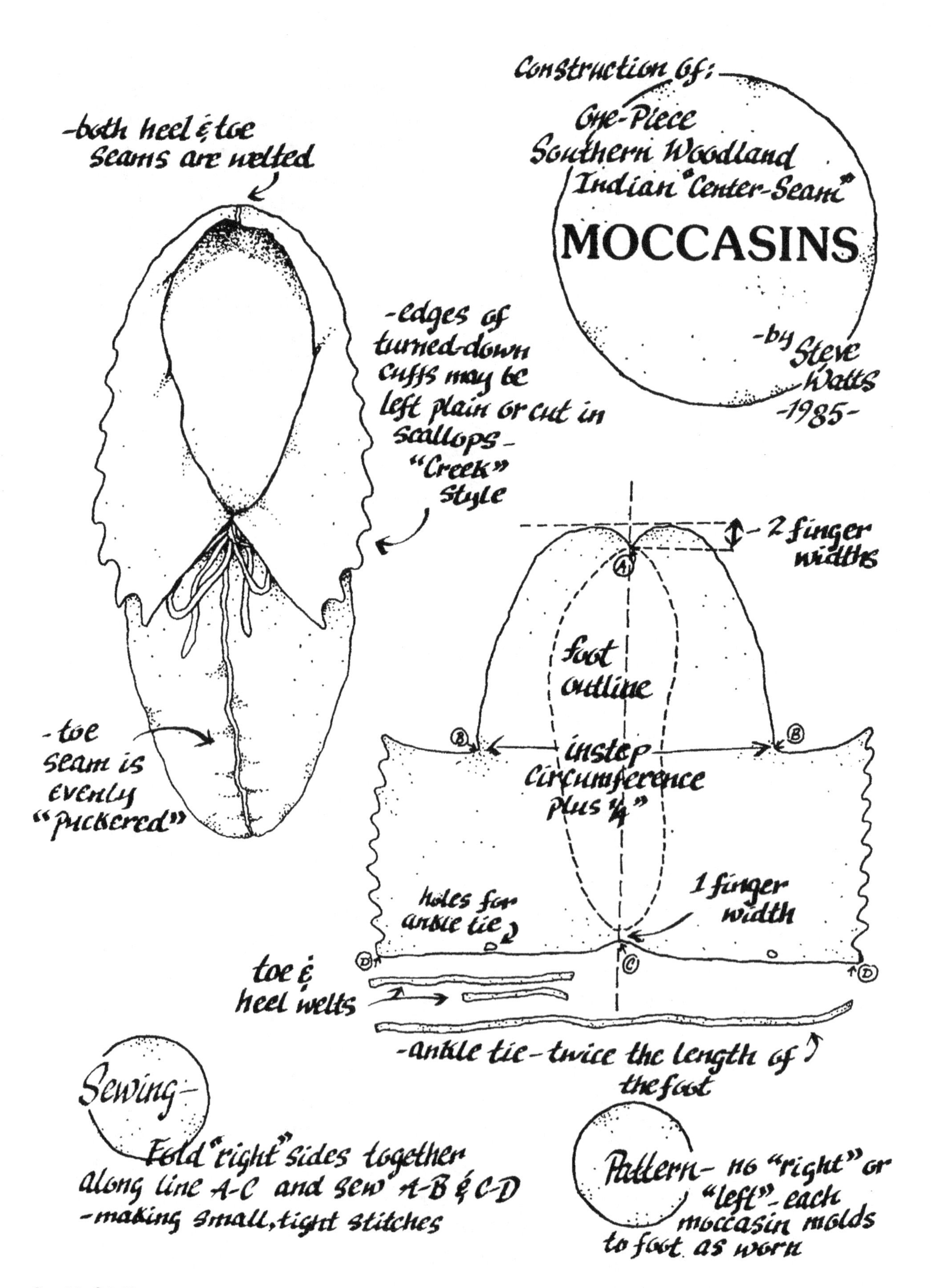
Construction of:
One-Piece
Southern Woodland
Indian "Center-Seam"
MOCCASINS
-by Steve Watts
-1985-
-both heel & toe
seams are welted
-edges of
turned-down
cuffs may be
left plain or cut in
scallops -
"Creek"
style
-toe
seam is
evenly
"puckered"
2 finger
widths
foot
outline
instep
circumference
plus ¼"
holes for
ankle tie
1 finger
width
toe &
heel welts
-ankle tie - twice the length of
the foot
Sewing -
Fold "right" sides together
along line A-C and sew A-B & C-D
-making small, tight stitches
Pattern - no "right" or
"left" - each
moccasin molds
to foot as worn

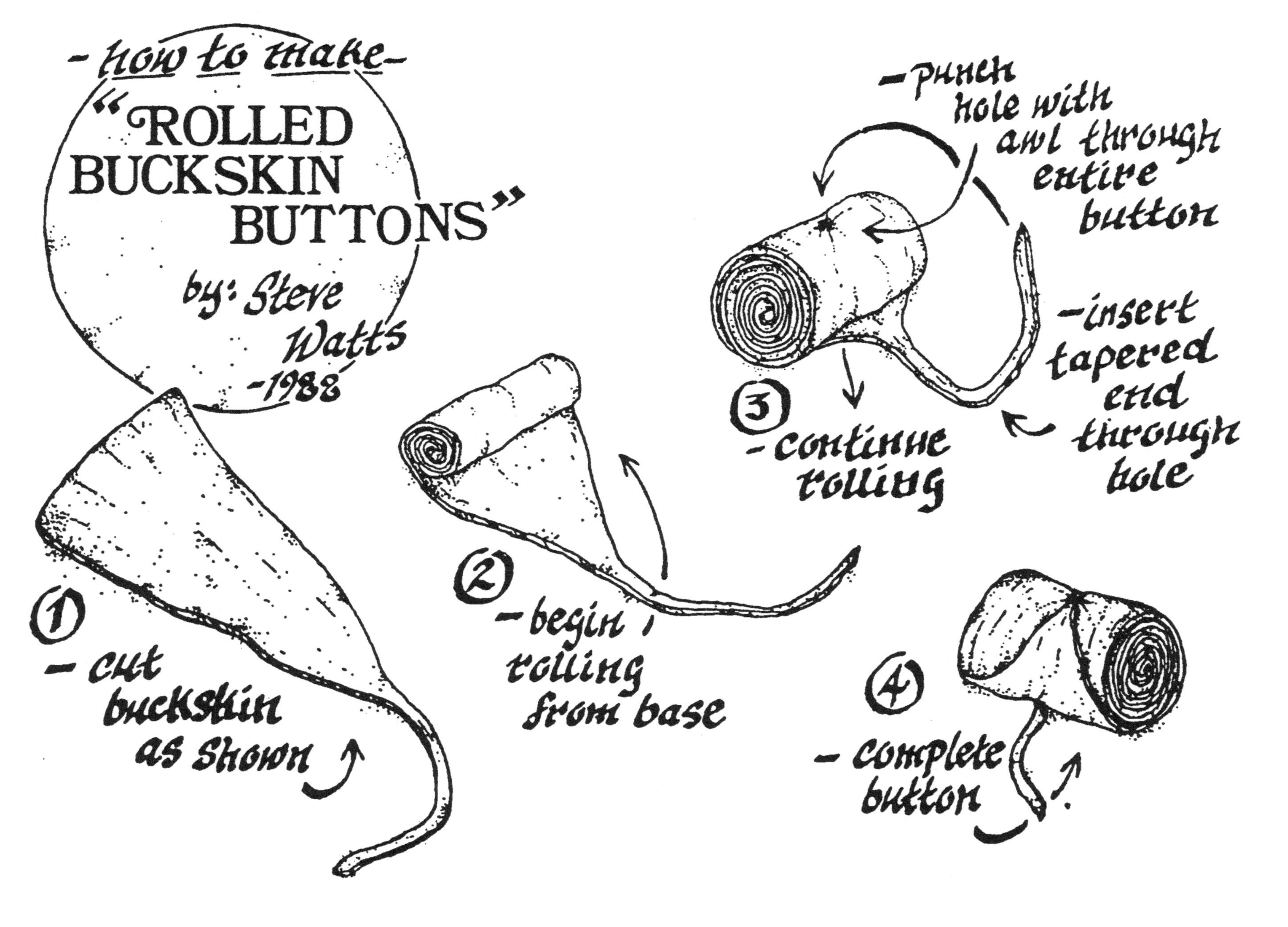

- how to make -
"ROLLED BUCKSKIN BUTTONS"
by: Steve Watts -1988
1 - cut buckskin as shown
2 - begin rolling from base
3 - continue rolling
- punch hole with awl through entire button
- insert tapered end through hole
4 - complete button

6

To Hunt and To Fish

Michael Eldredge

Agriculture developed only about ten thousand year ago. Until that time, our ancestors made their way by hunting, fishing and gathering. The domestication of plants and animals meant the domestication of people as well.

The old hunting and gathering technologies that sustained us for more than two million years became supplemental strategies. These activities which once so defined us as a species in relation to others, are today most often viewed as mere sport or senseless acts of brutality. The hunter/gatherer way of life was stable and proved itself successful by its longevity. With its loss, we are disconnected from much of our heritage. Yet, the "hunt" and the "search" still remain among our most powerful metaphors.

Will
hunt
& gather
for Food
© BIG CRANIAL COMIX 1994
SW '94

The Manufacture of Primitive Primitive Thrusting Spears

Our Homo Erectus ancestors possessed both flake and core stone tools. That much is certain. Beyond that, we can only speculate about the wood, bone, fiber and other technologies at their disposal. Our first evidence of wooden thrusting spears does not appear archaeologically until Neanderthal times. Yet, to envision Lower Paleolithic humans without a sharp stick in hand is pretty difficult. They were most likely there, and their use was probably multifunctional - for prying and digging up food and flakable stone, for defense against predators, and (even though our earliest ancestors were most likely scavengers, not hunters) for the occasional killing of a maimed, sick or dying animal. The requirements were simple - sturdiness and a sharp point or bevel.

Perhaps the first of these tools were not created by man at all. Wind and water can splinter saplings and tree limbs which can in turn become lethal weapons in the hands of humans. Whatever the circumstances, the thrusting/jabbing spear was born. It is both the ancestor of all piercing weapons that would follow and an important and viable tool for the primitive hunter still. (See "Reconsidering the Thrusting Spear")

Primitive Primitive Manufacture

"Primitive Primitive" as used here has both temporal and technological connotations. Temporal - as in "first first" - reflecting on the earliest possible prototypes and functions. And, technological - as in "basic basic" - exploring the simplest tools and techniques needed to manufacture such spears. Having already offered up the possibility of expedient/found thrusters, we turn now to three basic methods of primitive manufacture - methods available to us and to the men and women of the Old Stone Age.

Figure 1. A bent sapling explodes under the forces of bending, resulting in a properly splintered thruster.

The "No Tools" Method

The technique is simple: Bend it 'til it breaks. Select a dead standing sapling or an accessible limb on a larger tree. Finding just the right tree at just the right stage can be tricky. You are looking fore wood that will "explode" under the stresses of compression and tension, resulting in a splintery break (Fig.1). Green wood is too flexible for this technique, and wood that is too far gone will be either too weak or will simply snap off cleanly. Experiment with a variety of species to discover the possibilities. Your failed experiments can be used for firewood. Eastern Red Cedar (*Juniperus virginiana*) fills the need in my part of the country. It's plenty strong enough. It is not very heavy, but remember, we're looking for a thruster not a thrower. And, it splinters into some wicked points

Fig. 2. The "No Tools" method of thrusting-spear manufacture results not in a point, but a sharp bevel.

Figure 4. Supporting the tree as you chop helps to steady the vibration and keep the point from splintering out.

and bevels (Fig. 2). Break off the butt end to the desired length and you have created one of the most basic of weapons.

The Handaxe Method

Much has been written about the possible uses of flaked stone choppers and hand axes in the Lower Paleolithic. Like the thrusting spear, their use was most likely multifunctional: butchering animals, defense, bone breaking for marrow extraction, use as a prepared core for flake removal, etc. Some people have eliminated the use of the "axe" label, altogether, citing too much of an inference of wood chopping functions. But, chop wood they will! It's not a lot of fun, but hand axes can indeed by used to fell and trim trees.

Select a suitable sapling and begin chopping in a downward direction, working your way around the tree. You are in essence cutting down the tree and shaping the spear's point simultaneously (Fig. 3). Support the tree with your body as you work so that it will not fall under its own weight too soon and splinter or "fuzz up" the point (Fig. 4). Cutting it all the way to the last fiber will result in the desirable strength and sharpness. If you need it sharper, you can use the edge of the hand axe in

Figure 3. Chopping has progressed completely around the tree. Continuing in this same manner, the point is completed as the tree is felled.

Figure 5. Sharpening the point with the edge of the handaxe.

a scraping fashion (Fig. 5). Lay the downed tree on a log and chop it to the desired length.

Dead, seasoned wood will be harder to chop, but will produce a spear that is ready to go. Green wood cuts much easier, but will require seasoning or fire hardening to keep the point strong and sharp.

The Fire-and-Stone Method

This is basically a "burn and scrape" or a "burn and grind" technique. Select a standing dead sapling and either break it off or uproot it. The spear is sized by burning at the desired location. To create a point, rotate the blank as it burns. A little scraping with an unmodified flake (struck from your hand axe perhaps), or grinding on a coarse stone will remove the char and expose the hard wood underneath. Keep burning and scraping or grinding until satisfied. A very sharp point can result.

Three completed "primitive primitive" thrusting spears. Left to right: no-tools method, fire and stone method, handaxe method.

RECONSIDERING THE THRUSTING SPEAR

The standard progressive train of thought runs something like this: First, hunters used thrusting spears for the taking of large game. Sometimes these spears were thrown. Lighter and more flexible atlatl darts replaced the heavy spears, only to be replaced themselves by the even speedier arrow. And so, the lowly thrusting spear is left behind in the ever-evolving tool kit of the hunter.

Yet, if we look at the ethnographic evidence from hunter/gatherer cultures which survived into the twentieth century, we find that a place for the thruster remains in the arsenal - in spite of the presence of both atlatl and bow and arrow technology. Inuit hunters of the arctic used short thrusting spears for the dispatching of sea mammals taken by harpoon - much in the same way that a modern hunter may carry a pistol to dispatch an animal wounded by his rifle. Clubs and mauls of various designs were used for this "final blow" function in a multitude of other cultures.

Has the use of thrusting spears as dispatching weapons come and gone several times throughout prehistory? This question is raised by the sometimes confusing assemblages of "spear points" (of various sizes and edge angles) which occur together in a give n time period. Were some of these meant for "thrusting" only, while others were designed more specifically for cutting and/or aerodynamic flight? Or, have thrusting spears been there all along, becoming from time to time archaeologically invisible as they periodically alternate back and forth between stone tipped models and the all wooden Lower Paleolithic form?

"What we should be doing is trying to understand how a cultural system handled resources. . . Most people's thinking goes on the assumption that when something newer and better comes along, the people discard what they did before. This clouds a lot of the ways that tribal cultures are perceived."

John White *Early Man*, Archeological Quarterly Vol. 2, 1978

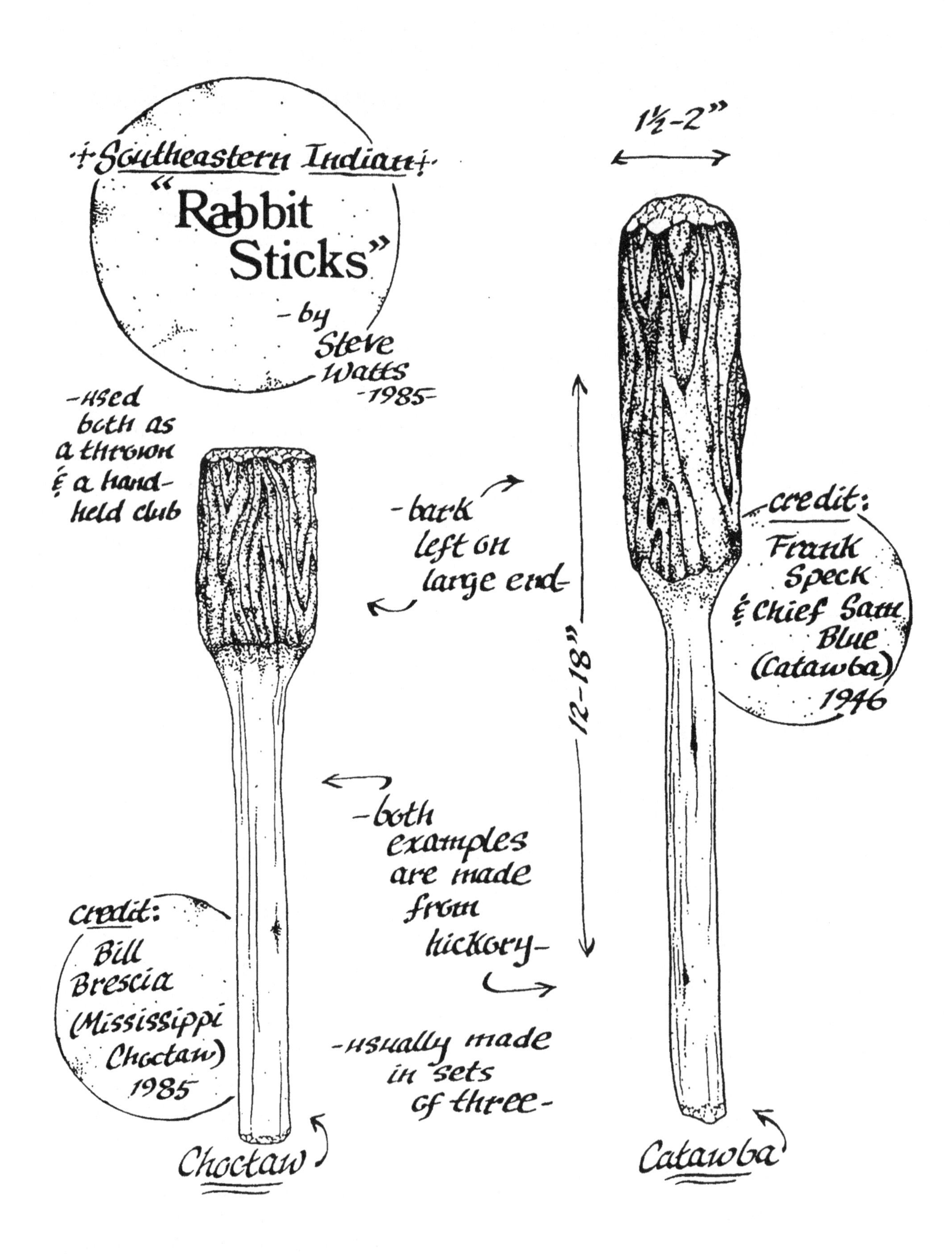

Southeastern Indian
"Rabbit Sticks"
-by Steve Watts -1985-
-used both as a thrown & a hand-held club
-bark left on large end-
1½-2"
12-18"
credit: Frank Speck & Chief Sam Blue (Catawba) 1946
-both examples are made from hickory-
credit: Bill Brescia (Mississippi Choctaw) 1985
-usually made in sets of three-
Choctaw
Catawba

The Southeastern Indian Rivercane Blowgun: Legacy, Lineage, and an Aboriginal Approach to Manufacture

SW - 1991
Revised 1994

Partially published previously in *Woodsmoke: Collected Writings on Ancient Living Skills* by Richard and Linda Jamison. Menasha Press, 1994

Mike Peters

Photo 1: Rivercane blowgun and locust / thistle fletched hunting darts.

In the summer of 1954, I stood wide-eyed in the cool shade of the big trees and watched an unnamed Cherokee man shoot a thistle fletched dart from a rivercane blowgun. It sped from the muzzle in a blur, and before I could blink or think or try to understand; it was there - stuck firmly in a softwood log target. To him, the Cherokee, I was just another nameless seven year old boy. I was one of hundreds or perhaps thousands, of seven year old boys who had witnessed his demonstrations that summer on the Qualla Boundary in the Great Smoky Mountains of North Carolina. But to me he was a magician. With a few sticks and a tuft of dried plant fibers he had opened a door. A man, a boy and a rivercane blowgun - tied up tightly forever in a bundle of childhood memories.

Photo 2: Cherokee blowgun maker and traditionalist, Richard Crow.

The Legacy

To the historic Cherokee, Creek, Houma, Catawba, Yuchi, Choctaw, Seminole, Natchez, Chitimacha, Biloxi and other native peoples of the North American Southeast, the blowgun was an important and valued hunting weapon in the pursuit of small game. (Speck, 1938 & Swanton, 1946) To the Catawba, Choctaw and Cherokee it remains to this day a symbol of traditional values and cultural pride. (Blue, 1979, Crowe, 1980 & Brescia, 1985)

Old guns are carefully curated and even venerated - being passed down through extended families, generation after generation. Recently, I was privileged to inspect (and shoot!) a one hundred and fifty-plus year old Cherokee gun. The patina of its surface (literally golden) was surpassed only by the glass-like smoothness of it bore - the result of the passage of countless numbers of darts through its interior. Its owner had just recently obtained it. It was the blowgun that he had shot as a young boy under the tutelage of a man who hunted with it regularly in the 1920s and 30s. (Underwood, 1988) To the new owner it represents not only a piece of the Cherokee spirit and passion, but the memory of a valued teacher and friend as well.

Contemporary traditional Choctaws and Cherokees highly prize the blowgun's use as well as its survival. Blowgun competitions are fierce at annual fall and summer fairs and gatherings. Shooting long rounds of competition (often lasting several days and involving hundreds of shots at distances up to sixty feet) blowgun champions take great pride in their accomplishments. Their shooting skills and the craftsmanship of their guns and darts are common topics of conversation and debate.

Though few today rely on the blowgun as a means of providing meat for the table, Southeastern traditionalists are very conscious of the blowgun as a cultural trait - almost a standard. Some, such as the Catawba, who no longer manufacture blowguns on a regular basis still cling to it as a treasured tribal symbol. Others, such as the Waccamaw, who have no record of blowgun use in their written history, see it as essentially "Southeastern" and purchase guns of Cherokee manufacture for use, display and demonstration. Its importance as a living tradition - connecting the present with the aboriginal past - can hardly be overstated.

The Lineage

The prehistoric blowgun picture in the Southeast is unclear. Some doubt the blowgun's antiquity in the region. At this point in time, archaeology has not yet provided us with a pre-contact example. The fragility of the materials used in the manufacture of blowguns and darts makes their survival in the archaeological record difficult at best. Perhaps some southern cave or wet site will someday yield a prehistoric specimen. Accidental or intentional burning in the past could provide us with a charred fragment. There are questions yet to be asked. How would a charred rivercane blowgun fragment differ in attributes from a charred cane fragment used in wattle wall construction or bench seats in a burned house or free-standing cane within or near an occupation site burned in a clearing
operation ?

Kroeber (1948) believed the blowgun to be a late introduction from South America. Some have argued that its presence in the earliest historic accounts speak of more ancient roots. (Nash, 1963) Frank Speck (1938) concluded:

> *"The derivation of the blowgun in the Southeast remains for the present, after all, an open question. To my mind the case in favor of its being a diffused trait from South America is no stronger than that for its local invention."*

Whenever and however the rivercane blowgun came to the Southeast, it was firmly entrenched as an important part of the small game hunting arsenal by the Historic Period:

> *"(The Choctaw) are very skilled in the use of the blowgun . . . when they see something which they want to hit they blow it, and they often kill small birds." (Bossu, 1768) "The young savages . . . blow it so expertly as seldom to miss a mark fifteen or twenty yards off and that so violently as to kill squirrels and birds therewith. " (Romans, 1775) "(The Cherokee children) at eight or ten years old, are very expert at killing small animals and birds with a sarbacan, or hollow cane, through which they blow a small dart, whose weakness obliges them to shoot at the eye of the larger sort of prey, which they seldom miss. " (Timberlake, 1765) "This (the Yuchi blowgun) was almost exclusively used for bringing down small animals, squirrels and birds. " (Speck, 1909) "With other peoples of the Southeast, the Catawba shared the trait of using the blowgun or blowpipe exclusively for the purposes of hunting small animals and birds. It has had a desultory survival down to the present generation of older men and is known by the designation* ***wa'sa'pu'he****, 'cane blowing', or 'dart blowing'." (Speck, 1938)*

The list goes on. (See Swanton, 1946.)

The Material

Although elderberry stems are sometimes used in the manufacture of blowguns by the Houmas of Louisiana, it is rivercane (*Arundinaria gigantea*) that is most often associated with the traditional weapon made by most southern native peoples. It is the material of choice both from a utilitarian and a cultural point of view. Called "swamp cane" in the western southeast (Choctaws, Chitimachas, etc.) and "rivercane" in the eastern southeast (Cherokees, Creeks, Catawbas, etc.), Arundinaria is found growing most often in the bottomlands along rivers and streams.

Rivercane habitats are threatened in the Carolinas and other parts of the southeast. The rich "bottoms" are perfect for agriculture as well as rivercane. Consequently, cane has been driven to the edges of fields and streams by more than two hundred years of cultivation. This is of much concern to blowgun makers in the area. Cherokee craftsmen often travel long distances to obtain proper blowgun cane. Trips to Alabama, Georgia and Kentucky from their North Carolina mountain homes are not unusual. The search for good blowgun cane is ongoing, and a Cherokee maker—no matter where he travels—is ever on the lookout.

Some have speculated that rivercane is "hybridizing" with bamboo, an Asian import. (Medford, 1988) Evidence of this is said to result in shorter lengths of sections between the joints and deeper flutes at the branch junctures. These attributes along with the tendency of bamboo to split when drying, have made bamboo itself an unsatisfying substitute for the native material. Traditional blowgun makers seek out the long-section canes in search of "pure stock".

Michael Eldridge

Photo 3: The author heating a blowgun blank to straighten it.

-An Aboriginal Approach-

Making The Rivercane

"Blowgun"

by: Steve Watts -1989-

-Choose a well seasoned piece of rivercane - 1/2 to 1 inch in diameter.

-Straighten by heating over hot coals & bending.

1. Blank - straightened & cut to length (4 - 8 feet)

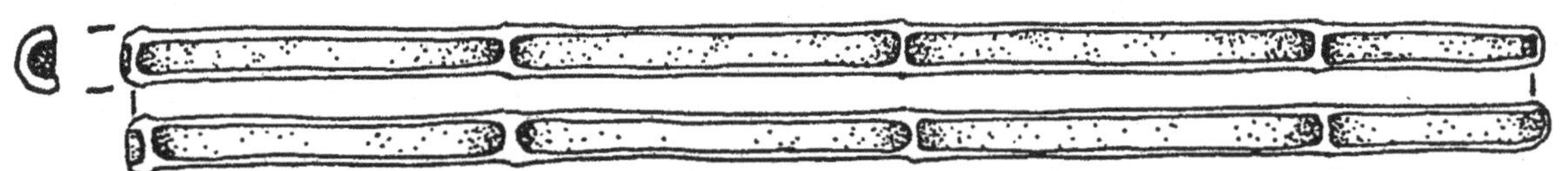

2. Split into two equal halves - use a stone flake or thin wooden "blade"

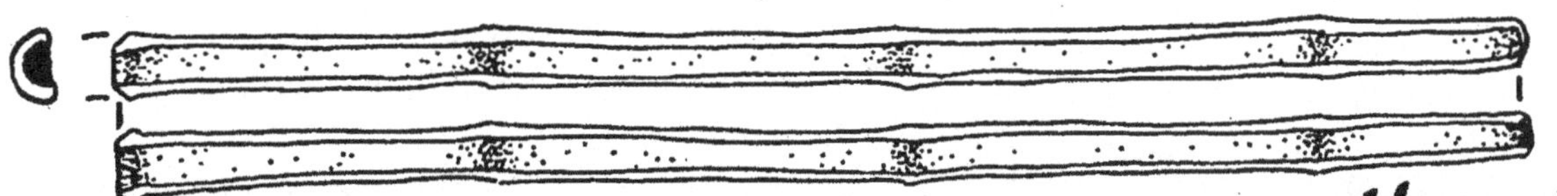

3. Interior walls at joints are cut/ground away using flakes and/or grinding stones

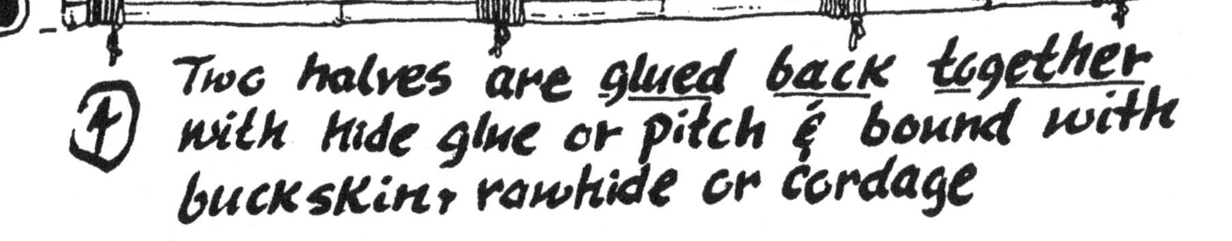

4. Two halves are glued back together with hide glue or pitch & bound with buckskin, rawhide or cordage

Second year growth is chosen for blowgun making. First year growth rivercane is weak and never seems to dry out firmly enough to produce a good gun. Craftsmen scan the canebrakes for plants of their favorite diameters and lengths. Some are chosen for serious hunting or competition, and some for sale to tourists. Yet, the traditional blowgun maker chooses each cane carefully, scorning others that clearcut a patch and use canes of mixed or inferior quality.

Historic Manufacturing Techniques

All of the known accounts of blowgun manufacture which we have from the Historic Period refer to the use of metal tools for hollowing and smoothing the weapon's bore. It must be remembered that European contact in the North American Southeast occurred more than four hundred years ago with the Spanish invasions. Access to simple metal tools no doubt quickly altered aboriginal blowgun manufacturing techniques.

Once the cane has been cut, bundled and allowed to dry, the blowgun maker begins the process of straightening. A cane which looks "straight as an arrow" in the field will reveal all kinds of kinks, curves and wiggles when later examined. Fortunately, rivercane responds well to heat straightening techniques as are commonly used with wood. The blank (the cane cut to length) is heated over flames or coals and bent at "the crooked places" over the maker's knee or the edge of a log, stump or rock. There are two "straightenings" (Lossiah, 1980) which must occur - curves in the sections between the joints, and bends which occur at the joints. At-the-joint bends require more care as the cane is likely to snap at this juncture if too much pressure or too little heat are applied. Straightening can be a frustrating process. An experienced blowgun maker can straighten a blank in a matter of minutes. Less experienced folks can spend hours working to straighten while trying to avoid undoing sections already dealt with.

Once the blank is straight, it's time to turn attention to the blowgun's interior. Now the joints must be removed and the walls of the joints reamed flush with the interior of the already hollow sections between the joints. It is this reaming process which is critical to making a good blowgun. Failure to adequately reduce the interior joint walls will result in an excessively slowed dart or, even worse, a stuck one.

The historic method for penetrating the joint walls most often involves the use of a heated metal rod. An experienced blowgun maker will likely have several different diameters of metal rods on hand to accommodate various cane sizes. The more joint wall material that can be removed in this boring/burning process, the less remains for the next step of reaming. Yet too large a diameter rod can burn through a wall or split the blank at the narrower muzzle end.

For reaming, the traditional historic era tool is the homemade rasp. This consists of a slender piece of split hardwood - hickory or locust - at least half the length of the intended blowgun. Once sized and smoothed so as to work freely back-and-fourth within the cane's interior, the last few inches of the forward end are wrapped with a roughened piece of metal. Strips of tin cans are often used for this with small holes punched in it to create many sharp edges not unlike the common kitchen cheese grater. It is truly remarkable how well these homemade rasps get the job done, quickly removing the remaining joint walls inside the gun. Once reamed, the interior is smoothed further by sanding or burnishing with a hardwood rod to remove any remaining splinters or rough spots which may catch or slow a dart. Truly well made blowguns exhibit polished interiors which become even smoother with the passage of time and darts.

Trimming and smoothing of the mouthpiece and muzzle ends complete the blowgun. Exteriors may be polished at this stage and, on rare occasions, decorated by sooting patterns of rings or spirals. Even less common is the practice of sooting the whole exterior surface - resulting in a totally black blowgun. (Medford, 1988)

Blowguns may vary in length from as short as three feet to as long as ten feet or more for serious hunting or competition. Longer guns provide more accuracy - all other things being equal. Yet, longer guns are much more difficult to manufacture. Five to seven foot guns are most common. The Choctaw even distinguish between five to six foot guns for nighttime hunting in the brier patch and eight to nine foot guns for daytime hunting on open ground. (Nash, 1963)

Before leaving this consideration of historic era techniques, it must be remembered that this is an ever-evolving craft among contemporary Cherokees, Choctaws and others. Even though the blowgun is an important symbol of their past, it is also alive within the culture of the present. And, even though the simple hand tools described above are considered "traditional" at this point (and completely adequate to get the job done) many present-day native craftsmen employ more "modern" substitutes. The commercial round wood rasp is sometimes substituted for the punched tin variety. Drill bits attached to long metal rods are sometimes used for boring instead of the older burning method. And, sandpaper often substitutes for a hardwood burnishing tool. The techniques change but the blowgun remains.

Speculations on Aboriginal Methods of Manufacture

For those wishing to understand how southeastern rivercane blowguns may have been manufactured prehistorically, or for those seeking to manufacture such a weapon themselves using only aboriginal style tools and techniques, questions remain. How the boring and reaming operations necessary for blowgun making were accomplished prior to the introduction of metal tools is still a matter of speculation. Various suggestions and traditions have been offered. The Choctaw believe that the joints were "knocked out" using a sharpened piece of cane of a smaller diameter, and the remaining joint wall fragments were reamed using a stone point/drill hefted to a long shaft. (Nash, 1963) The Catawba version cites the same "knocking out" method followed by rasping with sand and a hardwood shaft. (Blue, 1979) These methods are indeed workable, especially if one works the cane while it is green. "Drilling" out the joints with a stone drill becomes fairly simple (on short cues) if the cane is not excessively dry. This is perhaps the most direct and obvious solution to the prehistoric manufacturing question. Another possible method has been experientially tested (Watts, 1989) and is offered below. In short, it involves a splitting and rejoining technique. This approach corresponds to South American Indian methods and is alluded to in at least one historic Creek reference:

> *"The blowgun was made of a cane stalk about as long as a man is tall. To remove the pith it was sometimes necessary to section the cane, then bind it together again. " (Speck, 1907)*

Does this sketchy Creek account reflect a personal or tribal idiosyncrasy or is it an echo of a widespread technology which predates the iron rod? (Figure 1)

To begin - rivercane is gathered, bundled and allowed to dry. Cane can be harvested and cut to length with unmodified stone flakes or with more formalized bifaces. Choose a length of between four and seven feet for your first attempt. Once dry (give it at least a month if possible) the blank must be straightened using heat as in the historic technique. Rivercane tapers in diameter from the bottom to the top. The mouthpiece end (the larger diameter end) is trimmed and smoothed. It is best to locate the mouthpiece directly on or near a joint for strength. The muzzle end is likewise trimmed and smoothed. This end should have an inside diameter near to the diameter of your thumb or index finger. Trimming of the ends can be easily accomplished using unmodified stone flakes and smoothed using a fine sanding/grinding stone. A smooth mouthpiece allows for comfort and a tight no-leak seal with the shooter's lips. A smooth muzzle end insures speedy release of the dart from the end of the gun.

Next, the blank is split from end to end beginning at the smaller muzzle end. Splitting is relatively easy if care is taken. A flake makes a cut in the direct center of the muzzle end to begin the split. The flake itself or a thin sliver of hardwood is then pushed down the length of the blank. This splitting results in two halves, exposing the inner joint walls in cross-section. These interior wall halves are then cut away using flakes or bifaces and the remnant material ground smooth using properly sized grinding stones. No grinding or smoothing of the walls between joint sections is required. All that now remains to do is to rejoin the two halves. Hide glue, pitch or beeswax can be used. The important thing is to insure an air-tight seal between the two halves from mouthpiece to muzzle. Once the chosen adhesive is in place and the seams properly joined, the blowgun is bound at points along its length using buckskin, rawhide or lengths of plant fiber cordage. South American Indians often wrap the entire gun with bark after rejoining. (Wyatt, 1989) A final interior treatment is the passage of a hardwood shaft back a forth through the bore to remove any adhesive which may have seeped to the inside.

1999 Postscript - This experimental model is now on display at the Schiele Museum, Gastonia, NC (since 19940. It is periodically inspected by the author. For the first year or so, all was fine. But, slowly, over time, the interior shape has deformed from round to oval due to drying. Perhaps a complete wrapping (in South American style) would have prevented this - perhaps not. Further experimentation is needed.

This is but one possible aboriginal-style method of blowgun manufacture. There are of course many others. One craftsman I knew, for instance, accomplished the successful construction of a blowgun by knocking out the joint walls with a hardwood shaft and then reaming the interior with a rasp made of a long cattail stalk with quartz sand attached to

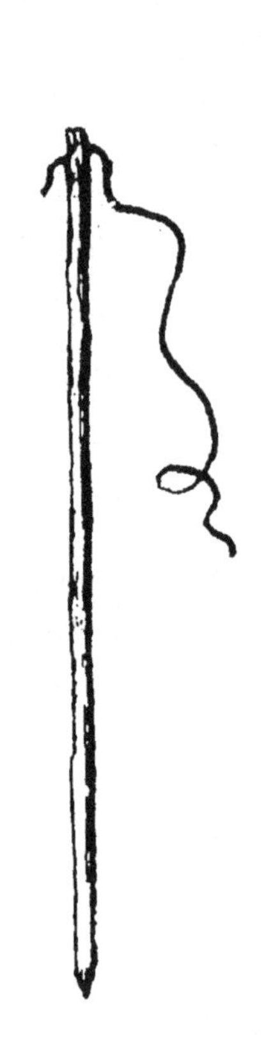

Whittle and smooth hardwood shaft 8-12" long and up to 1/8" in diameter. Insert thread into split cut in butt end.

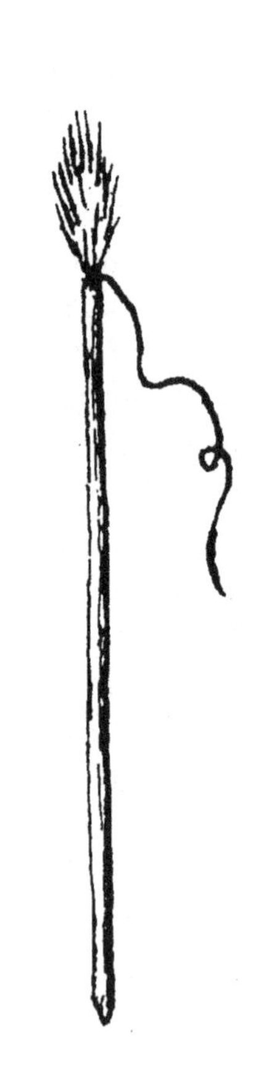

Begin wrapping thistle down to shaft in spiral of overlapping layers.

Cover 2-4" of shaft with down, ending with a few wraps around the shaft. End with overhand knot.

Completed dart - blunt

cut or burn end of thistledown even with the butt end of shaft.

the working end with hide glue. I sure didn't think it would work, but it sure did. (McDaniel, 1988) Other alternatives wait to be tested.

The Darts

Of course, no consideration of blowguns can be complete without giving attention to the ammunition - the darts. The Southeastern Indian blowgun dart is a rather large affair when compared to those used by their South American cousins. Unlike in South America, no poison was used in blowgun hunting, so the southeastern dart must carry a little more heft to complete the task of shock and penetration. It works in many ways like a small arrow. In fact, the Catawba word for arrow and dart are the same-*"wa"* . (Speck, 1938)

The shafts of these darts were historically constructed of a variety of materials. Split out pieces of hardwood, eight to ten inches in length, up to an eighth inch in diameter, shaved to a round cross-section and pointed on one end were most common. (Speck, 1938) Black locust is the wood of choice among Cherokee today. Chitimacha dart shafts were sometimes constructed from a rivercane splinter which, after being subjected to heat, was twisted into a "corkscrew" shape. The Choctaw also manufactured such shafts. (Nash, 1963) Longer shaft lengths were found as well. There are Cherokee darts in collections which exceed twenty-one inches in length. (Underwood, 1988)

Likewise, the fletchings found on these darts are made from a variety of natural materials. The fletching material must fill the inner cavity of the gun so as to "catch" the air and send the dart on its way. Yet, it must be of a material that is flexible enough to expand at the large mouthpiece end and contract at the small muzzle end of the blowgun. It must be fairly durable, yet light enough so as not to slow the dart's flight once it has left the gun.

Although cotton was preferred as a fletching material among the Gulf Coast tribes and feathers and fur were used by Catawba, the fletching of choice among the Cherokees and others was - and still is - thistle (*Carduus L.*). This plant, viewed by most today as a pest, is still found growing along roadsides and in open fields throughout the south. The flower heads are gathered in the late summer and early fall by craftsmen and stored for a winter of dart making. Once dry, the thistle "down" (the soft inner fibers of the flower) are removed and they alone are used for fletching. Left unattended thistle flowers allowed to dry will open up and send these fibers flying in all directions. To prevent this, dart makers wedge the freshly cut flower heads between two strips of hardwood or within the cleft created by splitting a piece of rivercane (Photo 5). In this way the thistle can be stored, allowing one flower head at a time to be removed and the fibers processed. Proper cleaning and manipulation of

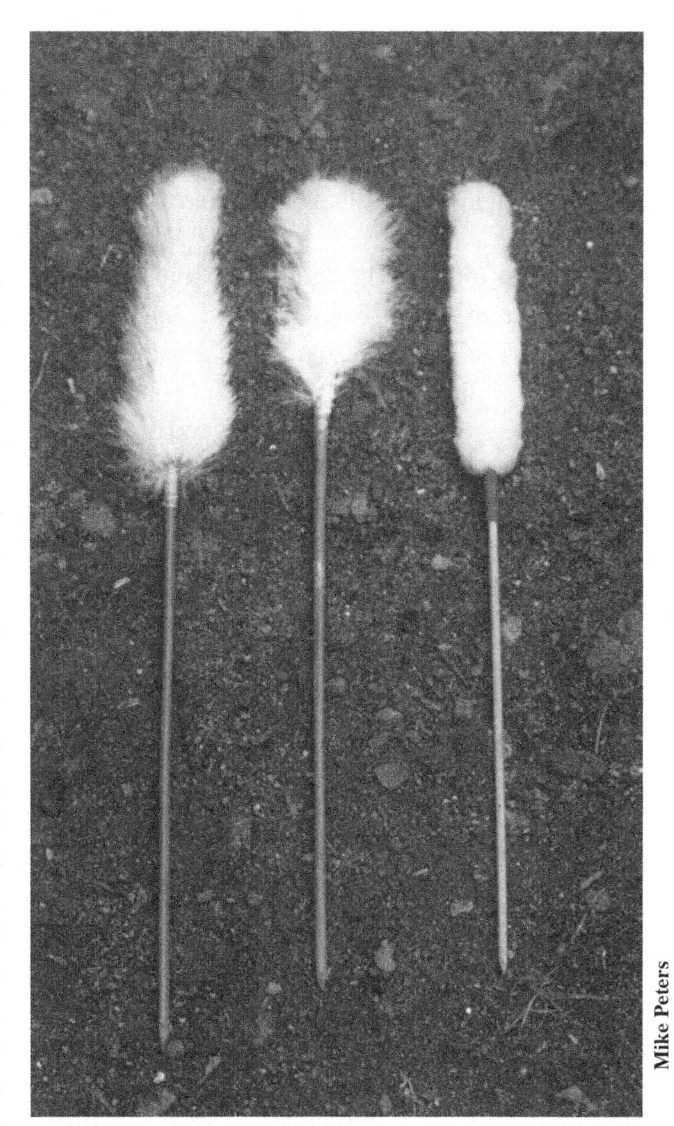

Mike Peters

Photo 4: Southeastern Native American blowgun dart styles (left to right): thistle fletched (Cherokee); feather fletched (Catawba); cotton fletched (Choctaw).

these fibers is crucial to successful dart making. It is a craft that can only be learned with much trial and error. It is without a doubt a technique that is best learned firsthand from an experienced dart maker.

A split is made in the blunt end of the dart shaft and a length of fine thread is inserted. A few twists of the shaft binds the thread in place without a knot. Today most dart makers use cotton thread. The Cherokees say that in the past milkweed or stinging nettle cordage was used. (Crowe, 1985) The free end of the string is held in the teeth. A bundle of prepared thistle down is held in one hand fanned out into a row which lies between the outstretched thumb and index finger. The other hand holds the shaft, and with its upper end lying on the index finger with the down, it is simultaneously rotated clockwise and moved up and in toward the base of the thumb. The result of this is that thistle fibers are caught at their base between the string and the shaft, creating a continuous spiral of attached fibers. When completed, the fletching appears to be a uniform gathering of down with the string being hidden. Once two to four inches of fletching has been applied, the end of the string is wrapped several times to catch the base of the last fibers and an overhand knot is tied. The fibers on the upper end are trimmed or burned flush with the blunt end of the shaft. The completed dart is then spun between the palms fluffing it out and releasing any unattached down. The dart is now complete.

If all this sounds like some kind of impossible magic trick requiring more hands than most of us have, then you've come close to the feeling a beginner dart maker has as he attempts to juggle shaft, string and thistle. At the same time one is doing this, he is trying to judge just how much down to feed into the process (and in what concentrations) so as to wind up with a fletching that is full enough to do the job, but not so large as to cause the dart to become stuck in the blowgun's bore. It is the skilled dartmaker who through much experience consistently matches the "caliber" of his dart with his gun. To watch a master Cherokee craftsman "roll" darts at a rate of one every couple of minutes is to experience the elegance of primitive technology in action.

Mike Peters

Photo 5: Dried thistle pods stored in split rivercane (above), dried thistle pod (left), thistle fibers cleaned and ready for fletching (right).

In the fall of 1554, a very young Catawba boy stood wide-eyed in the cool shade of the big trees on the edge of an open field and watched a hunter shoot a thistle fletched dart from a rivercane blowgun. It sped from the muzzle in a blur, and before the boy could blink or think or try to understand; it was there - stuck firmly in the chest of a rabbit now lying still in a patch of blue-stemmed grass. To the hunter, this boy was not just any boy. This boy was his son. The only son who would carry on the practice of making and using this blowgun. The only one who would be entrusted to pass on this way and teach his son who would follow. To the boy, this man was a magician. With a few sticks and tuft of dried plant fibers he had opened a door as only a father can do. A father, a son and a rivercane blowgun - tied up tightly forever in a bundle of survival and living tradition.

REFERENCES

Blue, Gilbert (Catawba)
1979 *Personal communication.*

Bossu, Jean Bernard
1768 ***Nouveaux Voyages Aux Indes Occidentales*** *. . . Paris.*

Brescia, Bill (Choctaw)
1985 *Personal communication.*

Crowe, Richard (Cherokee)
1980 *Personal communication.*

1985 *Personal communication.*

Kroeber, A.L.
1948 ***Anthropology,*** *Harcourt Brace, New York.*

Lossiah, Hayes (Cherokee)
1980 *Personal communication.*

McDaniel, Roger
1988 *Personal communication.*

Medford, Claude (Choctaw)
1988 *Personal communication.*

Nash, Charles H.
1963 *Choctaw Blowguns, Ten Years of the Tennessee* ***Archaeologist,*** *Vol. II, 1954-1963.*

Romans, Bernard
1775 ***A Concise Natural History of East and West Florida,*** *Vo.1 . . . New York.*

Speck, Frank G.
1907 ***The Creek Indians of Taskigi Town,*** *Mem. American Anthropological Association, Vol. II, Pt.2.*

1909 ***Ethnology of the Yuchi Indians,*** *Anthropological Publications of the University Museum, University of Penn., Vol. I, No.1.*

1938 *The Cane Blowgun In Catawba and Southeastern Ethnology,* ***American Anthropologist,*** *Vol. 40.*

Swanton, John R.
1946 ***The Indians of the Southeastern United States,*** *Bureau of American Ethnology, Bulletin 137.*

Timberlake, Lieut. Henry
1765 ***The Memoirs of Lieut. Henry Timberlake (who accompanied the three Cherokee Indians to England in the year 1762) containing . . . an accurate map of their Over- hill Settlement*** *. . . London.*

Underwood, Tom
1988 *Personal communication.*

Watts, Steven M.
1988 ***Making the Rivercane Blowgun: an Aboriginal Approach,*** *manuscript.*

Wyatt, Bonnie
1989 *Personal communication.*

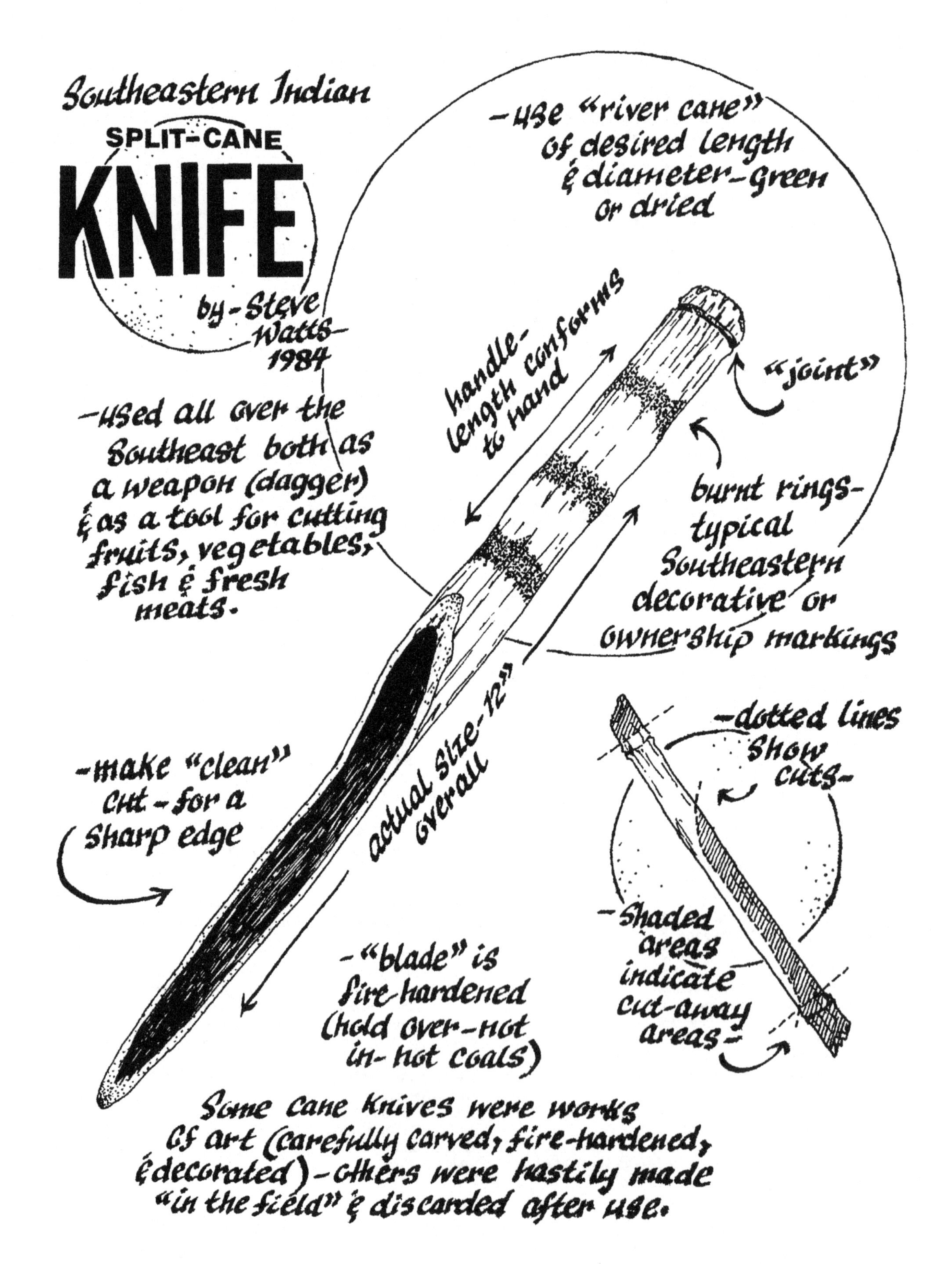
Southeastern Indian
SPLIT-CANE
KNIFE
by-Steve Watts-1984
-use "river cane" of desired length & diameter-green or dried
handle-length conforms to hand
"joint"
-used all over the Southeast both as a weapon (dagger) & as a tool for cutting fruits, vegetables, fish & fresh meats.
burnt rings-typical Southeastern decorative or ownership markings
actual size-12" overall
-dotted lines show cuts-
-make "clean" cut-for a sharp edge
-shaded areas indicate cut-away areas-
-"blade" is fire-hardened (hold over-not in-hot coals)
Some cane knives were works of art (carefully carved, fire-hardened, & decorated)-others were hastily made "in the field" & discarded after use.

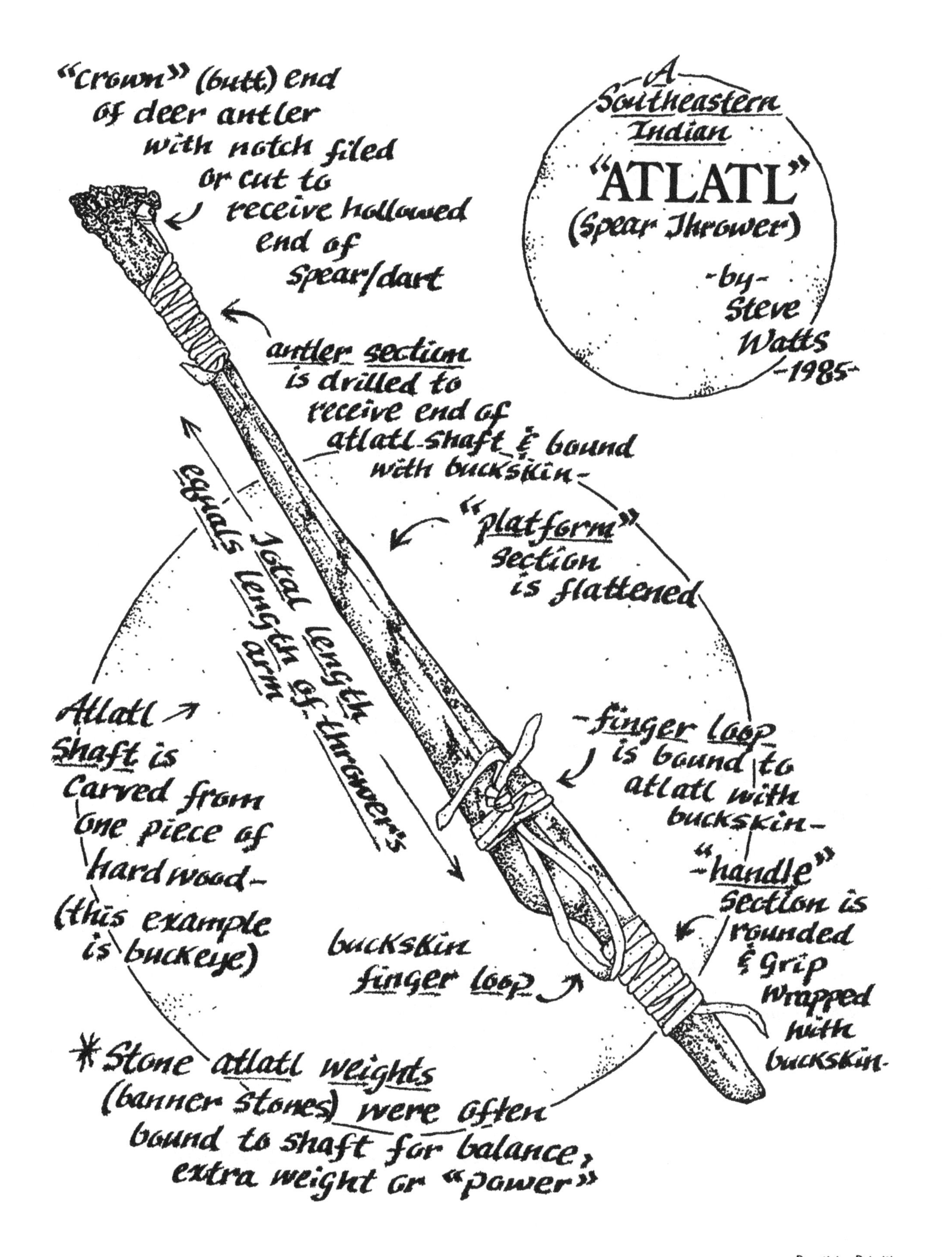
A Southeastern Indian
"ATLATL"
(Spear Thrower)
-by-
Steve Watts
-1985-
"crown" (butt) end of deer antler with notch filed or cut to receive hollowed end of spear/dart
antler section is drilled to receive end of atlatl shaft & bound with buckskin-
"platform" section is flattened
Total length equals length of thrower's arm
-finger loop is bound to atlatl with buckskin-
"-handle" section is rounded & grip wrapped with buckskin-
Atlatl shaft is carved from one piece of hardwood-
(this example is buckeye)
buckskin finger loop
* Stone atlatl weights (banner stones) were often bound to shaft for balance, extra weight or "power"

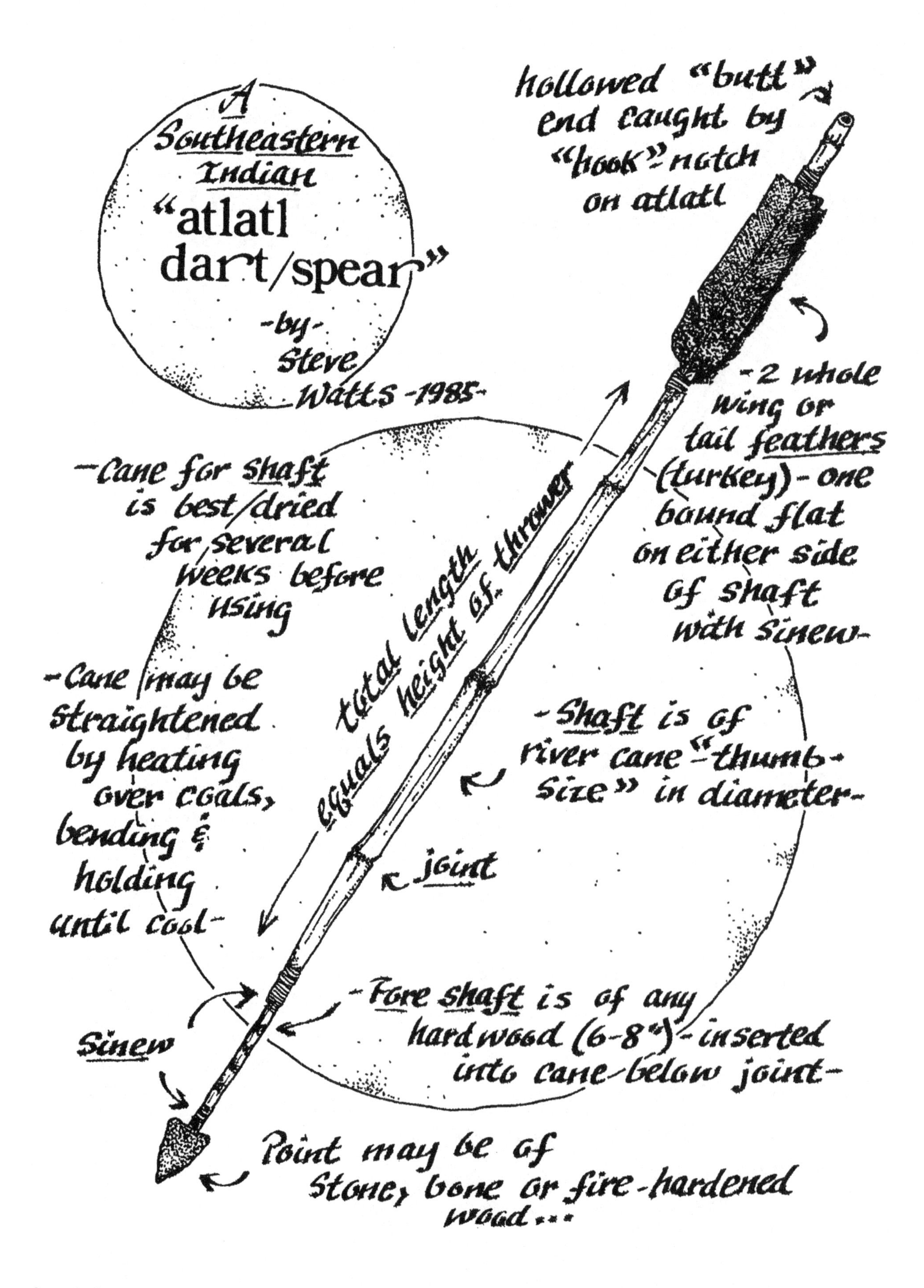
A Southeastern Indian
"atlatl dart/spear"
-by- Steve Watts -1985-
hollowed "butt" end caught by "hook"-notch on atlatl
-2 whole wing or tail feathers (turkey)-one bound flat on either side of shaft with sinew-
-Cane for shaft is best/dried for several weeks before using
total length equals height of thrower
-Cane may be straightened by heating over coals, bending & holding until cool-
-Shaft is of river cane "thumb-size" in diameter-
joint
Sinew
-Fore shaft is of any hardwood (6-8")-inserted into cane-below joint-
Point may be of Stone, bone or fire-hardened wood...

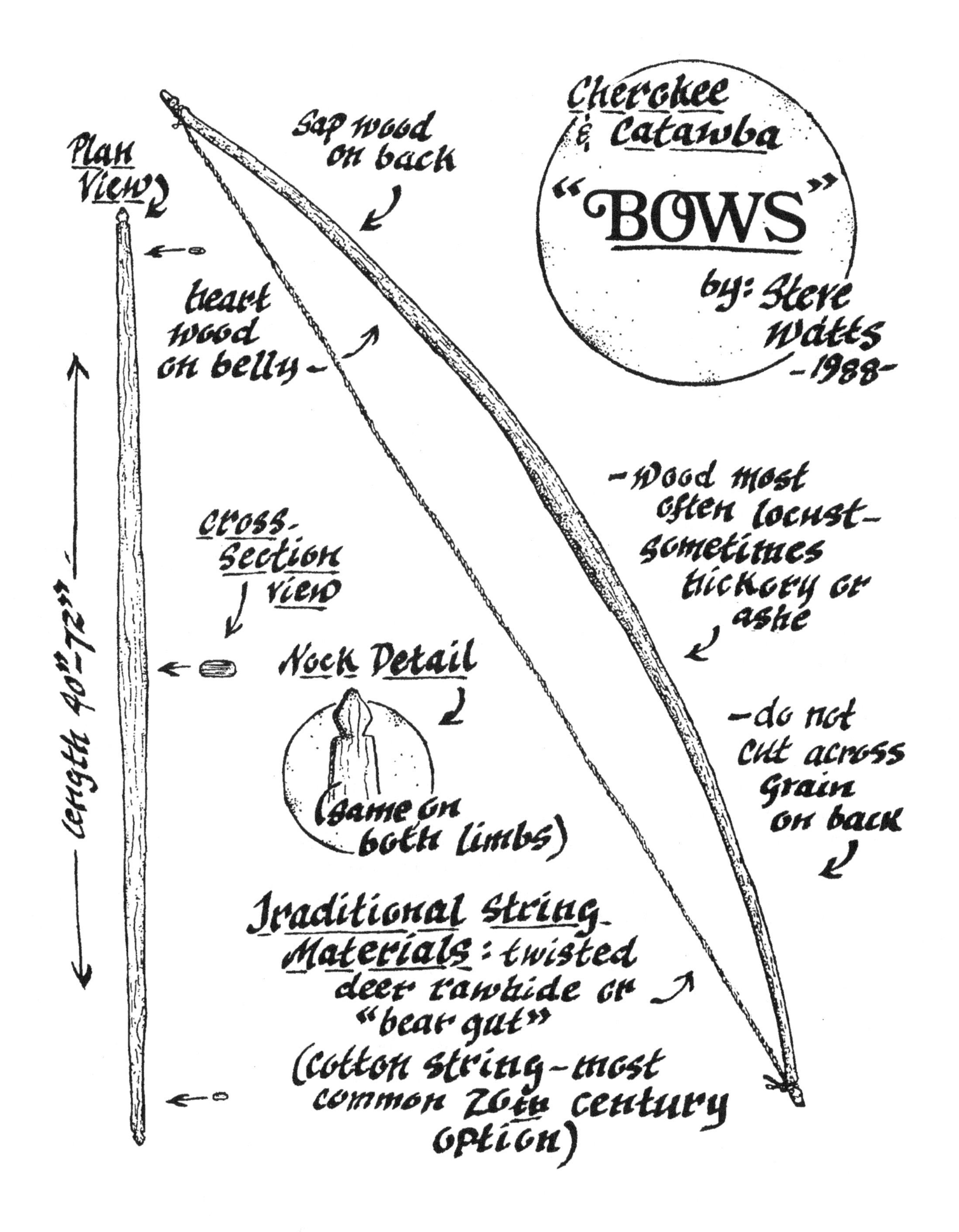
Cherokee & Catawba
"BOWS"
by: Steve Watts
-1988-
Sap wood on back
Plan View
heart wood on belly
Cross-Section view
Length 40"-72"
Nock Detail
(same on both limbs)
-Wood most often locust- sometimes hickory or ashe
-do not cut across grain on back
Traditional String Materials: twisted deer rawhide or "bear gut"
(cotton string-most common 20th century option)

Southeastern Rivercane Arrow Notes

Let us begin with homage to the plant itself - "Rivercane" (*Arundinaria sp.*)

"Cane supplied one of the most important of all raw materials. Besides the use of its seeds (for food), it was employed in making baskets and mats; as building material; in making fishing crails and traps, spears, and arrows; as backing for wattle walls; in making beds in houses and in the construction of corncribs; as a substitute for the shuttle in weaving; as knives and torches; in the 'spiral fire' at Creek councils; in making boxes and cradles, sieves, fanners, hampers, blowguns, blowgun arrows, shields, stockades and fences, rafts, litters, flageolets, counters, drills, and tubes through which to blow into the medicines; as pipes to blow the fire in burning out mortars and in smoking; and sometimes a section was employed to hold braids of the hair."

John R. Swanton, The Indians of the Southeastern United States.
Smithsonian Institution Bureau of American Ethnology, Bulletin 137, 1946.

It's pretty easy to see how those of us here in the North American Southeast find it difficult to conceive of a world without rivercane. It was surely an ace among raw materials for the Native peoples of our area, and remains so for the modern practicing primitive. I believe we could fill an entire book with rivercane projects and philosophy. . . but for now, we'll focus on a few brief thoughts about the rivercane arrow.

The Plant and the People

Rivercane is the traditional arrowshaft material of the historic Southeastern tribes: the Cherokee, Catawba, Creek, Yuchi, Seminole, Natchez, Choctaw, etc. Although hardwood shafts were sometimes used - cane was, by far, the material of choice. It is a true North American native hard-shelled giant grass - not to be confused with "reed grass" (*Phragmites sp.*) or the many varieties of imported oriental bamboos.

Rivercane grows across the southeastern United States from Texas, east to northern Florida, and north to the Virginia/Carolina border. It thrives in the rich bottom lands of the area. These are also prime agricultural plots, which have been under almost constant cultivation since the Late Prehistoric. Consequently, rivercane is often pushed to the edges - hanging on along the borders of fields and on the banks of rivers and creeks. To find an unmolested stand of arrow cane, is to find a treasure.

Attractive Characteristics

Arundinaria possesses a combination of attractive qualities that make it suitable for use in arrow manufacture: light in weight, yet adequately rigid with a wide range of flexibility. Much of this is due to its hollowness and woody, hard shell. These are characteristics that the makers of modern aluminum and fiberglass arrows have attempted to duplicate. And, although extremely well matched arrow shafts can be produced with these contemporary materials, few materials in the bush meet the criteria as well as rivercane.

The abuse these arrows can take is remarkable. I have witnessed them taking violent hits, both head-on and glancing, and come springing back from situations that would have left many a wooden shaft in splinters.

Perhaps one of rivercane's most attractive characteristics as a shaft material is its ease of preparation - no bark to remove, no manipulation of the circumference and its remarkable ability to hold a straightening - being seemingly less responsive to changes in weather than are most hardwoods.

Selection and Gathering

Seek out second-year growth canes without the sheaths which cover new growth. Cut several inches longer than needed, and begin straightening, or bundle to dry. Only when dry will you be able to test for spine - either by feel or with standard spine test apparatus. Remember that with rivercane, rigidity is deter mined not only by the overall diameter of cane, but by the wall thickness as well. Not all rivercane is created equal. Cut a good selection to choose from. This stuff makes serious arrows. You will be able to find rivercane that can take the power of the most serious aboriginal-style big game hunting bow.

Straightening

Though it may appear "straight as an arrow" in the patch, once it is cut, rivercane requires straightening. During the early stages of drying (complete drying will take a couple of weeks in the typically humid southeast) you can periodically straighten with hand and finger pressure alone. Completely dried cane will need heat to do the job. Heat the cane over the coals until it becomes flexible. It can then be straightened in hand or over the knee. Hold until cooled. Be careful. Too much heat can cause the air trapped between joints to explode.

Shaft Surface Treatments

Trimming of the joint areas is done by some arrowmakers, but once again exert caution. Excessive trimming can weaken the shaft. Just a slight abrading, sanding or no treatment at all is more typical of Native arrowmakers.

The surface of rivercane can be brought to a smooth luster with a piece of wet buckskin and extra-fine sand used as an abrasive. A mirror-like finish can be created by burnishing with a bone, antler or joint of cane.

The one drawback to rivercane when it comes

Michael Eldredge

Claude Medford in a stand of rivercane.

to fletching and binding is its slick outer surface. This "skin" gives cane much of its strength and spring. However, it is not very porous and does not accept glue as well as do wooden shafts. It therefore becomes necessary to scrape away this skin in any areas to which you may be applying glue—the shaftment area (where attaching feathers) or the nock or pile end where sinew bindings may be applied. But, you should not scrape the whole surface of the cane. It will weaken the arrow and destroy its liveliness.

Nock and Foreshafts

The hollow and jointed nature of rivercane works in your favor when cutting nocks or inserting foreshafted points. Nocks should be cut directly behind the joint for strength. I have never found it necessary to insert a hardwood nock reinforcement as is sometimes done with Phragmites arrows. A good, strong rivercane arrow can accept a nock by itself. With a little bit of sinew wrap reinforcement, I have often cut nocks in the middle of a section without the added support of the joint wall.

The hollow stem is also perfect for accepting hardwood foreshafts. Cut several inches past a joint if possible, reinforce the cut end with a sinew wrap, shave the foreshaft to fit, and insert.

Final Thoughts and Thanks

Many thanks go out to Richard Crowe, Hayes Lossiah, Walker Calhoun, Eddie Bushyhead, Eva Bigwitch and the other Cherokees who have shared their love and understanding of rivercane with me over the years. Whether they use it for arrows, blowguns, baskets or flutes; these folks possess a familiar reverence for this plant from which we could all learn. And, to Claude Medford, Choctaw basketmaker and itinerant scholar of Native Peoples and Places. Thanks, Claude I know if there is a cane patch in the next world—that's where you are now.

Construction of "Old Time" Southeastern Indian

CANE ARROWS

by: Steve Watts -1983-

Gather cane several months in advance - to allow time for drying -

"V" cut just above joint in cane

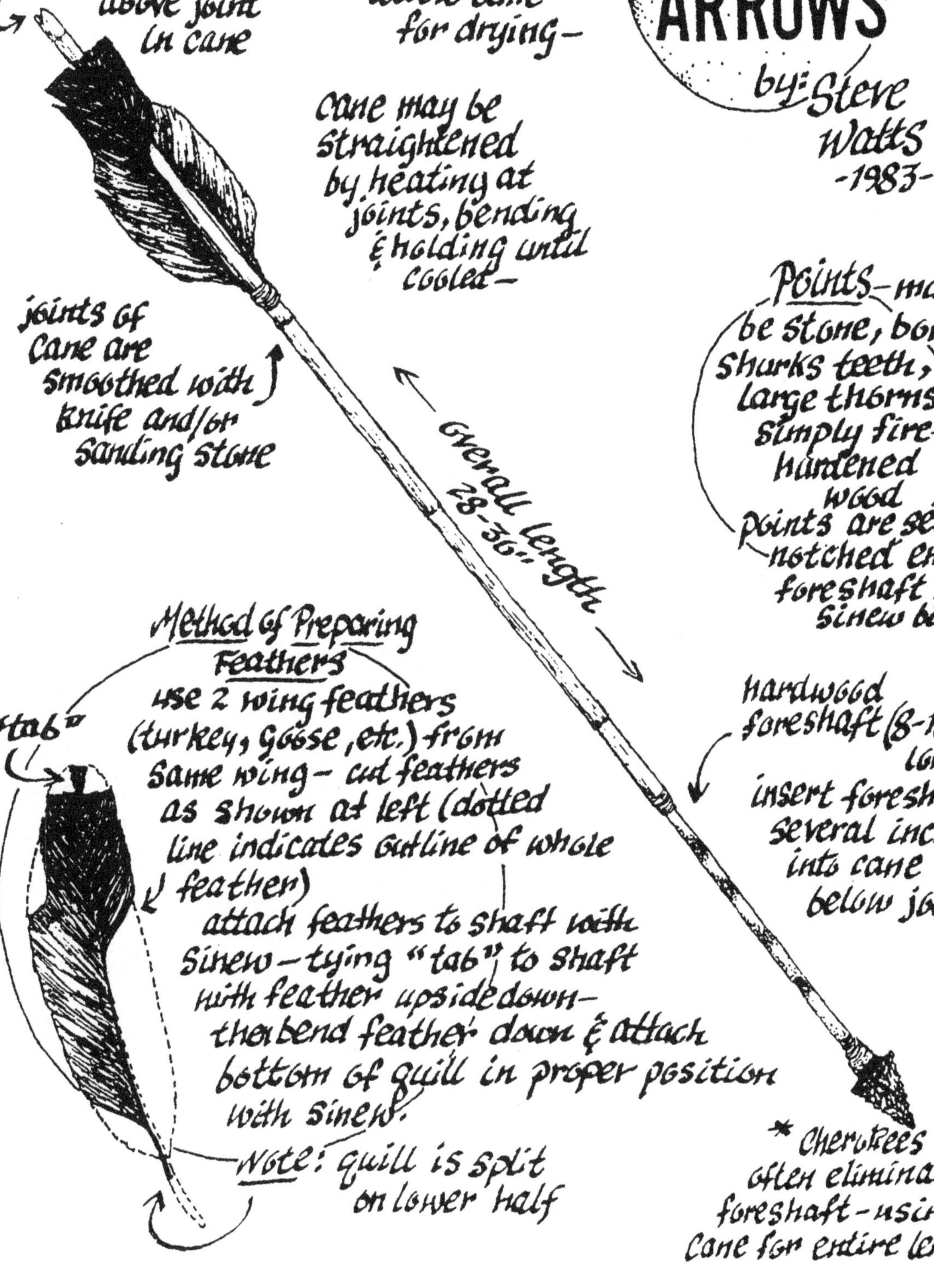

Cane may be straightened by heating at joints, bending & holding until cooled -

joints of cane are smoothed with knife and/or sanding stone

Overall length 28-36"

Points - may be stone, bone, sharks teeth, large thorns or simply fire-hardened wood

points are set in notched end of foreshaft with sinew binding

Method of Preparing Feathers

use 2 wing feathers (turkey, goose, etc.) from same wing - cut feathers as shown at left (dotted line indicates outline of whole feather)

attach feathers to shaft with sinew - tying "tab" to shaft with feather upside down - then bend feather down & attach bottom of quill in proper position with sinew.

"tab"

Note: quill is split on lower half

hardwood foreshaft (8-16" long)

insert foreshaft several inches into cane below joint -

* Cherokees often eliminate foreshaft - using cane for entire length

SW - 1989

Primitive Hook-and-Line Fishing Tackle Options

- **Line:** *2 or 3-ply cordage . . . 8-10 ft. long (yucca leaf, dogbane, milkweed or stinging nettle fiber)*
- **Hooks:** *"J" Hooks (bone, shell, wood or thorn) Gorge Hooks (bone, wood, shell, rivercane or antler)*
- **Sinkers:** *Tied or set into line (stone or ceramic)*
- **Floats:** *Corn cob, wood, bark, large leaf, feather, gourd or plant gall*
- **Poles:** *Light, springy wood (willow) or rivercane . . . 6-8m ft. long*
- **Bait:** *Worms, grasshoppers, grubs, wasp larvae, cornmeal, corn, minnows, frogs, crawfish, etc.*
- **Bait Containers:** *Gourd, basket, bark container, buckskin or rawhide bag*
- **Tools:** *Flake knife (general cutting, pole trimming, cleaning fish etc.) Grinding stone (hook sharpening) Digging stick (worm and grub grubbing)*
- **Stringers:** *3-4 ft. stout cordage with cross stick or hooked branch*
- **Extras:** *Spare line, hooks and sinkers*
- **Tackle Box:** *For carrying the above (minus pole)— basket, rawhide box, bark bucket, rolled mat or hide, string net bag or gourd.*

David Wescott

Primitive fishing tackle by Steve Watts: dogbane string, bone hooks, shell lures, corn cob bobber, and stone weights.

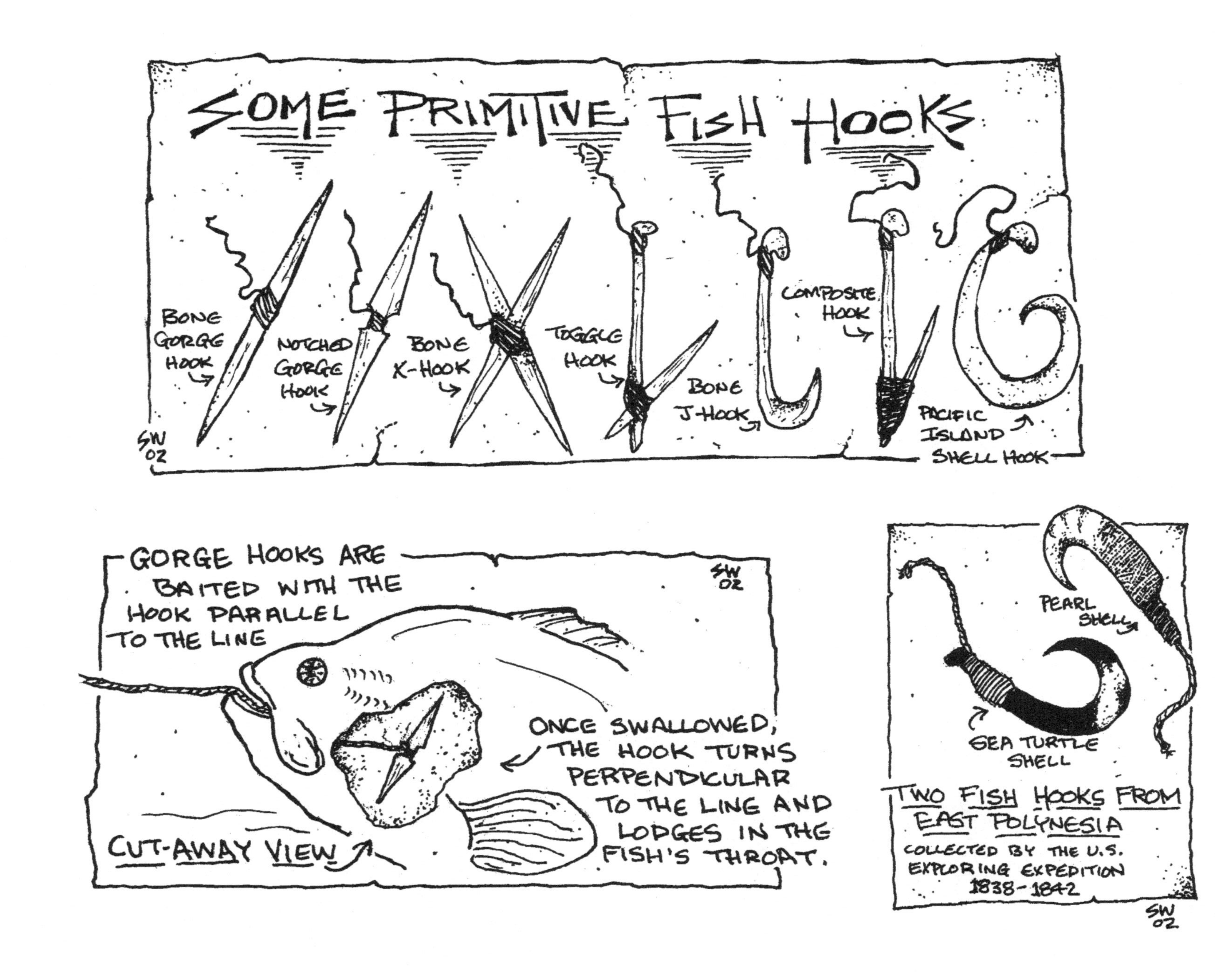
SOME PRIMITIVE FISH HOOKS
BONE GORGE HOOK
NOTCHED GORGE HOOK
BONE X-HOOK
TOGGLE HOOK
BONE J-HOOK
COMPOSITE HOOK
PACIFIC ISLAND SHELL HOOK
SW 02
GORGE HOOKS ARE BAITED WITH THE HOOK PARALLEL TO THE LINE
ONCE SWALLOWED, THE HOOK TURNS PERPENDICULAR TO THE LINE AND LODGES IN THE FISH'S THROAT.
CUT-AWAY VIEW
SW 02
PEARL SHELL
SEA TURTLE SHELL
TWO FISH HOOKS FROM EAST POLYNESIA
COLLECTED BY THE U.S. EXPLORING EXPEDITION 1838-1842
SW 02

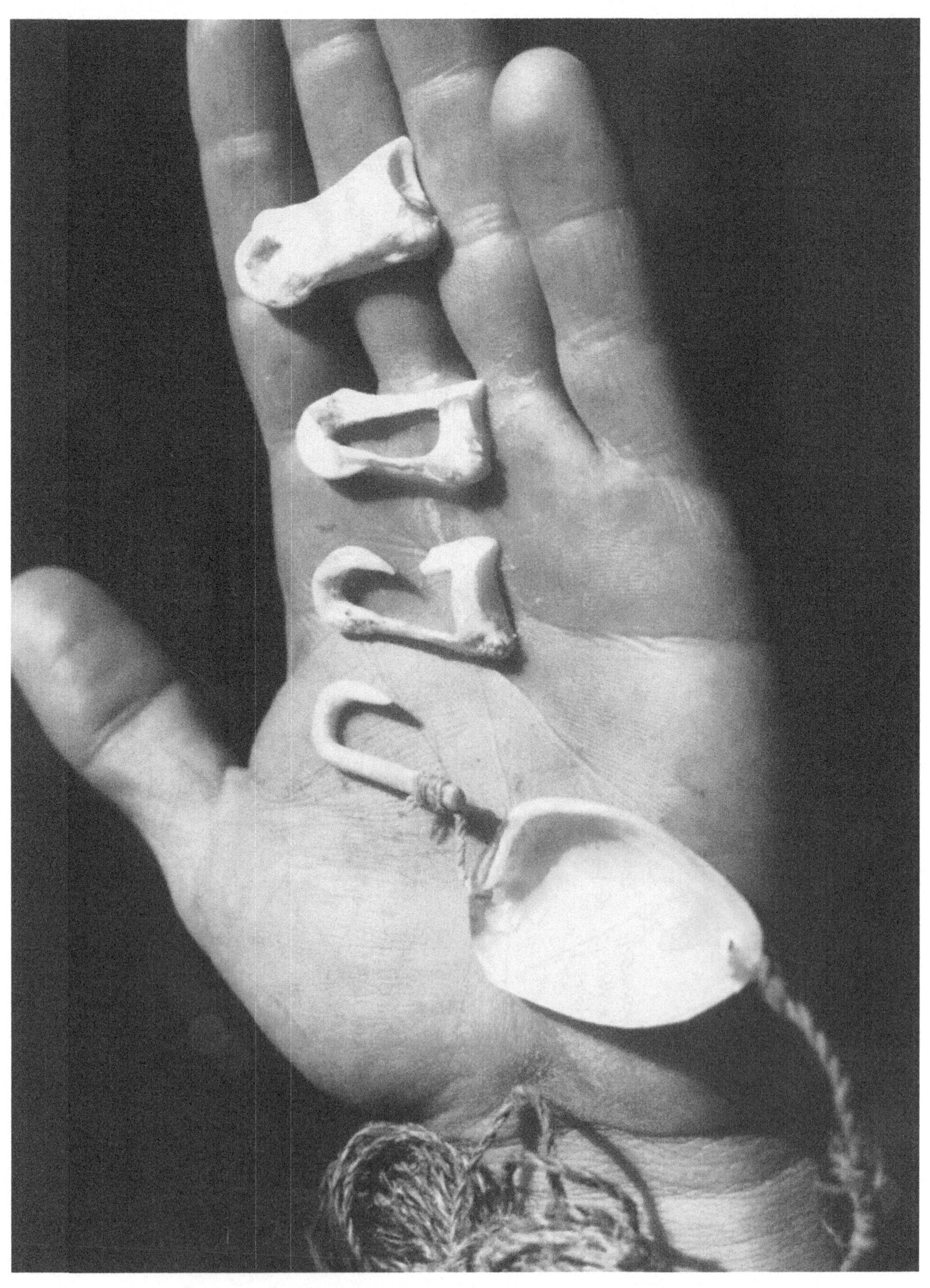

Sequential grinding process for making fish hooks from deer toe bones.

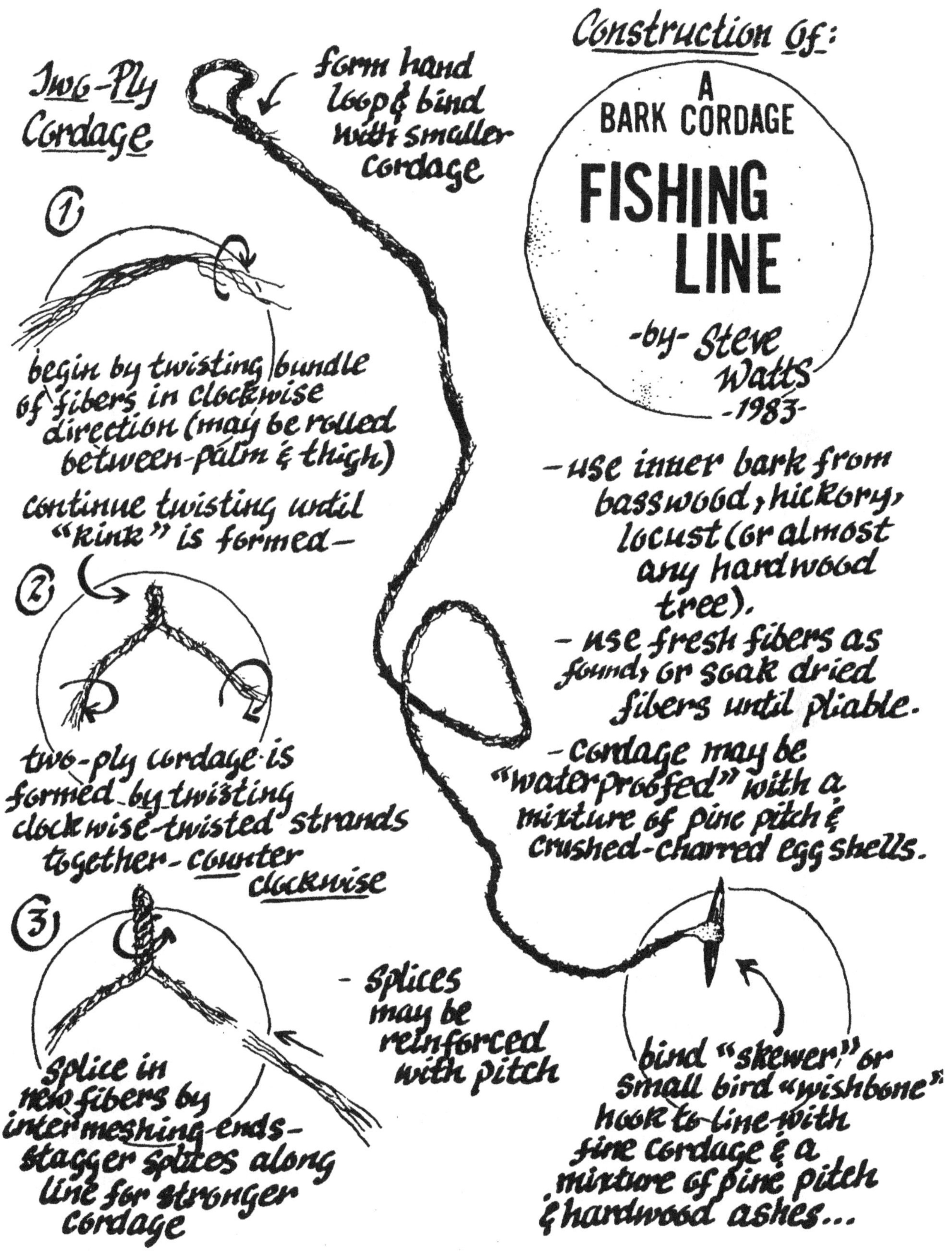

Construction Of:

A BARK CORDAGE FISHING LINE

-by- Steve Watts -1983-

Two-Ply Cordage

form hand loop & bind with smaller cordage

① begin by twisting bundle of fibers in clockwise direction (may be rolled between palm & thigh)

continue twisting until "kink" is formed-

② two-ply cordage is formed by twisting clockwise-twisted strands together-counter clockwise

③ Splice in new fibers by intermeshing ends-stagger splices along line for stronger cordage

- splices may be reinforced with pitch

- use inner bark from basswood, hickory, locust (or almost any hardwood tree).
- use fresh fibers as found, or soak dried fibers until pliable.
- cordage may be "waterproofed" with a mixture of pine pitch & crushed-charred egg shells.

bind "skewer," or small bird "wishbone" hook to line with fine cordage & a mixture of pine pitch & hardwood ashes...

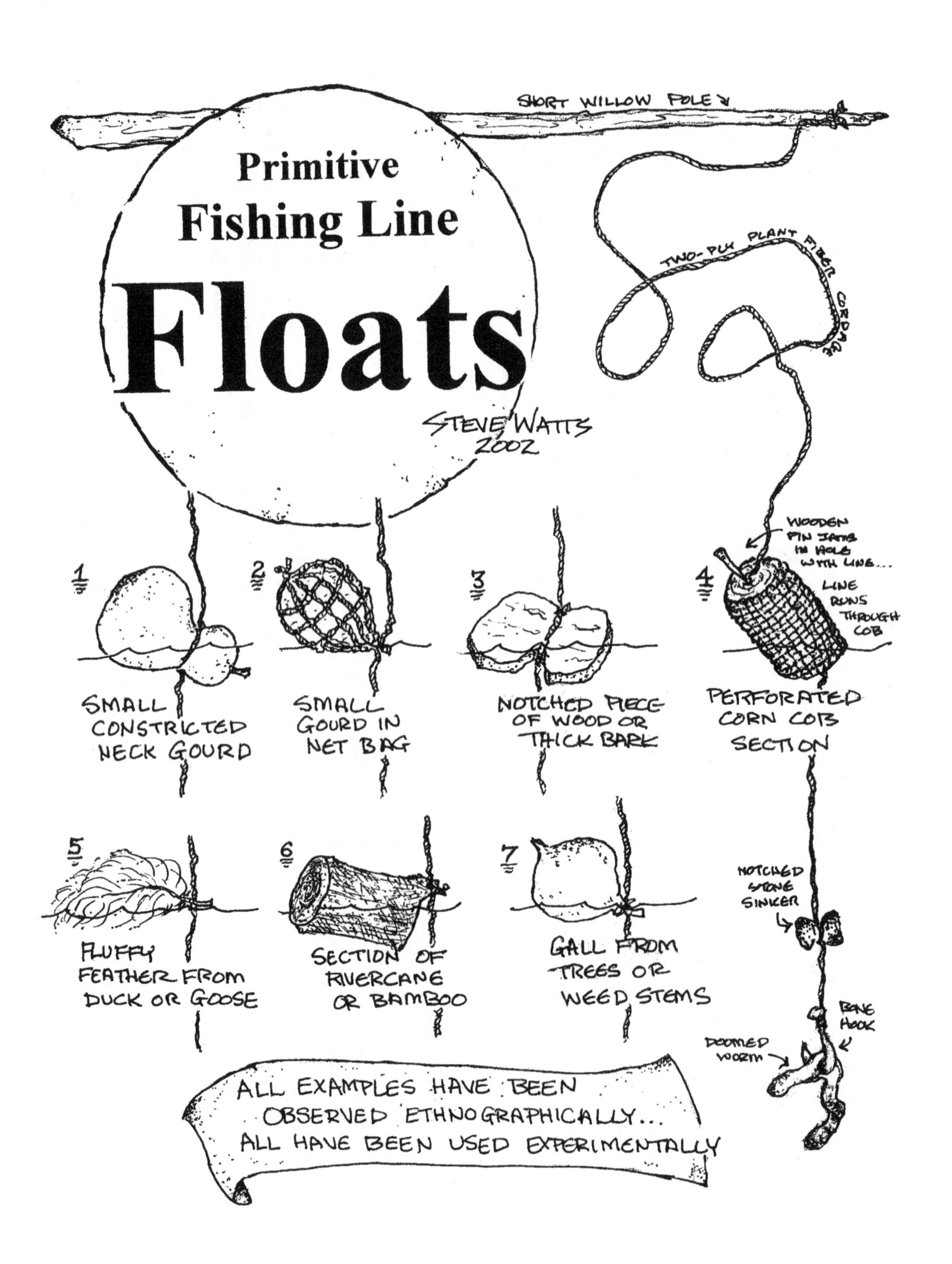

Primitive
Fishing Line
Floats
STEVE WATTS
2002
SHORT WILLOW POLE
TWO-PLY PLANT FIBER CORDAGE
1
SMALL CONSTRICTED NECK GOURD
2
SMALL GOURD IN NET BAG
3
NOTCHED PIECE OF WOOD OR THICK BARK
4
WOODEN PIN JAMS IN HOLE WITH LINE...
LINE RUNS THROUGH COB
PERFORATED CORN COB SECTION
5
FLUFFY FEATHER FROM DUCK OR GOOSE
6
SECTION OF RIVERCANE OR BAMBOO
7
GALL FROM TREES OR WEED STEMS
NOTCHED STONE SINKER
BONE HOOK
DOOMED WORM
ALL EXAMPLES HAVE BEEN OBSERVED ETHNOGRAPHICALLY...
ALL HAVE BEEN USED EXPERIMENTALLY

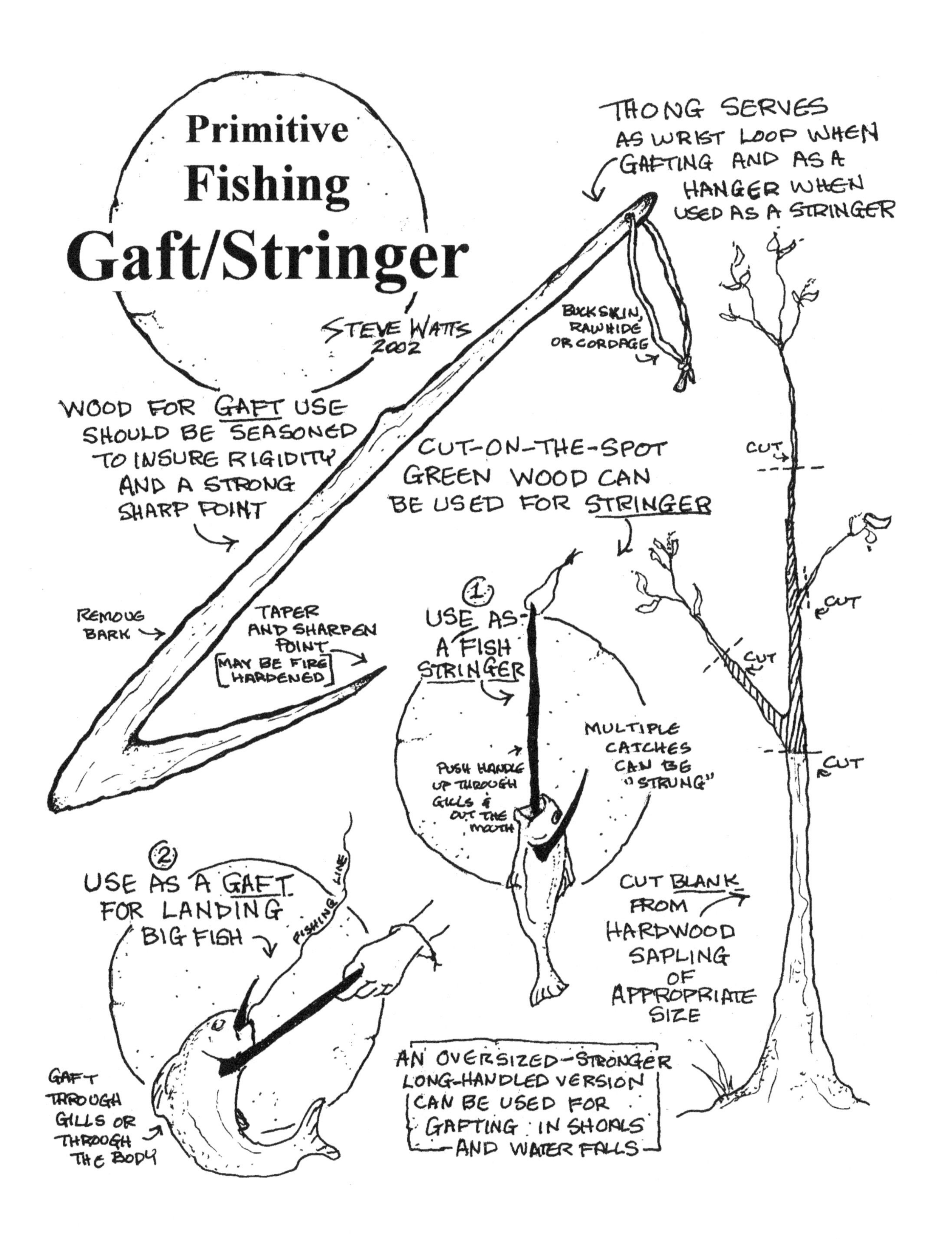
Primitive
Fishing
Gaft/Stringer
STEVE WATTS
2002
THONG SERVES AS WRIST LOOP WHEN GAFTING AND AS A HANGER WHEN USED AS A STRINGER
BUCKSKIN, RAWHIDE OR CORDAGE
WOOD FOR GAFT USE SHOULD BE SEASONED TO INSURE RIGIDITY AND A STRONG SHARP POINT
CUT-ON-THE-SPOT GREEN WOOD CAN BE USED FOR STRINGER
CUT
REMOVE BARK
TAPER AND SHARPEN POINT
MAY BE FIRE HARDENED
1
USE AS A FISH STRINGER
CUT
CUT
MULTIPLE CATCHES CAN BE "STRUNG"
CUT
PUSH HANDLE UP THROUGH GILLS & OUT THE MOUTH
2
USE AS A GAFT FOR LANDING BIG FISH
FISHING LINE
CUT BLANK FROM HARDWOOD SAPLING OF APPROPRIATE SIZE
AN OVERSIZED-STRONGER LONG-HANDLED VERSION CAN BE USED FOR GAFTING IN SHOALS AND WATER FALLS
GAFT THROUGH GILLS OR THROUGH THE BODY

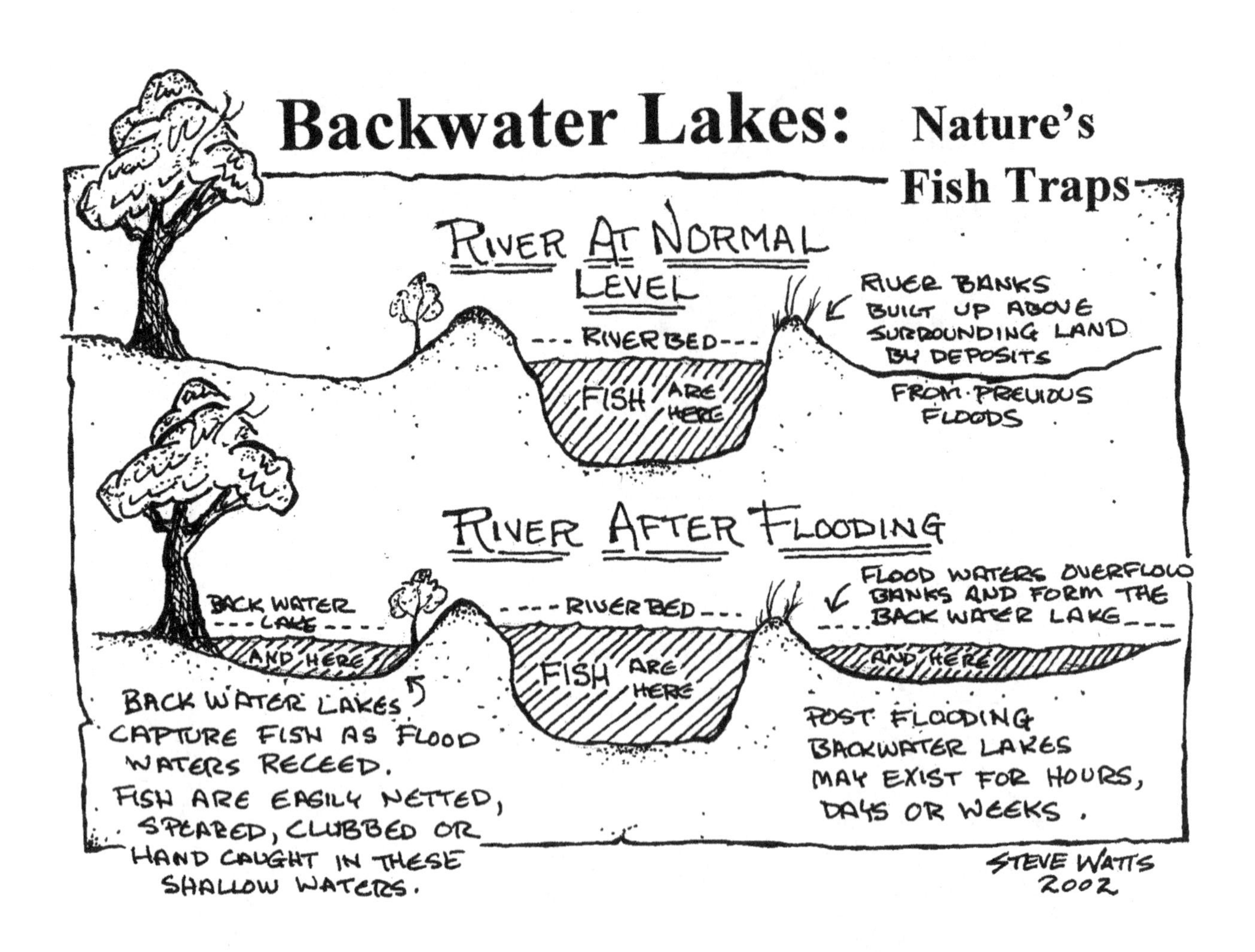

Left - Stone-weighted fish net with gourd floats. Right - A bait-and-tackle kit made from a small gourd includes bone hooks, a corn cob bobber, dogbane string, a stone knife, and shell lures. Net and kit made by the author.

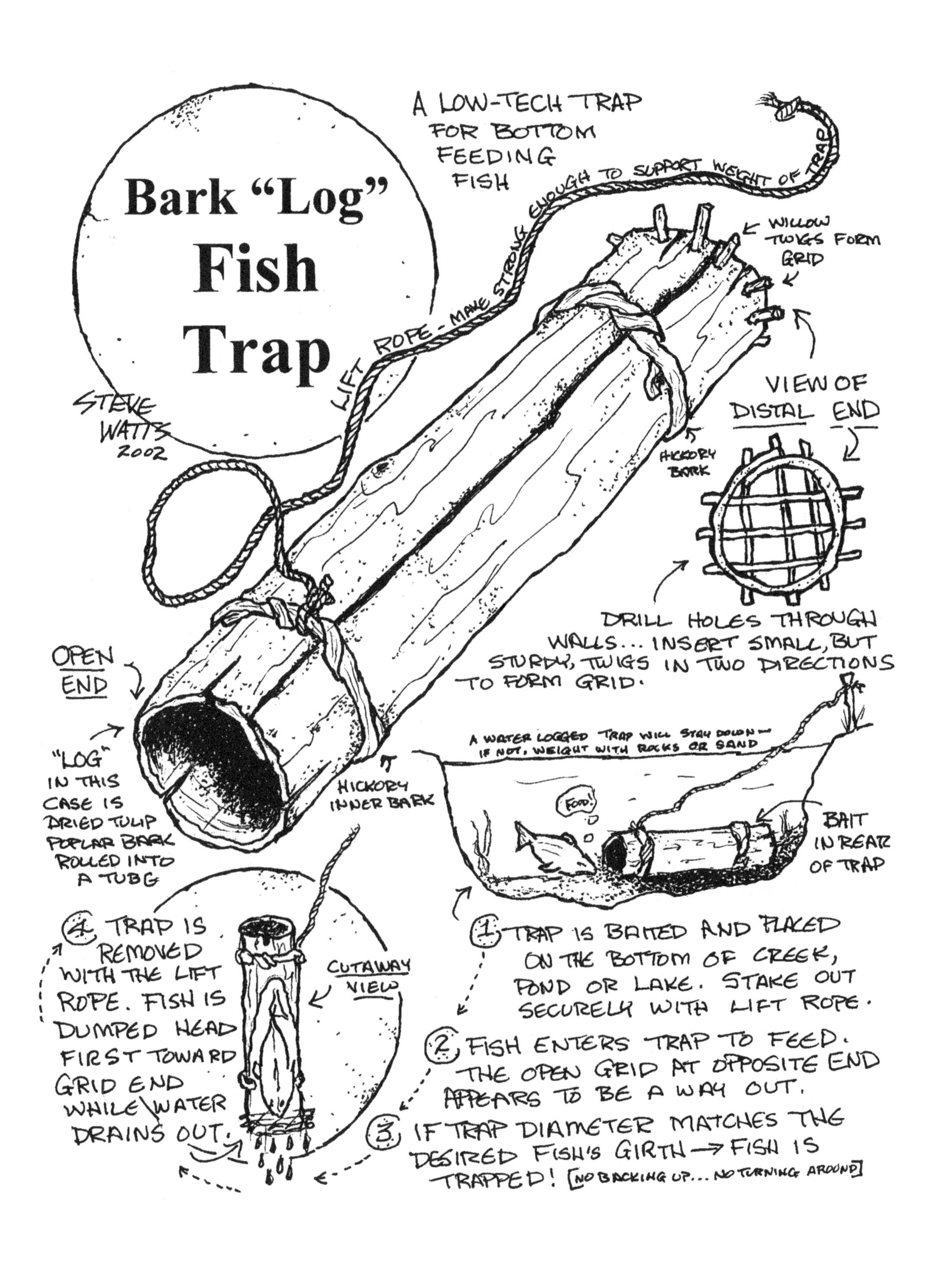

Bark "Log" Fish Trap
STEVE WATTS 2002
A LOW-TECH TRAP FOR BOTTOM FEEDING FISH
LIFT ROPE - MAKE STRONG ENOUGH TO SUPPORT WEIGHT OF TRAP
WILLOW TWIGS FORM GRID
VIEW OF DISTAL END
HICKORY BARK
DRILL HOLES THROUGH WALLS... INSERT SMALL, BUT STURDY, TWIGS IN TWO DIRECTIONS TO FORM GRID.
OPEN END
"LOG" IN THIS CASE IS DRIED TULIP POPLAR BARK ROLLED INTO A TUBE
HICKORY INNER BARK
A WATER LOGGED TRAP WILL STAY DOWN— IF NOT, WEIGHT WITH ROCKS OR SAND
FOOD!
BAIT IN REAR OF TRAP
CUTAWAY VIEW
4 TRAP IS REMOVED WITH THE LIFT ROPE. FISH IS DUMPED HEAD FIRST TOWARD GRID END WHILE WATER DRAINS OUT.
1 TRAP IS BAITED AND PLACED ON THE BOTTOM OF CREEK, POND OR LAKE. STAKE OUT SECURELY WITH LIFT ROPE.
2 FISH ENTERS TRAP TO FEED. THE OPEN GRID AT OPPOSITE END APPEARS TO BE A WAY OUT.
3 IF TRAP DIAMETER MATCHES THE DESIRED FISH'S GIRTH → FISH IS TRAPPED! [NO BACKING UP... NO TURNING AROUND]

Michael Eldredge Photos

Fish Trap Workshop
Schiele Museum
Aboriginal Studies Program, 1989

Kay Moss twinning the funnel of a willow fish trap, using willow bark.

Arlena Meek fishing with a willow pole, 2-ply dogbane line, corn cob float, and bone gorge hook. A rivercane fish trap leans against the fence.

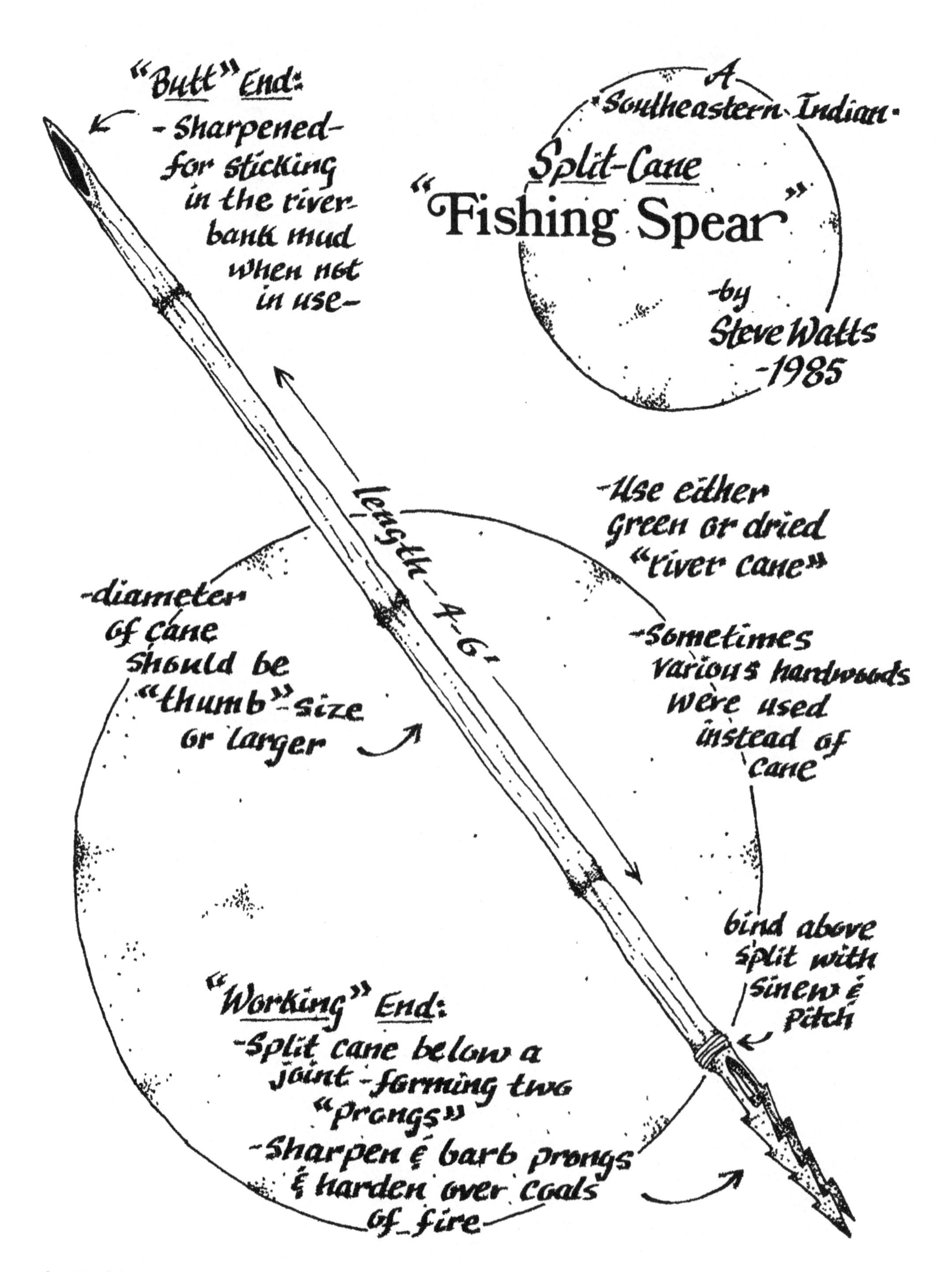
A Southeastern Indian
Split-Cane
"Fishing Spear"
-by Steve Watts -1985
"Butt" End:
- Sharpened-
for sticking
in the river-
bank mud
when not
in use-
length 4-6'
-Use either
green or dried
"river cane"
-diameter
of cane
should be
"thumb"-size
or larger
-Sometimes
various hardwoods
were used
instead of
cane
bind above
split with
sinew &
pitch
"Working" End:
-Split cane below a
joint - forming two
"prongs"
-Sharpen & barb prongs
& harden over coals
of fire

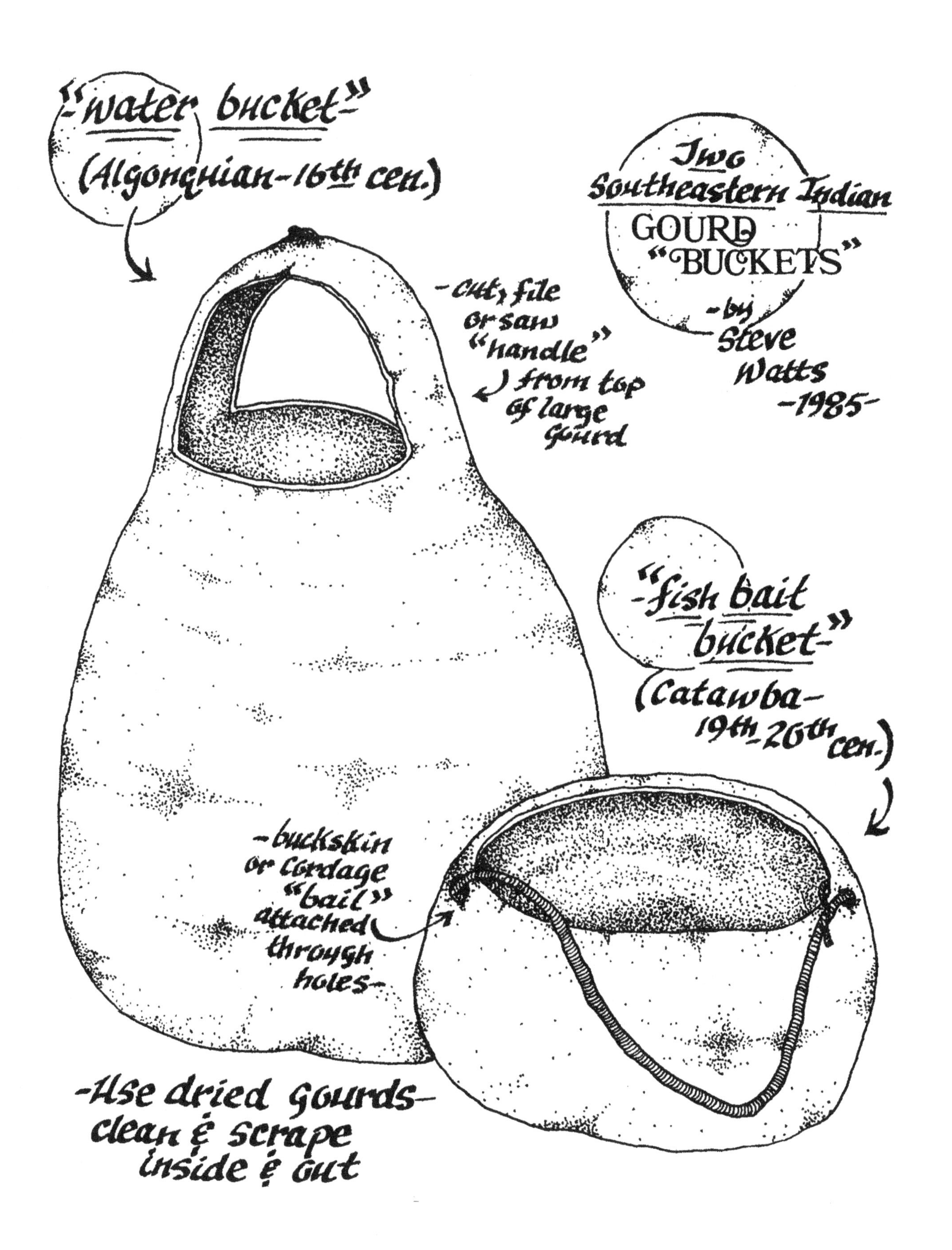
"-water bucket-"
(Algonquian-16th cen.)
Two Southeastern Indian
GOURD "BUCKETS"
-by Steve Watts -1985-
-cut, file or saw "handle" from top of large gourd
"-fish bait bucket-"
(Catawba-19th-20th cen.)
-buckskin or cordage "bail" attached through holes-
-Use dried gourds-
clean & scrape
inside & out

7
The Aboriginal Arts

Pam Perkins

Around thirty thousand years ago in the Upper Paleolithic, a great explosion of creativity occurred. Our ancestors began to paint on the walls of caves and on freestanding stones. They carved bone, stone, ivory, and antler into three dimensional representations of the animals they hunted. They pierced shells, teeth, claws, and bones to wear as ornaments. They painted and tattooed their bodies with signs of clan, tribe or personal vision. From bones, skins, plants, and shells, they fashioned instruments of music.

These expressions reflected a new way of thinking - a higher level of interpretation - a whole new technology of abstraction and symbolism.

"Images In Stone" Animals, Art and Anima

"Neither in body nor in mind do we inhabit the world of those hunting races of the Paleolithic millenia, to whose lives and ways we nevertheless owe the very forms of our bodies and the structures of our minds. Memories of the animal envoys still must sleep, somehow, within us; for they wake a little and stir when we venture into wilderness. They wake in terror to thunder. And again they wake with a sense of recognition, when we enter any one of those great painted caves. Whatever the inward darkness may have been to which the shamans of the caves descended in their trances, the same must lie within ourselves nightly visited in sleep."

Joseph Campbell,
The Way of the Animal Powers,

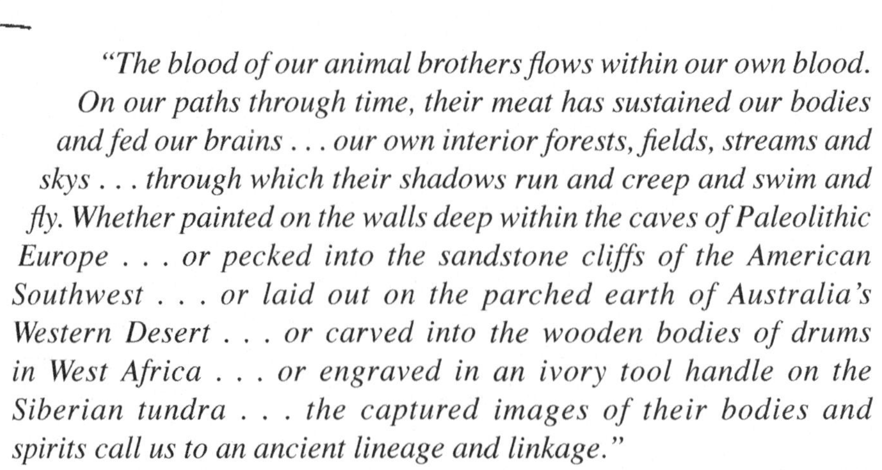

"The blood of our animal brothers flows within our own blood. On our paths through time, their meat has sustained our bodies and fed our brains . . . our own interior forests, fields, streams and skys . . . through which their shadows run and creep and swim and fly. Whether painted on the walls deep within the caves of Paleolithic Europe . . . or pecked into the sandstone cliffs of the American Southwest . . . or laid out on the parched earth of Australia's Western Desert . . . or carved into the wooden bodies of drums in West Africa . . . or engraved in an ivory tool handle on the Siberian tundra . . . the captured images of their bodies and spirits call us to an ancient lineage and linkage."

Steve Watts, 1991

"Rock Graphics"

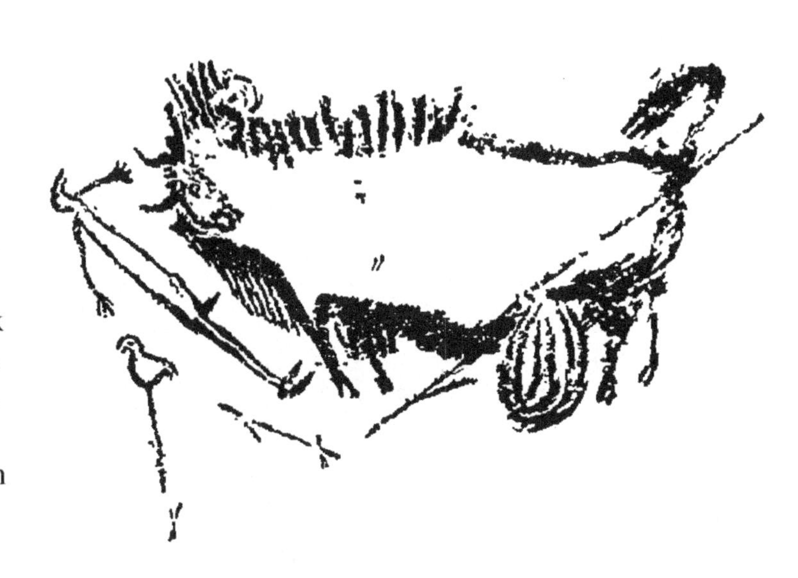

Pictograph

A pictograph may be created by any number of application techniques, using a wide variety of pigments, but is essentially an image painted on a rock surface. It may be a single image on a pebble, slab or free standing boulder . . . or it may take the form of a multi-imaged panel on a cliff face or canyon wall.

Petroform

Petroforms are images formed on the surface of the earth by the placement of stones in a pattern. These images may be simple outlines or massive placements resulting in effigy mound formations.

Petroglyph

Petroglyphs are images formed by cutting into the surface of a rock using one or a combination of techniques. The resulting image might be shallow or deep . . . made by scratching, grooving, drilling or (as most ofen) pecking. Once again, the number of images may vary from one to many and the size from pebble to cliff-face panel.

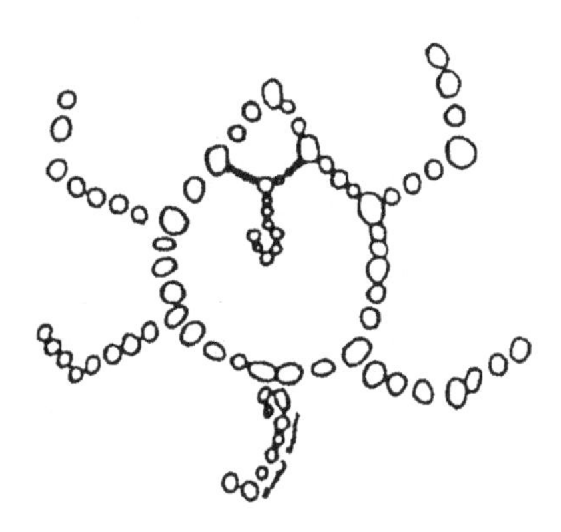

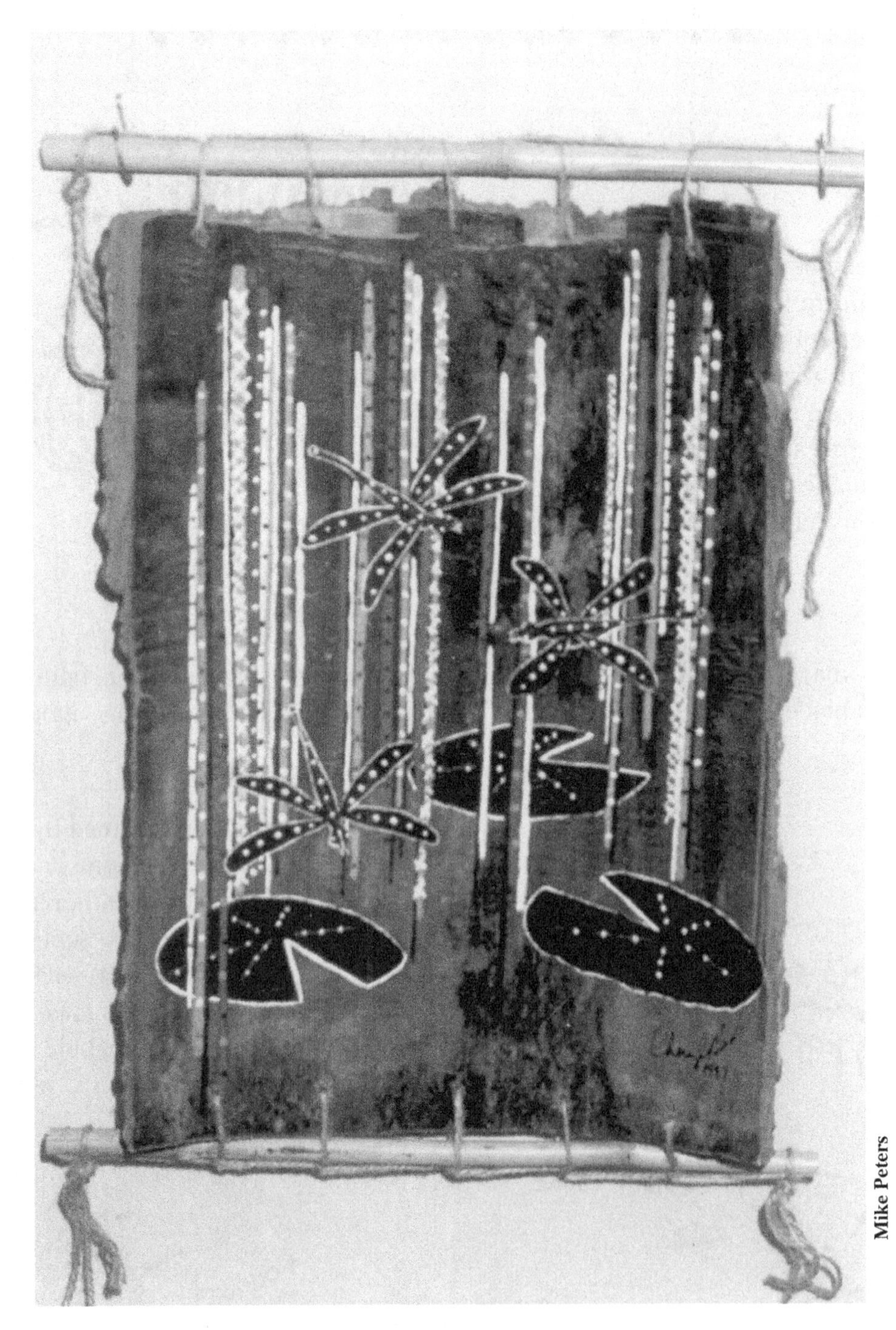

Bark Painting

By Cheryl Baskins

(Limonite, hematite, kayolin clay, and wood charcoal)

Aboriginal "Art Supplies"

Mineral Pigments

Red...Hematite
Yellow...Limonite
White...Kayolin Clay, Gypsum, Chalk, Bird Droppings
Black...Charcoal, Graphite, Manganese Ores

Vehicles and Binders

Water
Animal Fat
Plant Juices and Oils
Hide Glue
Egg Whites
Blood
Urine

Applicators

Hair and Fiber Brushes
Fingers, Hands
Chewed Twig Brushes
Split Bones
Soft Sticks
Fur, Moss, & Leather Bundles
Feathers
Charcoal "Pencils"
Ochre "Crayons"

Paint Containers

Turtle Carapice
Shells
Stone Bowls
Clay Pots/Fragments
Bark Trays
Large Leaves
Skulls/Fragments
Bone and Stone Pallets
Gourd Bowls

Paint Preparation and Storage

Mortar and Pestles
Grinding Stones
Water Containers
Cane & Bone Vials

"Phosphenes"

Certain images (circles, spirals, crosses, grids, etc.) seem to crop up again and again in aboriginal art. Is this merely coincidence or is there something else at work. Some have suggested that these images reflect the "hard wiring" of the brain . . . .actual viual representations of the inner life by peoples intimately familiar with that interior landscape . . .*"phosphenes."*

Petroglyph, Little Petroglyph Canyon, Coso Range, California

"Phosphene comes from the Greek word for "light shows", and they are produced by excitation of the retina. Everyone who has received a severe knock on the head has seen flashes of light that seem to originate within the head. Such light patterns can also be seen when falling asleep or meditating with eyes closed. Airplane pilots report seeing similar apparitions when flying across expanses of empty sky. Astronauts have reported viewing phosphenes so tangibly in outer space that they were first believed to be caused by heavy light particles. Phosphenes appear when the opened eyes have had nothing to see for an extended period of time. Delirium tremors, fasting, high fever, hyperventilation, migraine headaches, and simple eye pressure can produce variations on the basic set of fifteen patterns. From a scientific point of view, what are these inner light shows? Phosphenes are believed to originate primarily in the retinal-optical track and the brain. Scientists think they are images reflecting neural firing patterns in the visual pathways, which makes them very important cognitive images."

Robert Lawler, Voices Of The First Day, 1991

One version of the fifteen phosphene forms. From: "Phosphenes", Gerald Oster, Scientific American, Feb. 1970

Two other versions: Kellog, Knoll and Kugler, 1965 and Hedges, 1981

Primitive Oil Lamp Components

Containers

Stone...Natural Depressions
Carved Depressions... Soapstone, Lime-stone, Mud/Siltstone
Pecked Depressions... Granite, Eroded Quartzite, Sandstone,

Vesicular Basalt, Other medium-grained stones.

Fired Ceramics...Either formal vessels or curved fragments of vessels.

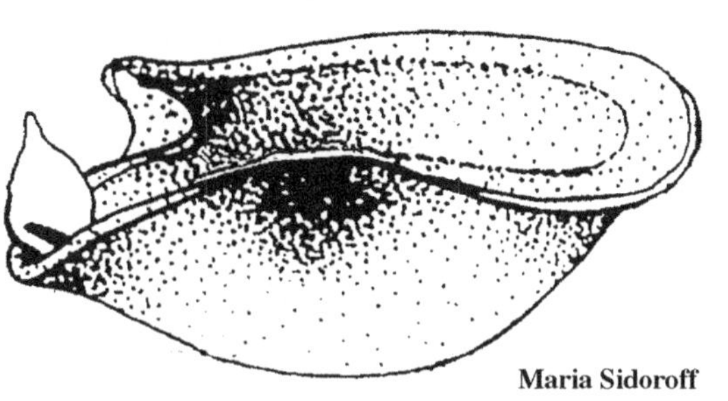
Maria Sidoroff

Wet Clay or Mud Vessels

Marine/Fresh Water Shells

Bone...Turtle Shells
Skull Caps
Long Bone Fragments

Even more flammable materials such as gourds, wooden bowls, coconut shells, etc. can be used if lined with sand, clay, etc. and flame is kept away from the rim.

Fuels

Vegetable Oil
Animal Fat
Animal Oil (rendered fat)
Marrow
Butter

Wicks

Twisted/Corded Wicks...Juniper or other inner barks of trees.
Lump Wicks...Mosses and Lichens
Dried Herbivore Dung
Cattails and Other Plant "Downs"
Rolled Dried Mullien Leaves
Cotton
Juniper Bark

WHAT KIND OF SOUND DOES A GOURD MAKE?

The Plant, the Process and the Possibilities

"Their chief instruments are rattles made of small gourds or pumpeons shells. Of these they have base, tenor, counter-tenor, mean and treble. These they mingled with their voices, sometimes twenty or thirty together . . ."

John Smith, 17th century, Virginia

GOURDS?

First . . . a little taxonomy for clarity's sake: The use of the term "gourd" in popular literature and common speech sometimes leads to much confusion. In England, if you were to ask for a "gourd" you might get a pumpkin or a squash. So called "ornamental gourds" (*Cucurbita pepo*), typically found on the decorated American Thanksgiving table, get the same label. "Loofah gourds" (*Luffa aegyptiaca*) - that utilitarian fibrous vegetable used historically for washing dishes and more recently for up-scale human bathing - is actually most closely related to the cucumber. In Middle and South America we find the "calabash" or "tree gourd" (*Cresentia cujete*) - a species unrelated to all of the above.

Photo 1. Gourd is mature and ready to harvest when vine is dead and stem is dry. (Gourd from Olin S. Watts garden - Fall, 1994.)

For the purposes of this article, the word "gourd" is used to refer to the so-called "hard-shelled gourd" (*Lagenaria siceraria* or *Lagenaria vulgaris* in the older literature). Lagenaria are members of the *Cucurbitacea* family. This large plant family includes cucumbers, pumpkins, squashes, watermelons, cantaloupes, ornamental gourds, etc. Hence, we discover some of the root of the confusion.

Distribution

Hard-shell gourds are found in the temperate and tropical zones of the Americas, Africa, Asia and the Pacific. Much has been written concerning their origin. The debate usually comes down to a choice between an African or American genesis theory. (For one of the best treatments of this question in the popular literature, see *The Gourd Book*, Charles B. Heiser, Jr., 1979, Chapter 7.) Whichever continent may ultimately lay claim to its birth, the fact remains that Lagenaria fragments appear in the American archeological record as early as 6 to 7,000 years ago. Recently, identifiable gourd seeds were found in Florida in preserved mastodon dung!

For the modern primitive gourd crafter, distribution may be as near as the backyard garden (see *"Gourds: Their Culture and Use"*, Hamlin, The American Gourd Society, Mt. Gilead, Ohio for cultivation information) or a commercial grower/distributor (Lena Braswell, Braswell's Gourd Farm, Wrens, Georgia is a first-class contact).

Properties and Preparation

Gourds were perhaps most likely used by early humans for containers or a less than tasty food source. Additionally, *Lagenaria* possess certain properties which make them ideal for the manufacture of a variety of musical instruments. And, variety itself is one. Hard shell gourds come in sizes which range from just a few inches in diameter to bushel basket size. And, the shapes - globular, elongated, spherical, flattened, tubular, hourglass, goblet and bottle-shapes are only some of the forms - forms which can compete favorably with the human imagination.

A good, mature gourd is "woody" and extremely durable to a point, yet can easily be worked using stone-age tools. Being hollow, gourds serve as a natural resonating chamber, so important in the magnification of sound. Only bamboo rivals the gourd as the choice material for the construction of primitive musical instruments worldwide.

Preparation of gourds for instrument manufacture is simple once a mature gourd is obtained. Gourds have reached maturity when the vine has died and dried (Photo 1). Cutting a gourd from the vine prior to maturity will result in a rotted, not a dried, end product. Depending on the gourd's size, it will dry (preferably outside in cold weather) in a few weeks to several months. When dry it will be relatively light in weight and one can hear either the seeds or a large lump rattling around inside when shaken.

During the drying process, the outer skin (a thin layer which covers the thicker shell) will flake, mold, mildew and generally begin to look like a leftover science project gone bad. Have no fear. The transformation now begins. After wetting down the gourd's skin to soften it, begin to scrape

Photo 3. Mature dried gourds . . . a field full of music, awaiting release

away the offending matter with a knife, shell or stone flake (Photo 3). The skin will peel away and you will be rewarded with a beautiful, smooth, cream to amber colored shell. This preparation serves more than an aesthetic function, by the way. The cleaning of the shell's outer surface (like the removal of the pithy material inside the gourd) will aide in the prevention of future deterioration. An unscraped gourd will continue to draw moisture, even from the air in humid climates. And, if your are looking for a resonator here, be assured that improved appearance equals improved performance. You are now ready to cut, empty, interior scrape, perforate, oil, decorate or otherwise modify the gourd to suit your purposes.

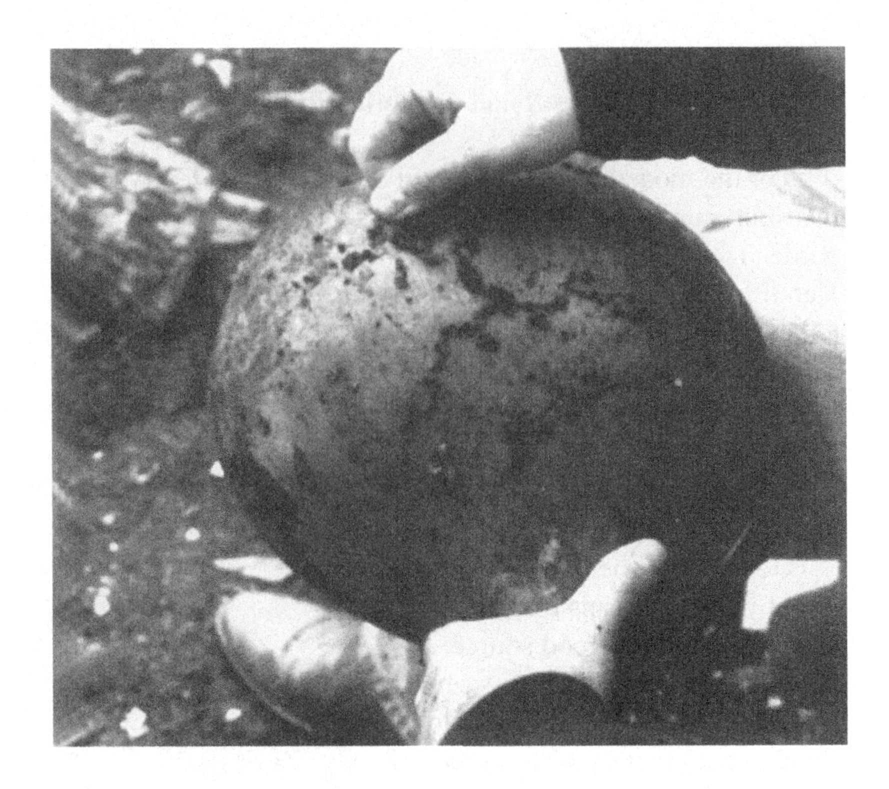

Photo 3. Scraping away outer skin with a stone flake.

THE INSTRUMENTS

What follows is a sampling of the variety of musical instrument forms which can be created from the hard shelled gourd (Photo 4). There are many others. Only historically/ethnographically based examples are cited here. Your imagination and creativity alone define the limits.

What kind of sound does a gourd make? Using the traditional ethnomusicological classifications of instruments, let us begin to explore.

Idiophones

Pick up a mature dried gourd and shake it. You have just discovered (as did many an ancestral musician) one of the most wide-spread of all idiophones - the rattle. Gourd rattles may take either the simple or the composite form - ie. the whole intact gourd with seeds inside (sometimes perforated to "let the sound out") or, a cut gourd with a handle attached and stones or seeds added to create the desired sound. African and Native American examples abound, from which you may choose. *"Shakere"*-type rattles derive their distinctive sound not from objects within but from the netted arrangement of seeds, shells or beads which hit and rub against the gourd's hard outer surface.

The concussion "drum" of Hawaii - the *ipu* - is simply a large bottle gourd with the top removed, which is sounded either by slapping with the hand or by being dropped/ thumped on the padded ground. This is a true idiophone not a drum in the classic sense (see membranophones below).

Rasps, or friction idiophones (known as *guiros* in Latin America) are created by cutting a sound hole or removing the end of an elongated gourd and cutting grooves across its surface. Sound is produced by rubbing across these grooves with a wire or thin wooden stick.

Gourds also serve as separate resonators in some composite idiophonic instruments - the "thumb piano" of Africa and the wooden keyed xylophones or marimbas of Africa and South America are often amplified with the addition of gourds.

Aerophones

Cut both ends from an elongated gourd, blow in one end bugle-style, and you have the simplest of gourd aerophones. Traditional Africa is filled with a variety of horn-like instruments either made from gourds entirely, or in which gourds are used as a component. These include trumpet-type horns (either transverse or end-blown) along with double and single-reeded oboe and clarinet "snake charmer" types.

Simple gourd whistles and nose flutes have been reported from Polynesia and the Native North American Southeast. These are single to triple-holed affairs made from small pear-shaped gourds and blown "bottle-neck" fashion. The long necks of dipper gourds have also been fashioned into multi-holed flutes (see *"Gourds of the Southeastern Indians"*, Frank G. Speck, 1941).

Perhaps one of the most unusual of aerophones is the "swing top" from Hawaii (see *Hawaiian and Other Polynesian Gourds*, Dodge, 1978). This musical amusement is made from a small gourd with its top removed and swung by a string around the head in a bullroarer fashion. It produces a high-pitched whistling sound which one can interpret as soothing or annoying depending on your mood and taste.

Membranophones

Stretch a wet rawhide over the cut off end of a gourd and you have a drum. It seems obvious enough, considering the hollow resonating structure of the gourd form. Yet, I find ethnographic examples only from Africa - none in Asia or the Americas. I trust that there are readers who can enlighten me further. I do know that I've seen a few nice gourd drums made by modern practicing primitives, of both the single and double-headed variety. (I'm referring here to the drums, not to the makers.)

Chordophones

From the most simple of musical bows (like the *berimbaus* of Brazil) to the most elaborate of sitars and vines from India, the gourd functions to amplify the sound of the plucked string. Various forms of lutes, zithers, harps and harp-zithers are found throughout Africa - many with one or more gourd resonators. (See *African Music: A People's Art*, Bebey, 1969 for excellent examples.) The birthplace of the Afro-American banjo is disputed. But, whether its inventor was a free man of West Africa or a slave in the Americas, gourds were there at its inception.

What kind of sound does a gourd make?

Perhaps it's the quiet, mellow sound of a single-holed flute in the woods of the tidewater Virginia Rappahanock . . . or the deep throated booming sound of a whole orchestra of gourd drums in Africa's Upper Volta . . . or the sensual wave of sound that flows from an ancient classical Indian rage . . . or the soft but sure sound of the healer's rattle from deep within the Amazon Basin.

Or maybe, it just might be the sound that you make . . . from where you are. . . here and now.

continued . . .

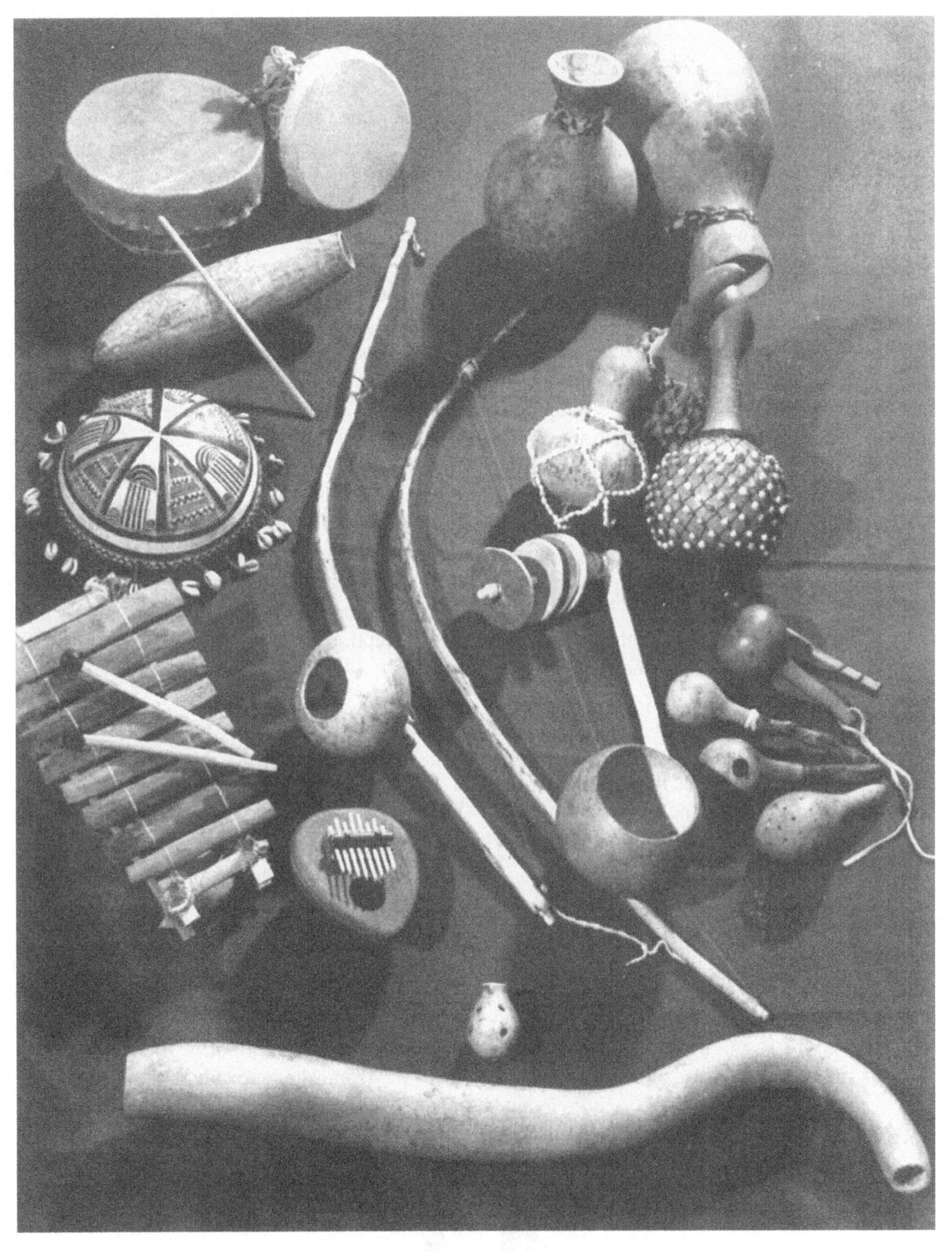

Photo 4. A variety of gourd-based musical instruments (Clockwise - beginning at upper right): two "Ipu" concusion drums, three "shakere"-style rattles, gourd disk sistrum, five gourd rattles (simple and composite), two musical bows with gourd resonators, gourd trumpet, three-holed whistle, thumb piano with gourd resonator, "balafon" with gourd resonator (suspended under keys), gourd and cowrie-shell tambourine/ bowl, "guiro" rasp, two gourd drums.

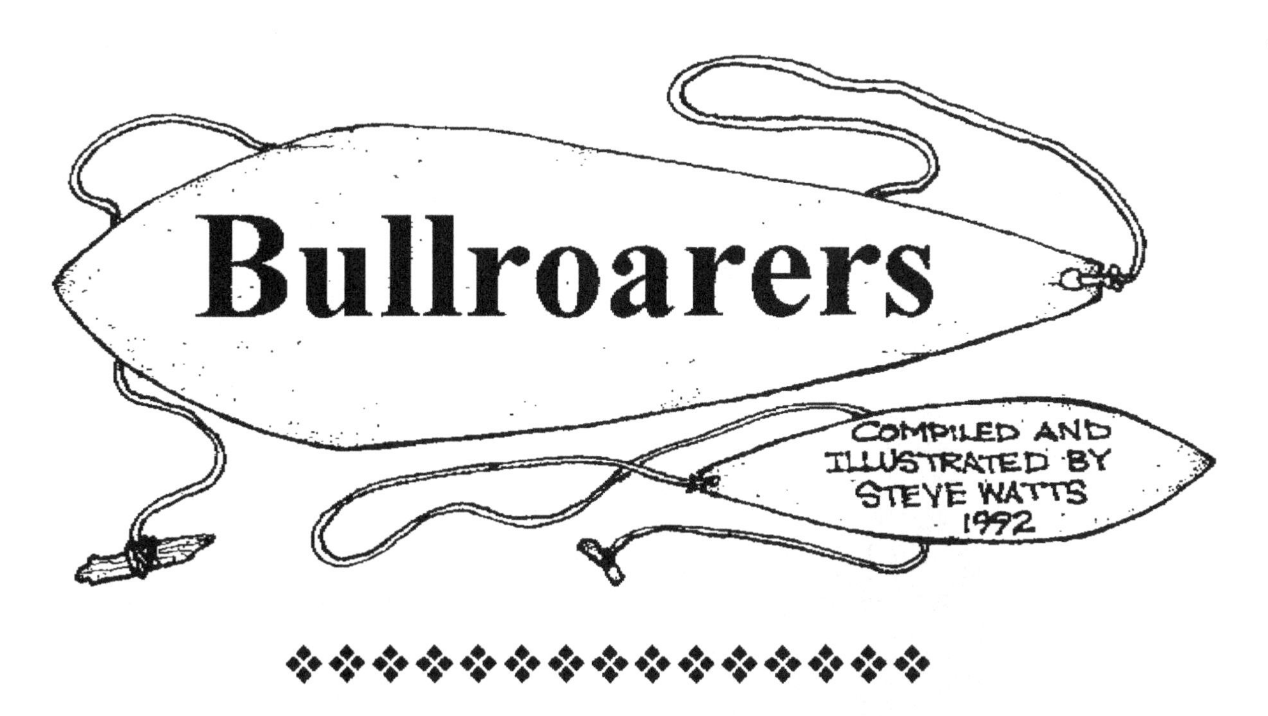

The Bullroarer has sounded from Paleolithic Europe to the traditional cultures of the Americas, Africa and the Pacific. Reduced to the status of a child's toy in most cultures today, it's former form and function survive in bullroarer lore found from the Carolina Piedmont to the Western Desert of Australia

Bullroarer (Fr. rhombe; Ger. Schwirrholz). An instrument made from a spatulate piece of wood tied to a string which is knotted into a hole close to one end. It is classified as a whirling aerophone. To produce sounds the player whirls the blade through the air. holding it by the free end of the string. Blades vary in size (15 to 75 cm), shape, material and decoration. The shapes range from lanceolate to narrowly rectangular, with straight, sometimes waisted, or often serrated edges . . . . The most common material is wood, but stone, bone and similar materials (and very rarely iron) are also used . . . In general smaller bullroarers give a high noise when whirled, while larger specimens sound low in pitch. The speed of rotation and length of the string also affect volume and pitch . . . The oldest surviving specimen is presumably the prehistoric bullroarer from a site in the Dordogne, carved from reindeer antler.

Haddon (1898) reported that the word 'bull-roarer' was itself of English folk origin. Other terms recorded by him in England and from various countries in Europe are 'bummer', 'buzzer', hummingbuzzer', 'thunderbolt', 'thunder-spell' and 'swish'. The term 'bullroarer ' was universally adopted in 1880 as the technical term in English. In ancient Greece the bullroarer was used in the Dionysian mysteries. It's Greek name, rombos, possibly the source of the geometrical term 'rhomvus', survives in the French term 'rhombe'.

***The New Grove Dictionarv of Musical Instruments*, 1984, pp. 283-2X4**

"Swing one over your head for ten or fifteen minutes and a globe of sound will form with you as the vortex. Whenever I did this I caught glimpses of animals and sometimes lost track of time altogether."

Mickey Hart
***Drumming At The Edge of Magic*, 1990**

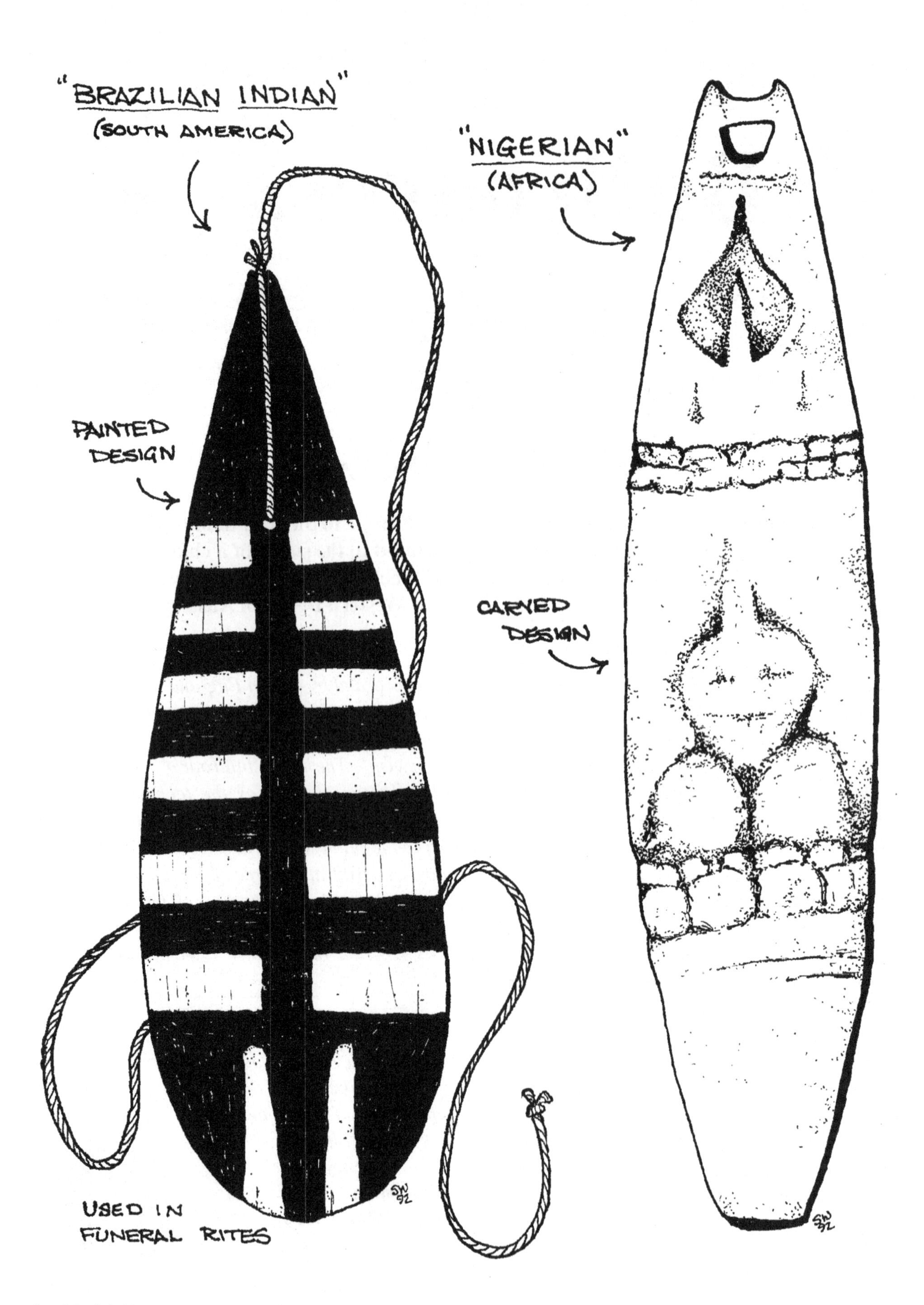
"BRAZILIAN INDIAN"
(SOUTH AMERICA)
PAINTED DESIGN
USED IN FUNERAL RITES
SW 92
"NIGERIAN"
(AFRICA)
CARVED DESIGN
SW 92

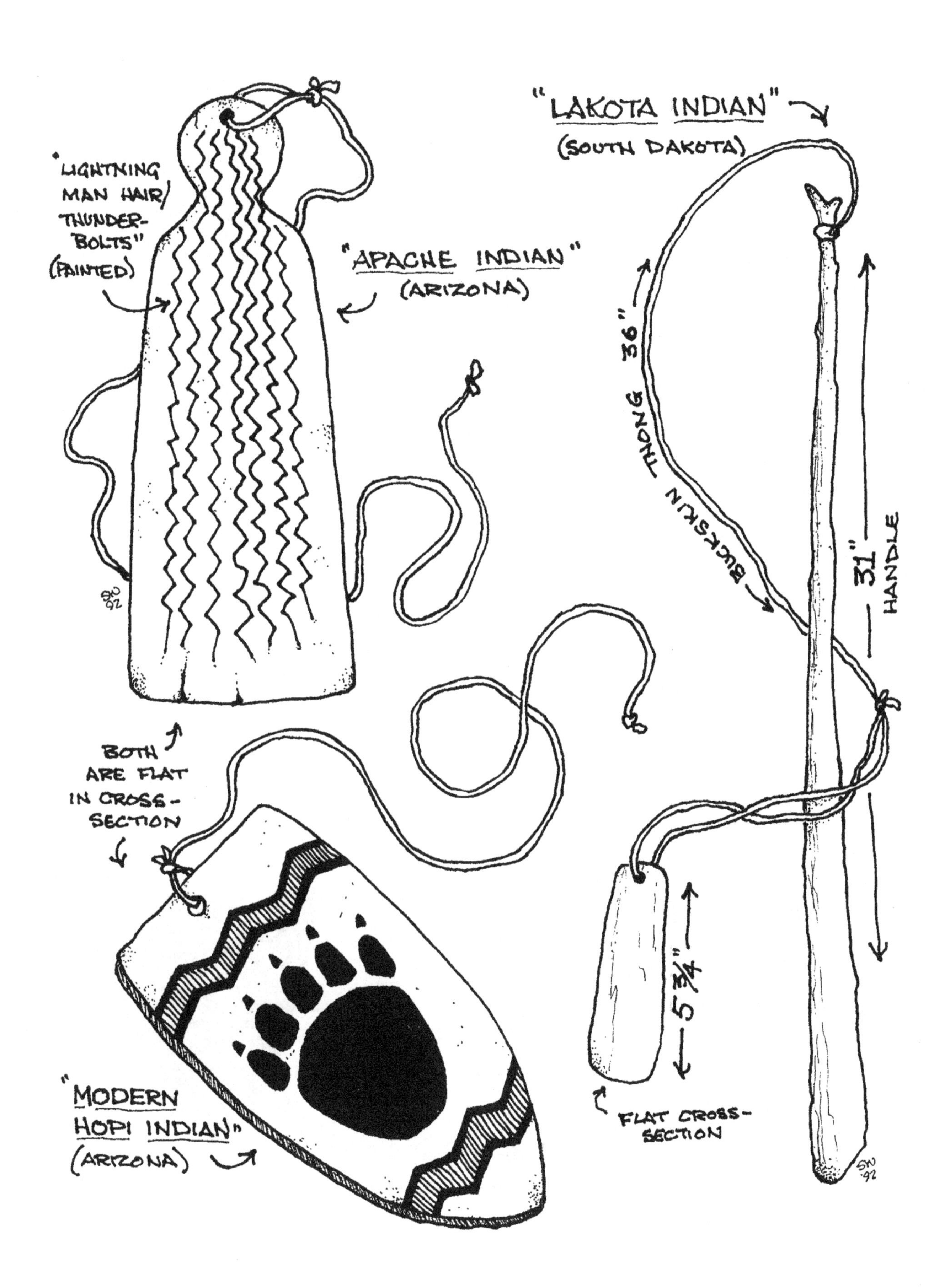
"LIGHTNING MAN HAIR/ THUNDER-BOLTS" (PAINTED)
"APACHE INDIAN" (ARIZONA)
"LAKOTA INDIAN" (SOUTH DAKOTA)
BUCKSKIN THONG 36"
31" HANDLE
BOTH ARE FLAT IN CROSS-SECTION
5 3/4"
FLAT CROSS-SECTION
"MODERN HOPI INDIAN" (ARIZONA)
SW '92

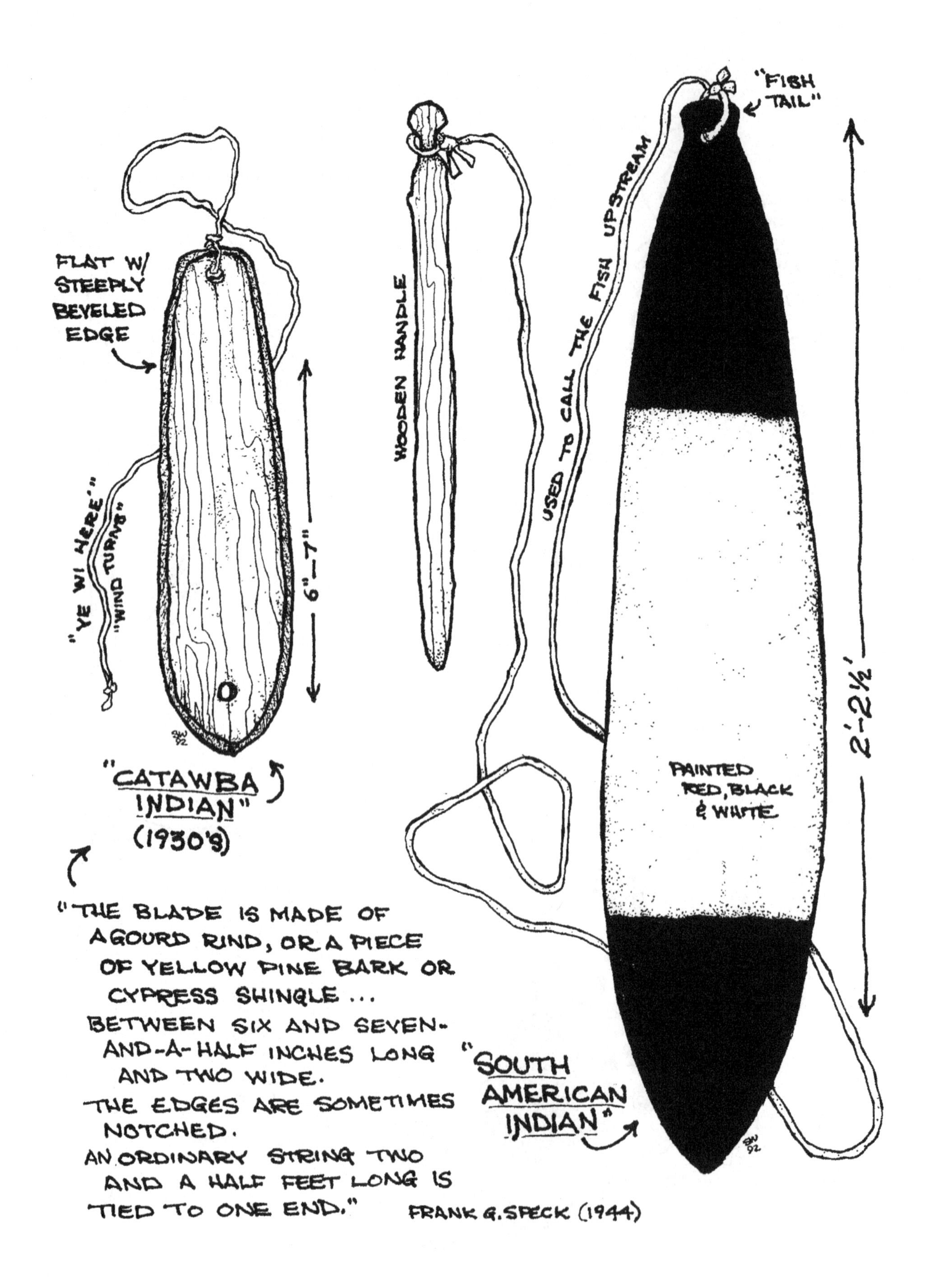

"THE BLADE IS MADE OF A GOURD RIND, OR A PIECE OF YELLOW PINE BARK OR CYPRESS SHINGLE ... BETWEEN SIX AND SEVEN-AND-A-HALF INCHES LONG AND TWO WIDE. THE EDGES ARE SOMETIMES NOTCHED. AN ORDINARY STRING TWO AND A HALF FEET LONG IS TIED TO ONE END." FRANK G. SPECK (1944)

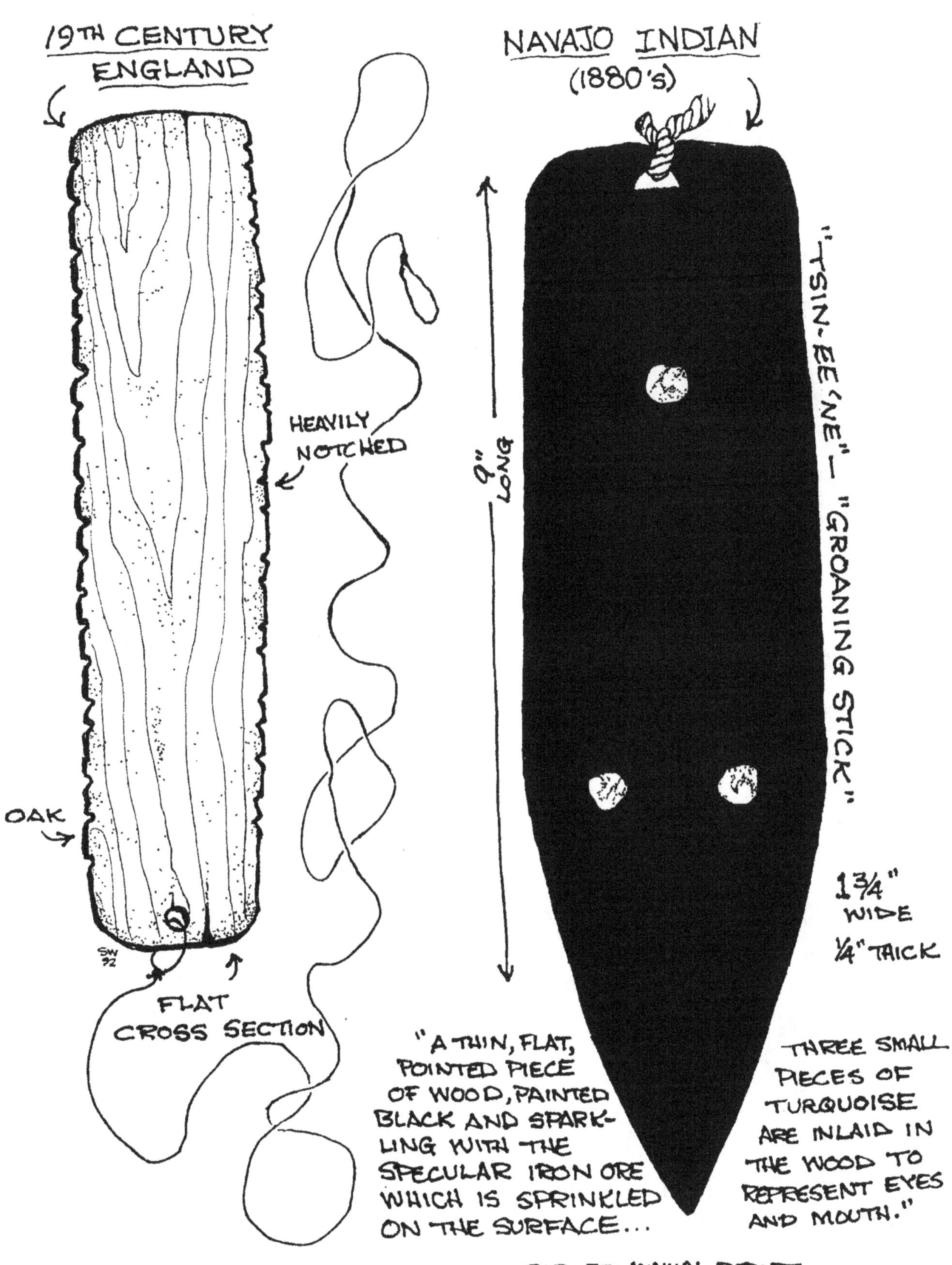
19TH CENTURY ENGLAND
HEAVILY NOTCHED
OAK
SW 92
FLAT CROSS SECTION
NAVAJO INDIAN (1880's)
9" LONG
"TSIN-EE'NE" — "GROANING STICK"
1¾" WIDE
¼" THICK
"A THIN, FLAT, POINTED PIECE OF WOOD, PAINTED BLACK AND SPARKLING WITH THE SPECULAR IRON ORE WHICH IS SPRINKLED ON THE SURFACE...
THREE SMALL PIECES OF TURQUOISE ARE INLAID IN THE WOOD TO REPRESENT EYES AND MOUTH."
BAE, 5TH ANNUAL REPORT 1887

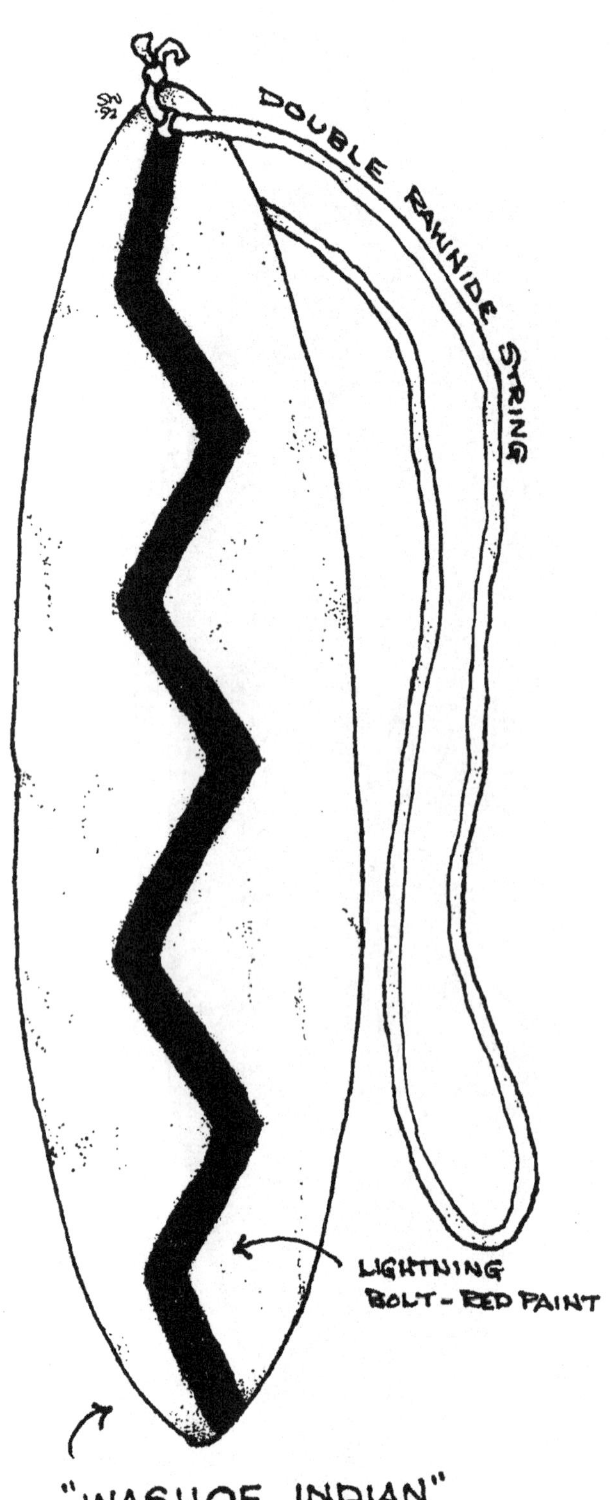
SW '92
DOUBLE RAWHIDE STRING
LIGHTNING
BOLT - RED PAINT
"WASHOE INDIAN"
(CALIFORNIA)
..."LIGHTNING STICK"
USED FOR RAIN MAKING

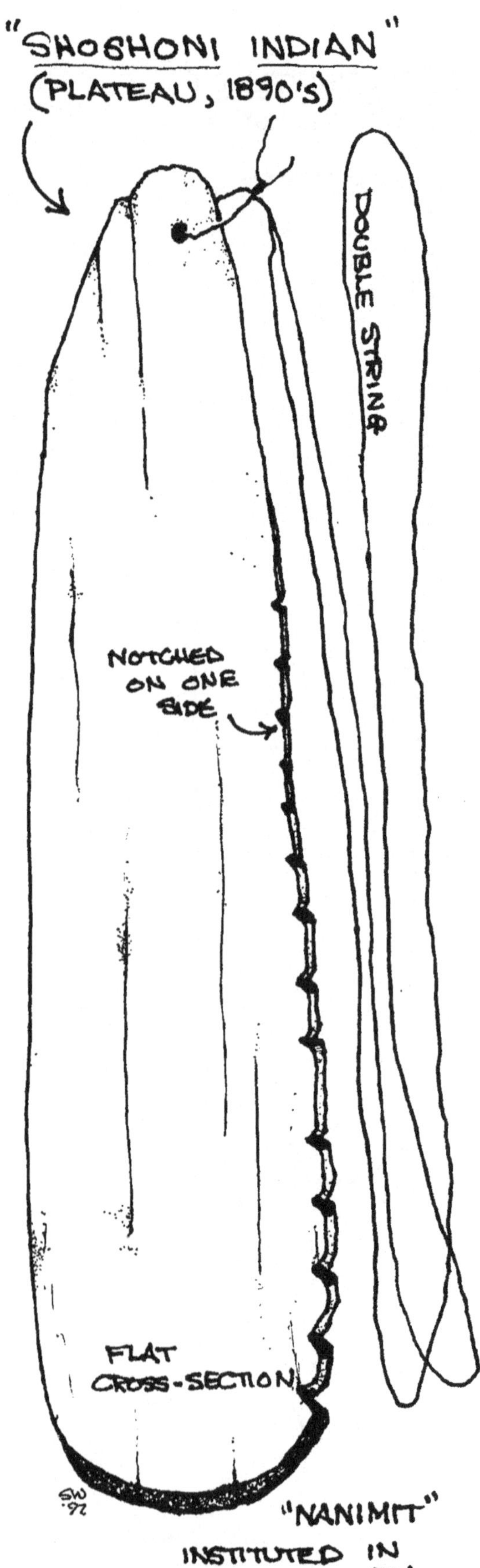
"SHOSHONI INDIAN"
(PLATEAU, 1890'S)
DOUBLE STRING
NOTCHED
ON ONE
SIDE
FLAT
CROSS-SECTION
SW '92
"NANIMIT"
INSTITUTED IN
MYTHOLOGY BY
THE WOLF

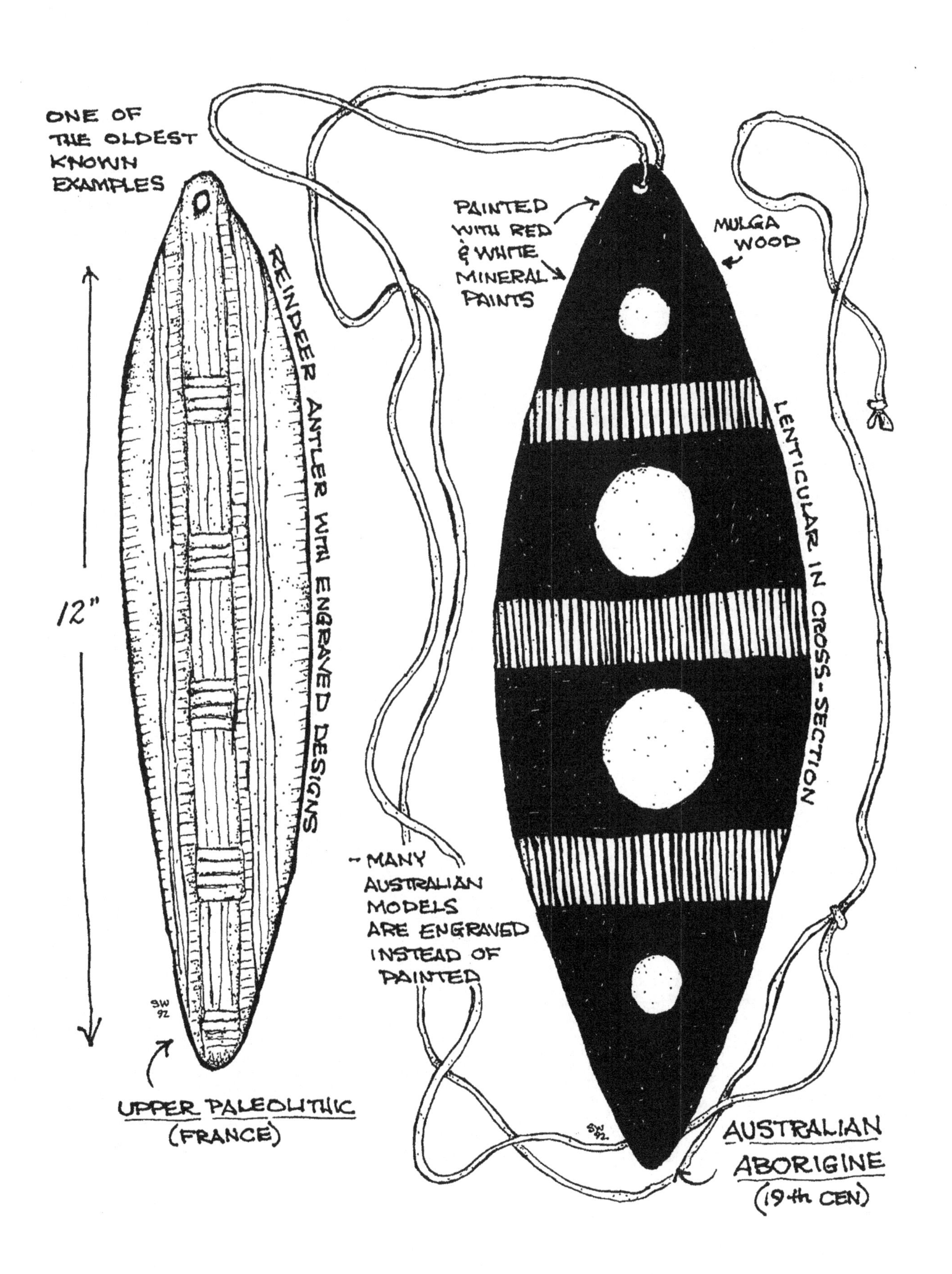

ONE OF THE OLDEST KNOWN EXAMPLES
12"
REINDEER ANTLER WITH ENGRAVED DESIGNS
SW 92
UPPER PALEOLITHIC (FRANCE)
PAINTED WITH RED & WHITE MINERAL PAINTS
MULGA WOOD
LENTICULAR IN CROSS-SECTION
MANY AUSTRALIAN MODELS ARE ENGRAVED INSTEAD OF PAINTED
SW 92
AUSTRALIAN ABORIGINE (19th CEN)

John Lathem

Large marine gastropod shells are easily converted into simple trumpets. Grind the apex until you have opened up a mouthpiece-sized hole. Break out an inch or so of the interior whorl, and you're ready to go. If the hole winds up to be too big, fashion a didjerido-type mouthpiece using beeswax or gum (as with the large horse conch specimen shown at the top). These trumpets are found archaeologically and ethnographically throughout the Pacific and the Americas. Shell trumpets made by the author.

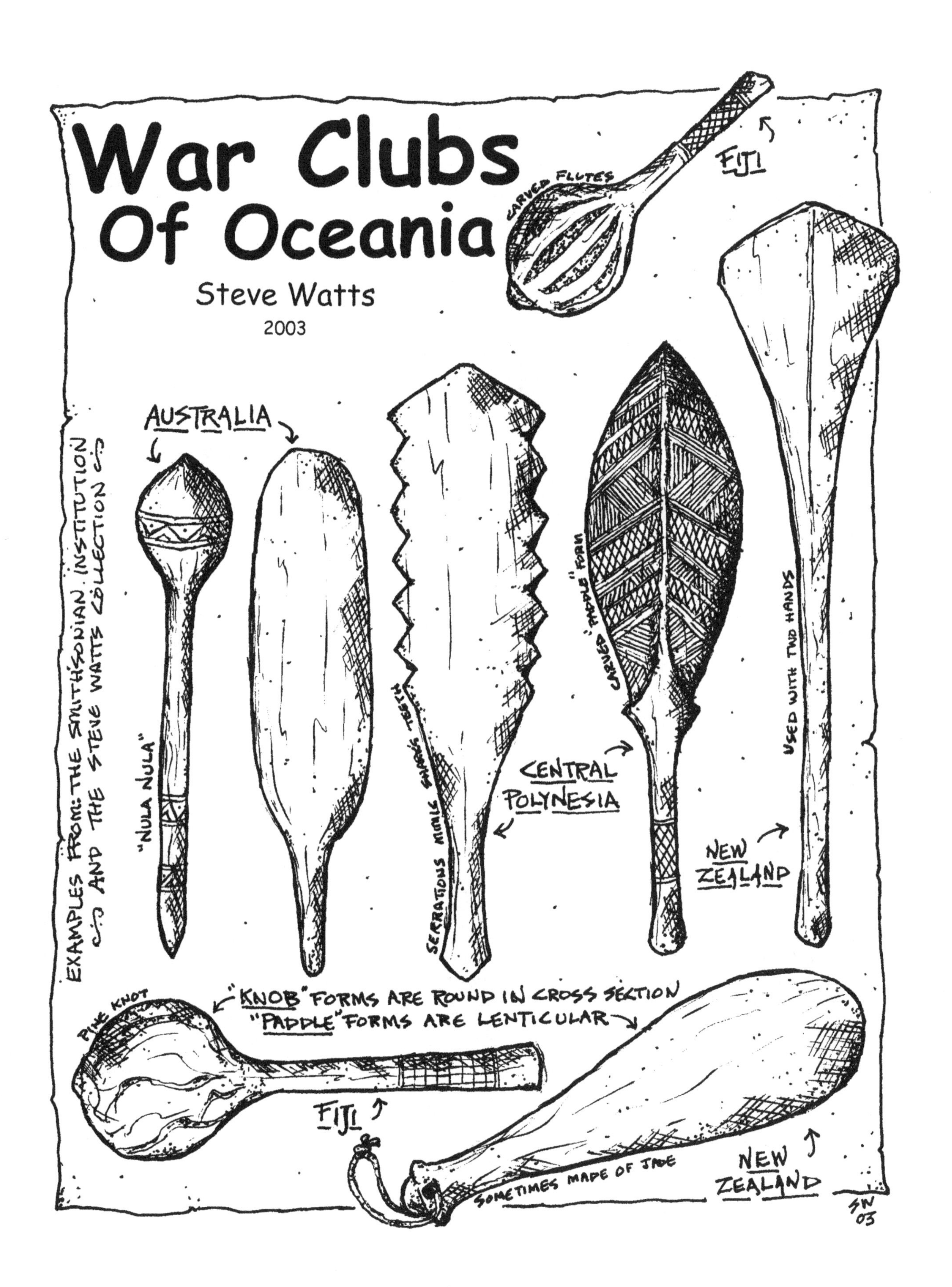
War Clubs
Of Oceania
Steve Watts
2003
FIJI
CARVED FLUTES
AUSTRALIA
EXAMPLES FROM: THE SMITHSONIAN INSTITUTION AND THE STEVE WATTS COLLECTION
"NULA NULA"
SERRATIONS MIMIC SHARK'S TEETH
CENTRAL POLYNESIA
CARVED "PADDLE" FORM
USED WITH TWO HANDS
NEW ZEALAND
"KNOB" FORMS ARE ROUND IN CROSS SECTION
"PADDLE" FORMS ARE LENTICULAR
PINE KNOT
FIJI
SOMETIMES MADE OF JADE
NEW ZEALAND
SW 03

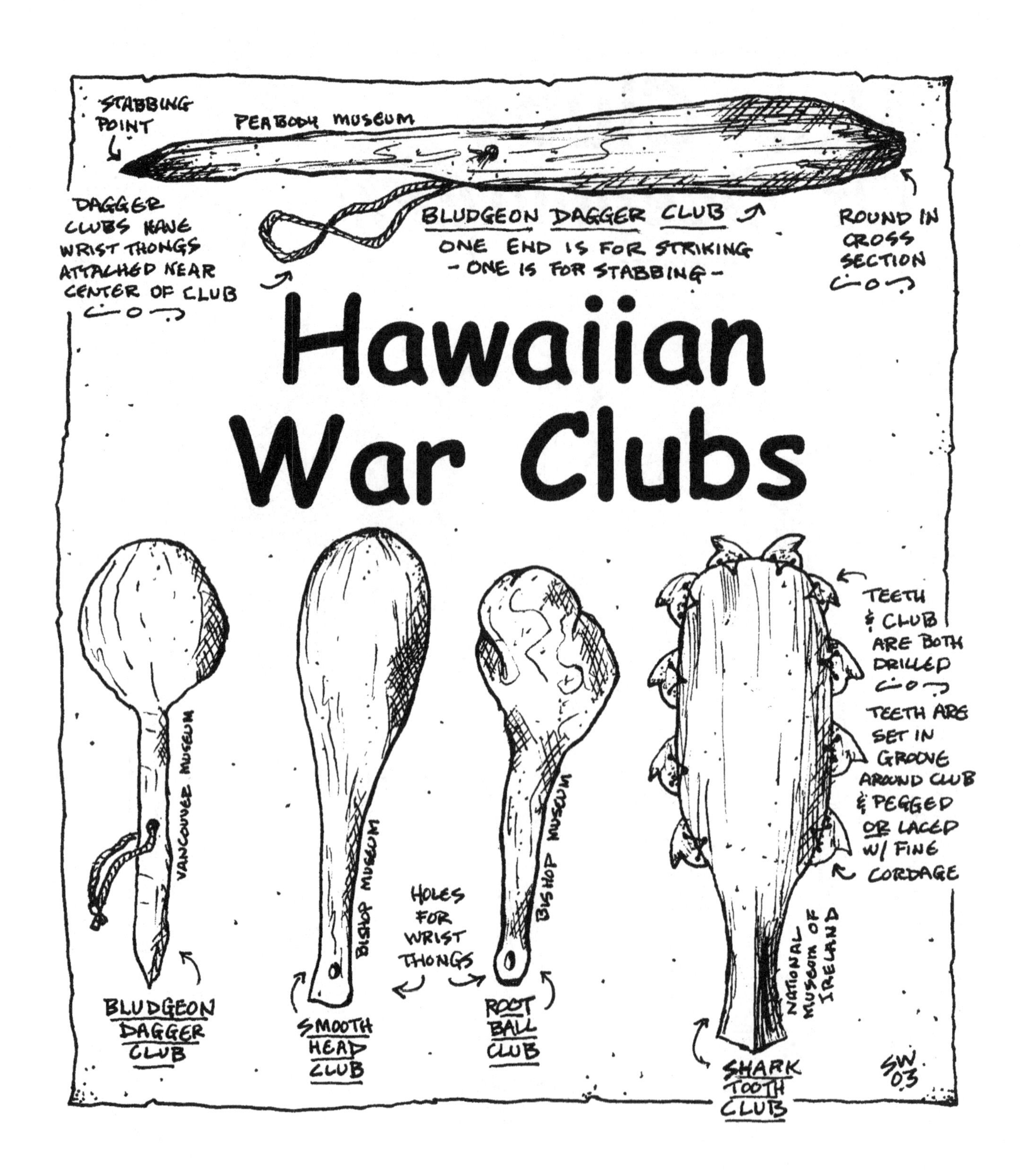
STABBING POINT
PEABODY MUSEUM
DAGGER CLUBS HAVE WRIST THONGS ATTACHED NEAR CENTER OF CLUB
BLUDGEON DAGGER CLUB
ONE END IS FOR STRIKING
- ONE IS FOR STABBING -
ROUND IN CROSS SECTION
Hawaiian War Clubs
VANCOUVER MUSEUM
BISHOP MUSEUM
BISHOP MUSEUM
HOLES FOR WRIST THONGS
TEETH & CLUB ARE BOTH DRILLED
TEETH ARE SET IN GROOVE AROUND CLUB & PEGGED OR LACED W/ FINE CORDAGE
NATIONAL MUSEUM OF IRELAND
BLUDGEON DAGGER CLUB
SMOOTH HEAD CLUB
ROOT BALL CLUB
SHARK TOOTH CLUB
SW 03

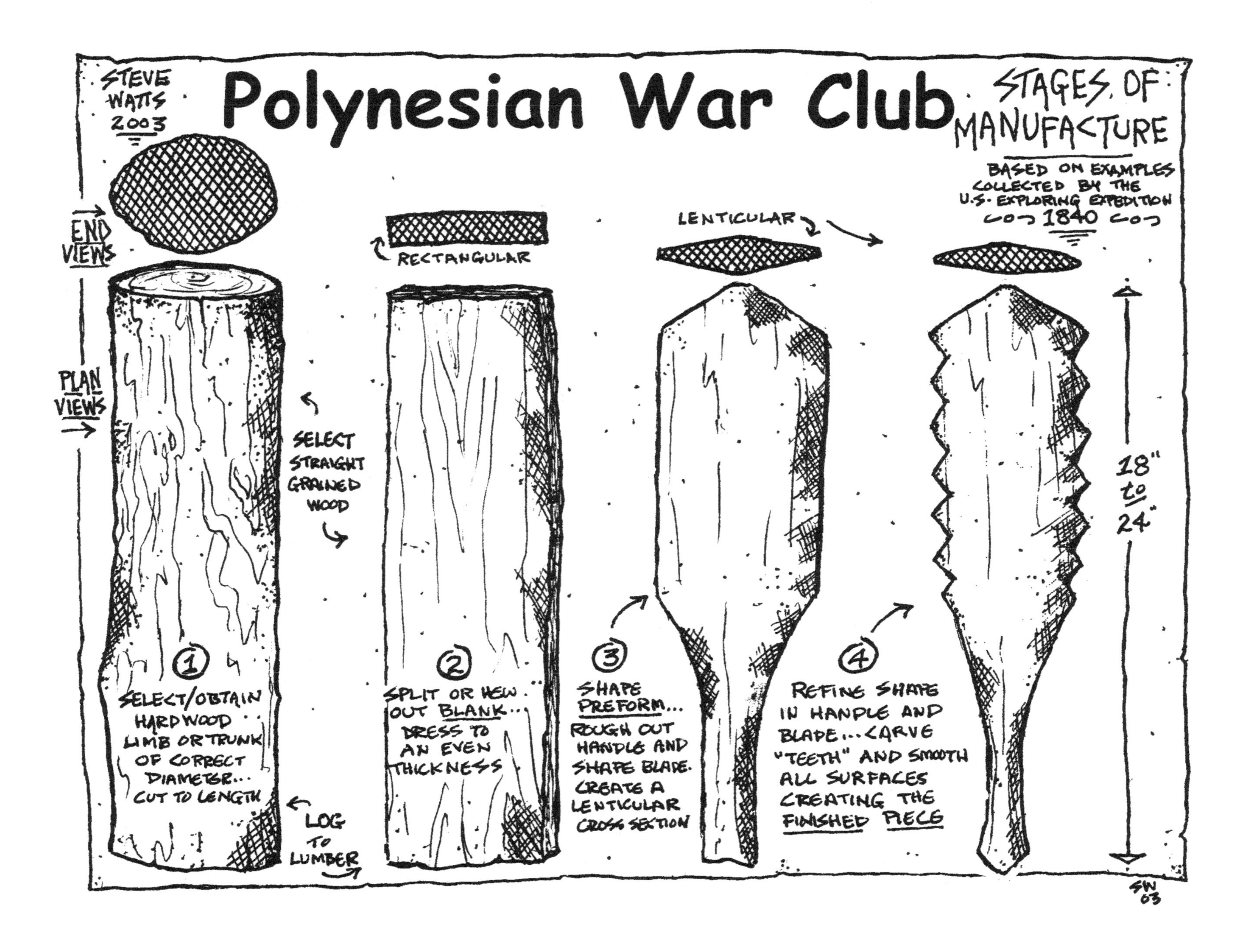
STEVE WATTS 2003
Polynesian War Club
STAGES OF MANUFACTURE
BASED ON EXAMPLES COLLECTED BY THE U.S. EXPLORING EXPEDITION 1840
END VIEWS
PLAN VIEWS
RECTANGULAR
LENTICULAR
SELECT STRAIGHT GRAINED WOOD
LOG TO LUMBER
1 SELECT/OBTAIN HARDWOOD LIMB OR TRUNK OF CORRECT DIAMETER... CUT TO LENGTH
2 SPLIT OR HEW OUT BLANK... DRESS TO AN EVEN THICKNESS
3 SHAPE PREFORM... ROUGH OUT HANDLE AND SHAPE BLADE. CREATE A LENTICULAR CROSS SECTION
4 REFINE SHAPE IN HANDLE AND BLADE... CARVE "TEETH" AND SMOOTH ALL SURFACES CREATING THE FINISHED PIECE
18" to 24"
SW 03

8

Applied Primitive Skills

Michael Eldredge

Applied Primitive Skills, 1990.

The application of aboriginal skills to a field situation opens up a whole new dimension in learning. Using tools and techniques from the past must never be confused with recreating the past—yet the field application of primitive technologies can open new doors of understanding about our heritage.

Over the years the Aboriginal Studies Program at the Schiele Museum of Natural History has offered a series of short applied primitive skills field courses. Each course was an attempt to not only put these skills to the test in a real world situation, but to find ways to increase the learning. Going camping with stone age tools is fun and challenging, but can we make it more than that?

What follows is a reprint of the handbook from our 1993 course. It is offered as a simple example of an attempt to combine experience and experiment. Perhaps it will inform and inspire.

Aboriginal Studies Program

Applied Primitive Skills '93

Participant Handbook

Schiele Museum of Natural History, Gastonia, North Carolina

Applied Primitive Skills '93

An Inspiration

"If, moreover, I am at times seemingly too personal in style of statement, let it be remembered that well-nigh all anthropology is personal history; that even the things of past man were personal, like as never they are to ourselves now. They must, therefore, be both treated and worked at, not solely according to ordinary methods of procedure or rules of logic, or to any given canons of learning, but in a profoundly personal mood and way. If I would study any old, lost art, let us say, I must make myself the artisan of it - must, by examining its products, learn both to see and to feel as much as may be the conditions under which they were produced and the needs they supplied or satisfied; then, rigidly adhering to those conditions and constrained by their resources alone, as ignorantly and anxiously strive with my own hands to reproduce, not to imitate, these things as ever strove primitive man to produce them. I have virtually the same hands he had, the same physique, generally or fundamentally the same activial and mental functions too, that men had in ages gone by, no matter how remote. If, then, I dominate myself with their needs, surround myself with their material conditions, aim to do as they did, the chances are that I shall restore their acts and their arts, however lost or hidden; shall learn precisely as they learned, rediscovering what they discovered precisely as they discovered it. Thus may I reproduce an art in all its stages; see how it began, grew, developed into and affected other arts and things."

Frank Hamilton Cushing
***The American Anthropolocist*, Vo. F71, 1895**

"Fully embracing them all."
Steve Watts, 1992

A Caution

"To go out for a few days, knowing that one can return to comfort if things don't work out-and to make generalizations from the experiences learned thereby - is to fall victim to deceptively convincing but incredibly naive cliches. One must stay with the land long enough to wash out his old systems (both physical and cultural) in order to fall into the rhythm of the natural. This, I believe, cannot be done in less than a two-week period, and I am coming increasingly to suspect that a full year cycle may be necessary to arrive at 'complete' breakthrough. The ultimate test of experimental or living archaeology must await such a thorough investigation."

Errett Callahan
***The Old Rag Report: A Practical Guide to Living Archaeology*, 1973**

A Simple Middle Ground

"Seeking the evidence and experience of life."

John Coles
***Experimental Archaeology*, 1979**

David Wescott

Steve absorbing inspiration at Callahan's landmark Pamunkey Museum exhibit.

Aboriginal Studies Program
Applied Primitive Skills '93
Schiele Museum of Natural History
Gastonia, North Carolina

Official/Genuine/Approved/Legal/Allowed
Gear List

Individual Aboriginal-Style Gear (Required)

__ ***Stone Biface/Knife***...make, buy or trade for (or one will be supplied)

__ ***Sheath For Above***...neck, belt or free (raw-hide, buckskin, bark, fiber, etc.)

__ ***Six Unmodified Stone Flakes***...in small buck-skin bag

__ ***Shoulder Bag***...buckskin, rawhide, bark, fiber, etc. (Special note: No pockets will be allowed during the course. Forget you've got 'em, sew 'em closed, cut 'em out, what ever. This shoulder bag thereby becomes very important. It will carry tools, cordage, trail food, etc.)

__ ***Cordage***...20 ft. (no more, no less - exactly 20) hand-laid fiber cordage, brain tanned or rawhide thongs). Cordage carried may be of different lengths and diameters - to be used for tools bindings, trap triggers, bundle tying, etc. Of course we will make additional cord age during the course as needed.

__ ***Gourd Water Bottle/Canteen***...with carrying strap usable for potable water

__ ***Bowl & Cup***...gourd, ceramic, shell, etc.

__ ***Spoon***...wood, horn, gourd, etc.

__ ***Rabbit Stick***..."don't go anywhere without a rabbit stick" - sling or bola

__ ***Digging Stick***...good sound hardwood (oak, hickory, locust, etc.)

__ ***"Pack"***...basket, hide, abo-style pack frame, etc. (all individual gear must be securely packed in or fastened to your "pack")

__ ***Sleeping Pad***...abo-style (woven or twined fiber, fur, etc.)

__***Personal Medicine Kit*** (in buckskin bag, bark container, or small basket)—perscription drugs, amulets, contacts or extra glasses, etc.

Individual Aboriginal-Style Gear (Allowed)

__ ***Stone Axe, Celt or Chopper***...consider real need, weight.

__ ***Archery Gear***...bow, arrows, quiver, extra string, etc.

__ ***Blowgun Gear***...gun, darts, quiver, etc.

__ ***Bone Needles/Awls***...for repairs or construction of field projects.

__ ***Personal Abo-style Ornaments***... beautification of the beasts.

__ ***Musical Instruments***...abo-style.

__ ***Netting***...as carrying bag, trapping, etc.

__ ***Baskets***...as "inner pack" containers, multi-use.

__ ***Knapping Tools***...a pressure flaking tool (antler) perhaps borders on the necessary.

> ***Note:*** *This "allowed" category can quickly get out of hand. Don't bring it just because you have it. Seriously consider the need. Any other item(s) than those listed must be approved no later than one month prior to the Field Session.*

Individual Non-Aboriginal-Style Gear

__ *Clothing*...sans pockets...dress and plan for the weather..don't forget headgear and gloves

__ ***Raingear***...poncho or rain suit

__ ***Bed Roll***...sleeping bag, blankets, etc.

__ ***Ground Cover***...waterproof (plastic, coated nylon, etc.)

__ ***Personal Items***...drugs, toiletries, glasses/ contacts, etc. (no personal food allowed...no non-abo tools).

__ ***Data Gathering Tools***...notebook and pen, camera, ruler/tape, watch, small tape recorder, etc. (some or all of these may be required to record data from your research project...be sure to bring what you need...remembering that these projects are an important part of the course.) These are carried in your "Field Bag"...see "Thoughts on Preparation" section.

> ***Note:*** *As above, any other item(s) than those listed in this category must be approved no later than one month prior to the Field Session.*

David Wescott

Individual Gear Lists Worksheet

The individual gear lists are designed to provide a standard from which to work in preparation for the Field Session. Remember you have 10 months to prepare. The construction/acquisition of the above items is an important part of this course and will provide you with many pre-Field Session learning opportunities. Now is the time to begin. This worksheet can help you take an inventory and plan ahead. Use it if it seems useful.

Items I already have on hand (as of Jan.1993) . . . Complete . . . Ready to go . . . Requiring no further modification . . . I am now putting aside so as not to use until the field session . . . I can check off my list today:

__________ __________ __________

__________ __________ __________

__________ __________ __________

Items I already have on hand (as of Jan. 1993) . . . Almost complete . . . Or needing some modification . . . Or I anticipate using at some time before the field session . . . I can complete easily and check off my list soon:

__________ __________ __________

__________ __________ __________

__________ __________ __________

Items I do not have on hand (as of Jan. 1993) . . . I need to construct & have the basic tools and knowledge to do so:

__________ __________ __________

__________ __________ __________

__________ __________ __________

Materials that I do not have on hand to complete these items . . . I need to gather or obtain in some other way:____________________

____

____

Items I do not have on hand (as of Jan. 1993) . . . I need to construct & feel that I need further help/ideas/research/tools/ knowledge, etc. to complete:

__________ __________ __________

Items I do not have on hand (as of Jan. 1993) . . . I do not plan to construct and need to buy, trade or barter for, or be supplied.

__________ __________ __________

Group Aboriginal-Style Gear (Provided by the Program)

__ ***2 cooking pots*** - ceramic for group cooking…one for "stew", one for "tea"
__ ***1 celt***…for group needs
__ ***1 friction fire kit***…hand drill
__ ***1 large gourd water bucket***…for bringing cooking water from the "spring"…for that use only!..individual gourd bottles will be used for drinking.
__ ***1 conch shell trumpet***…for signaling
__ ***group food supply***…meat and fruit

Group Non-Aboriginal-Style Gear (Provided by the Program)

__ ***tarps***…shelter
__ ***first aid kit***…for group use assigned to an individual

"I went to the woods because I wished to live deliberately to front only the essential facts of life, and see if I could not learn what it had to teach, and not, when I came to die, discover that I had not lived. I did not wish to live what was not life, living is so dear; nor did I wish to practice resignation, unless it was quite necessary. I wanted to live deep and suck out all the marrow of life, to cut a broad swath and shave close, to drive life into a corner, and reduce it to its lowest terms, and if it proved to be mean, why then to get the whole and genuine meanness of it, and publish its meanness to the world; or if it were sublime, to know it by experience, and be able to give a true account of it in my next excursion."

Henry D. Thoreau

Applied Primitive Skills '93
Field Session Activities

The Field Session of this course is a combination of group activities (and individual activities aimed at a group task or tasks) and individual research projects (IRPs). During the four days and three nights of the field session, time will be divided roughly equally between the two. Each focus (group and individual) has its trials and rewards.

Group Activities

- ***Making and breaking camp***...Camp will be set up early on the first day and struck in the late afternoon of the fourth day...all hands will assist as needed.

- ***Firewood gathering***...An on-going activity. Initial firewood will be gathered during the camp set-up period and will continue throughout the session....think of firewood as your gift to camp each time you return from a trip away.

- ***Plant foraging***...An on-going activity. Using your knowledge of edible plants (which you can certainly add to in the months to come) you will gather wild edibles whenever possible for the camp larder....all question-able plant foods need to be cleared.

- ***Morning watch***...A group time together before starting the day's activities...place and setting to be determined in camp.

- ***Night Watch***...Each evening, two teams of two (one team on each end of camp) will sit all night watches. This provides you with an opportunity to experience the night in a totally different way, take responsibility for "watching" for the others, and (depending on how you and your partner work it out) spend time alone or getting to know another mem-ber of the group by sharing this unique experience.

- ***Evening campfires***...All three nights, after the evening meal . Time to reflect as a group on the day's activities ..music, stories, group discussions of group and individual projects.

- ***The cordage/knife/flakes data project***...Before, during and after the field session; all will participate in a simple data keeping exercise involving three tools from the "required" list. (See forms which follow)

- ***Cooking (evening meal)***...The food rap for the field session runs like this: Each morning, each individual will receive a daily ration of meat and fruit. This ration (plus individual foraging) provides you with the basic food for yourself for the day. You may eat it all, save it, trade it, add it back to the community larder, or whatever. In other words you're on your own as far as your eating schedule goes until the evening communal meal. By mid-afternoon, one third of the group (one woman + 1/3 of the men) will begin the planning and preparation of the evening meal for all. This meal will consist of a ration of meat from the community larder, foraged plant foods, and any meat successfully hunted during the day. This system will eliminate any one person getting stuck at the cooking hearth for more than an afternoon...thus freeing up time for IRPs and personal time. Note: Rations will be meager...hunting, trapping and foraging will be necessary.

• ***Group hunts***...Two hunts (a squirrel hunt in the woods and a rabbit drive in the field) will be organized on the second and third mornings

•***Food and Water***...We will be packing a supply of dried meat and seeds. This will be a group ration assigned to one of the participants for distribution. All other food will be gathered at the site and distributed by the hunters and foragers. No other food will be carried by participants. Even though there is a stream on the property we will be using, we face chemical pollution problems not encountered by our ancestors. Therefore water will be packed into the site ahead of time to create an artificial "spring" from which we can draw drinking water.

• ***Tools and Weapons***...There will be both group and individual sets of tools and weapons carried in. Other tools and weapons will be constructed as needed during the course. The attached list is complete. Please do not plan on bringing along any other tools or weapons. For those of us used to going nowhere without a pocket knife, this will be a learning experience.

Participant/experimenters in the Project will need to begin now making and/or accumulating many of the following tools, weapons etc. It will not be necessary for each participant to include all of these items in their own personal kit, but an effort must be made to insure that the cumulative collection is adequate.

The Cordage/Knife/Flakes Data Project

The "Cordage/Knife/Flakes Data Project" is a simple exercise in data collection to be completed by all participants. Data is recorded before, during and after the Field Session. Two work sheets follow:

1. Cordage: (Before Field Session)
Material:________________ Made By:_____________________
Length:_______ Approximate Average Diameter:______
(After Field Session)
Remaining Length:_____ Disposition of Missing Lengths (From Field Notes)____
____

2. Knife: (Before Field Session)
Blade Material:________________ Haft Material(if any):_______________
Bindings (if any):________________ Overall Length:_______________
Total Length of Blade:______
Width of Blade (widest point):______________
Made By:______________________________

Trace outline (actual size) using solid line:

(After Field Session)
Retrace outline over initial drawing using a dotted line. Comments on use, wear, breakage, repair, resharpening, etc. (from your Field Notes):

3. Flakes (Before Field Session)

Trace outline of all six flakes using solid line. Number drawings.

		Material	Made By
Flake	#1	TEXAS CHERT	WATTS
	#2	TEXAS CHERT	WATTS
	#3	CREASANT CHERT (ILL)	WATTS
	#4	TEXAS CHERT	WATTS
	#5	CREASANT CHERT (ILL)	WATTS
	#6	TEXAS CHERT	WATTS

(After Field Session)

Retrace outline over initial drawing using a dotted line.
Comments on use, wear, breakage, resharpening, etc. (from you Field Notes)

____

____

____

____

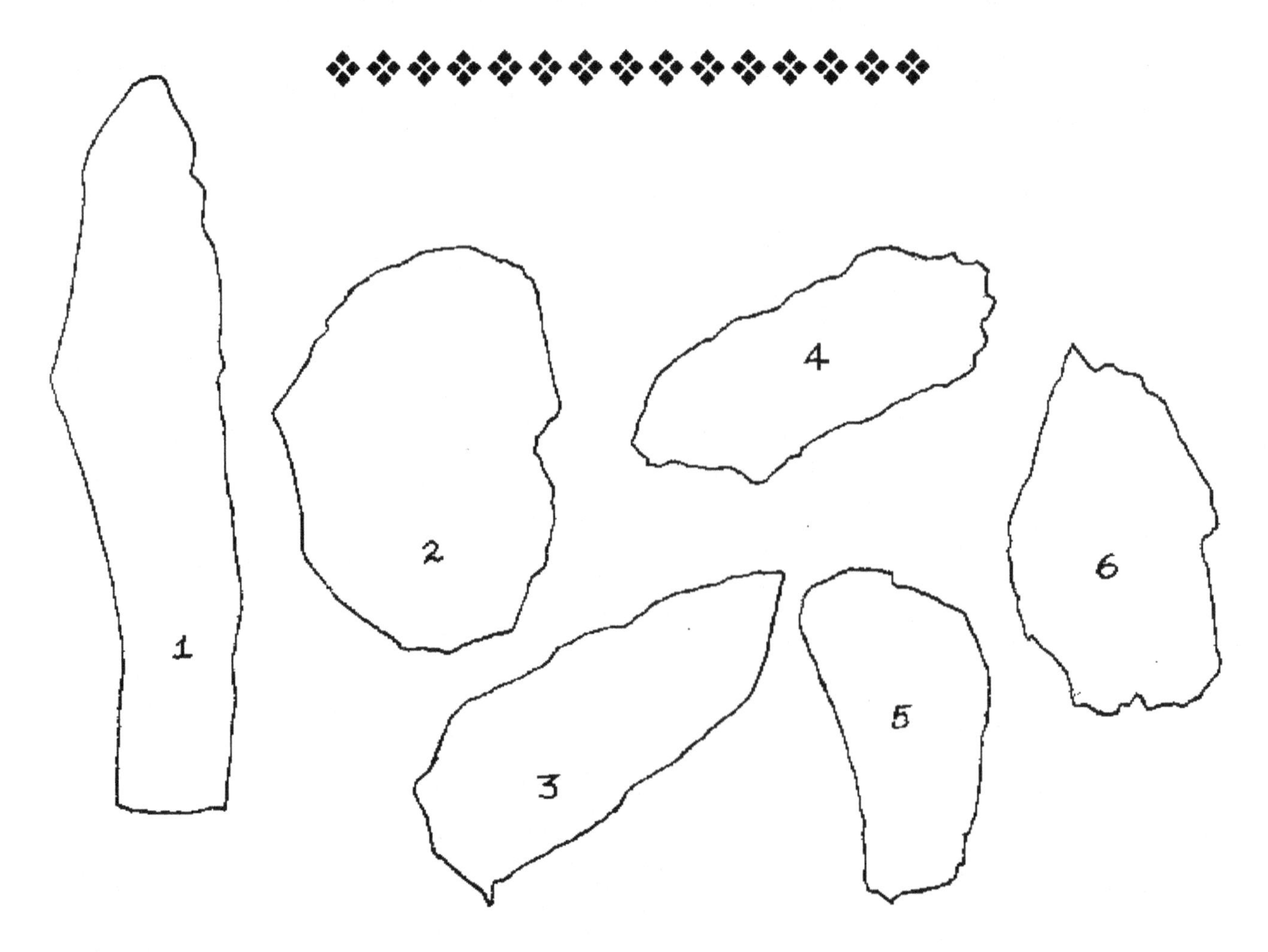

Individual Research Projects (IRPs)

The institution of Individual Research Projects in this year's workshop helps to set the course apart from a simple aboriginal-style camping trip or an exercise in short term survival. IRPs allow students to explore the application of primitive technologies in a field setting in a systematic way . . . and just as importantly, provide a framework for thinking through problems and questions relevant to our limited understandings of aboriginal lifeways.

The research activities and the data collection and evaluation methods presented are meant to be structured simply so as to maximize learning without sacrificing enjoyment. Those who may be more familiar with harder scientific approaches can relax a little with this model, and those who are more inclined toward raw unexamined experience may here find new tools for approaching the practice of primitive technology.

The idea is to choose a particular area of aboriginal technology (ie. stone working, pottery, basketry, whatever) that you are especially interested in - or that you would like to further explore in some way. It may be an area in which you have basic or advanced skills. Your choice of a subject does not demand, imply or in any way suggest your mastery of that subject! It simply reflects an interest which is yours to explore.

From that broad category you construct a project which can be tackled in the field within a four-day period . . . a project which relies on the field-available resources and setting for its completion. Think: activity, setting, resources. For instance, you might choose pottery. If you're thinking activity and setting only, you might carry in some clay and have the experience of ceramic construction in a field setting - a valuable learning experience. But, if you add resources to the mix . . . you add location, procurement and processing of available clays to the manufacturing process. All of a sudden we've got a very interesting project. What if your search for clays in the area was unsuccessful? What if the clays you found were unsuitable for pottery making once processed? These are questions which cannot be answered ahead of time. "Success" of a project does not always mean arriving at preconceived conclusions. What learning is available in this case about local clay resources? How can one predict where appropriate clay can be found? Can you? Are better search methods needed? What tools need to be created to follow a clay source into a bank in search of higher quality materials? And on and on.

Your job for the next two months (besides beginning your reading, researching, gear procurement, and mental/physical preparations) is to decide on and define an IRP so that you can begin to focus your thoughts and preparations for that part of the experience.

Following are some sample ideas which you are welcome to expand on and use . . . or they may simply inspire you to come up with another in the same or related area.

Sample Seed Thoughts for IRPs

- ***Lithics***...Locating and gathering local quartz . . . manufacturing and field testing a variety of tools from.
- ***Cordage***...Locating/gathering and processing a variety of local plant fibers suitable for cordage . . . manufacturing cordage and field testing the results.
- ***Ceramics***...Locating/gathering and processing local clay(s) and temper(s)... manufacturing and possibly firing small vessel forms.
- ***Bone Technology***...Locating/gathering bird, mammal, or reptile bones... manufacturing and field testing a variety of tools and ornaments made from them.

- ***Fire***...Locating/gathering and processing a variety of friction fire woods. . .manufac turing fire sets and making fire.
- ***Shelter***...Construction of a weatherproof shelter near the main camp...using only locally gathered materials...field testing for shade, wind protection, heat retention, waterprooffness, etc. (a good two person project)
- ***Hide Working***...Braintanning of a deer hide under field conditions...with stone and bone tools...no frame...hide and brains packed in...smoke if possible.
- ***Basketry***...Construction of one or more individual styles or sets of baskets...using only locally gathered and processed materials.
- ***Footgear***...Manufacture of a pair of sandals or slippers using only locally gathered materials.
- ***Trapping***...Establishment and maintenance of an intensive trap line—constructing a variety of traps using a variety of triggers manufactured only with locally gathered materials...experimentation with various sets, baits, etc.
- ***Fishing***...Construction and maintenance of fish trap or wier (or a series of such)...experiment with passive baiting, and driving options.
- ***Nutting***...Locating and gathering local nut resources...inventory of such...processing into food, ornaments, toys, etc.
- ***Bow Making***...Construction of small game bow suitable for rabbit/bird hunting using only axe/chopper and flakes (string may be packed in)...field test the bow.
- ***Lighting***...Experimentation with torches, grease lamps, etc...applied to shelter settings, open areas, signaling, etc.
- ***Ideas of Your Own (working notes)***____________________________________

  ____

"Theory without practice is empty; practice without theory is blind"
Immanuel Kant

The IRP Process

1. ***Definition***...Define your project...write it up (form enclosed)... submit to Watts for approval by March 1,1993..."approval" is a chance for a second opinion, suggestions, integration into or with other IRPs, etc...."approved" by March 15.

2. ***Research/Preparation***...Researching the relevant literature (literature support available) ...preparing your data collecting tools and materials...practice of skills...preparation of specialized tools, etc....periodic check-ins throughout the spring and summer.

3. ***Application***... Nov. 4-7, 1993... IRPs in the Field Session.... implementation and data collection.

4. ***Evaluation***...Compilation of data...drawing of conclusions...written report due by Feb.l, 1994.

5. ***Sharing***..."Published" versions of group IRPs by May 1, 1994

Applied Primitive Skills '93

Individual Research Projects

Proposal Form

Date: ______________________________

Name: ____

Address: ____
____

Phone #: _________________________________

Individual Research Project Title:

____

Project Description:

(Be as thoroughly descriptive as possible. Remember this is a proposal, subject to change and revision)

Rick Ward with completed Individual Research Project, Applied Primitive Skills, 1993.

Aboriginal Studies Program
"Applied Primitive Skills '93"
Some Thoughts on Preparation

Record Keeping

Record keeping during the course will happen on a variety of levels and serve a variety of functions. Keep in mind first of all that the course runs 10 months plus. Think of it as a rhythm which beats in the background of your everyday comings and goings. Considered in that way, there's certainly plenty of stuff to keep up with.

I would suggest a box, large folder, or a special comer on a shelf at home set aside for "Applied". This Participant Handbook is one of the first things to go there. You'll know where it is so you can refer to it easily. You'll need to read things over several times during the year. The Handbook is a skeleton upon which to build a body of information for and about the course. You'll flesh it out immediately during the Classroom Session with the addition of personal and group notes.

I would suggest a separate file folder for your IRP. Here you can keep a copy of your approved IRP proposal, the data collection materials you gather/develop, project related references, bits of specific information, etc.
Here will go the book or books you are reading related to the course . . . perhaps a notebook with your jottings, self-imposed checklists, quotes etc.

Remember that during the Field Session you will be recording information bits of many kinds . . . .p rsonal thoughts, data from your IRP, daily journal, drawings, etc. These are, I believe, best kept in one place to be sorted out later. A one volume "Field Notes" avoids keeping up with separate notebooks, loose papers, etc.

Cameras, small tape players, watches, measuring devices or whatever other data collecting tools you may need for your IRP, plus your Field Notes, should all fit into one "Field Bag". This bag is separate and apart from the shoulder bag used to carry your abo gear. It can be of any type materials.

Gear Preparation

The gear checklists are designed to help you prepare and/or acquire the necessary/required/allowed tools, weapons and gear for the Field Session. As you do so, meditate on the projected use(s) of each specific item. Is it well designed to do what you need it to do? If it breaks, how can you repair it? What is its "place" (physically and priority-wise)?, etc. Think about how each item may function multi-functionally. Hunter/gatherer cultures around the world did this on a regular basis (as we do today in fact—coins as screwdrivers, clothes hangers as car keys, shoes as hammers, etc.). How about a combination rabbit stick/digging stick? A bag or pouch as a hat? A basket as a hat (ala Great Basin/California)? Buckskin shirts, ponchos, robes or capes as burden carriers or sacks? Fur robes or capes as blankets? Tools as weapons ("knives" as "spear points", awls as daggers, etc.)? An emptied quiver as a gathering bag? A hand-drill shaft converted to an arrow - or vice versa?

This whole multi-purpose way of thinking can open up all kinds of possibilities. Explore all possible uses of all items beyond the standard "common sense" definitions. Really play with the alternatives. Try the most far out applications - not just mentally -but on an experiential functional level as well. As a good exercise - pick an item from your meager gear and brainstorm as wide a variety of uses as you can . . . and then try them out. You'll come up with a lot of 20th century hair-brained schemes, but in the process you may rediscover multifunctional attributes appropriate to the past. Stay with the technology and explore the boundaries.

Mind and Body

Physically: We'll be walking, packing, and moving around quite a bit during the Field Session. There will be no long marathon pack in and out, but life in the bush does imply lots of mobility (hunting, gathering, exploring, etc.). Do some extra walking, hiking, packing etc. to prepare. No superhuman feats or regimines are required- just take the opportunity of the coming months to become more active. You'll be hungrier than usual during the course. There will be adequate rations (no one's going to starve), but in smaller quantities and less readily available than is the norm for most of us. So, practice skipping a meal or two every once in a while to get the hang of it. Starving yourself in the weeks prior is probably not a good idea, nor is pigging out to "store up". Seek the middle ground.

Mentally: Review all that you have learned in our courses or elsewhere that you feel will be of use to you in the field. Anticipate the skills you may need and review, practice and inventory . . . especially the basic stuff . . . fire, cordage, traps and snares, etc. Besides the specifically oriented stuff aimed at your IRP, read generally (fiction and nonfiction) . . . not only for skills (past workshop materials, primitive skills books, etc.), but for inspiration as well. Set your thoughts on a positive primitive experience and make the best of this opportunity. Every once in a while, try to project ahead to the November Field Session. The more you think "abo", the better prepared you will be. Prepare, practice, project.

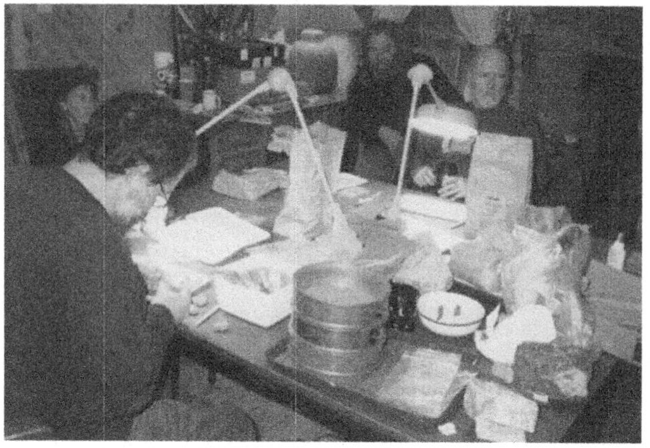

David Wescott

Steve and the "Old Rag" team catalogue discoveries from the first deep-time experimental project.

" . . . if one advances confidently in the direction of his dreams, and endeavors to live the life which he has imagined, he will meet with a success unexpected in common hours. We will put some things behind, will pass an invisible boundary; new, universal, and more liberal laws will begin to establish themselves around and within him; or the old laws be expanded, and interpreted in his favor in a more liberal sense and he will live with the license of a higher order of beings . . . . If you have built castles in the air, your work need not be lost; that is where they should be. Now put the foundations under them." **Henry D. Thoreau**

Supportive Services

"Supportive Services" are communication/information/evaluation /inspiration efforts you will receive from Watts/Aboriginal Studies Program in the coming months to help you make this course a learning-filled experience.

1. Suggested readings (general).
2. References to panted materials helpful in the planning and implementation of your IRP.
3. Consultations on your IRP.
4. Access to material resources.
5. Consultations on gear manufacture and/or acquisition.
6. Seasonal letters/communications updating the course's progress.
7. Aide in preparation of data collection materials.
8. Etc.

"The future is not to be found in the past. Yet, we know that the outermost bud on the upper most branch is fed by the deepest root. Ninety-five-plus percent of our history as humans cannot be ignored. 'Written' by scavengers, hunters, gatherers and early agriculturalists; the story of the Stone Age is our story. It is the great common denominator of humaness. Primitive technology is a way into that story. We are drawn to it as a to a fire . . . and, there we find others.

Armed only with Stone and Fire our ancestors faced the Big Cats of our shared past. The cats . . . with claws to climb and run and grab and hold . . . and teeth to crush and splinter . . . to stab and rip . . . sever and slice.

Today, the Big Cats no longer compete with us for food and territory, as now we struggle to protect the dwindling numbers of their descendants. The threats of contemporary life more often walk on two legs . . . on dark streets, in brightly lit corporate corridors, and even in the warm familiar glow of our neighborhoods and homes. Our 'boundaries of the unknown' take the form of microbes that defy our cleverness, and poisons we drink and breathe but cannot see. The dark domains of the late twentieth century lie not in the tall grass, but rather in our own interior landscapes, still so uncharted.

Stone gave our ancestors the Power and the Edge to compete with the Big Cats and the other environmental forces which threatened the future of our kind. Here, far down this path through time, we continue to seek the same . . . railing against the impotence and numbness which too often surround us. The Big Cats are gone, but We and the Stone remain."

Steve Watts, 1992

Applied Primitive Skills '93
"Readings"

"Readings" may take many forms during this course. There is general reading for inspiration and skills building . . . readings directly oriented toward your IRP . . . readings to help you with a specific piece of gear manufacture . . . readings (of several kinds) which will come from Watts . . . and readings during the Field Session at group meetings and campfires. So, what is "required" reading? Some I'll define here . . . some will be defined by your own needs and interests. Here are some suggestions divided up into different areas.

Ishi **-** Ishi gets a category all to himself. The unintentional father of the modern primitive technology movement, his story continues to inspire and inform.

"The Ishi volumes should occupy a place of honor on every abo bookshelf, as the memory of Ishi must surely shape the thoughts and actions of Neo-Aboriginals for all time." **Steve Watts, 1990**

"If you consider yourself an "abo" and haven't read Ishi, turn in you membership card."
Dave Wescott, 1990

"He (Ishi) looked upon us as sophisticated children, smart but not wise . . . knowing many things but much that was false . . . but he knew nature who was always true." **Saxon Pope, 1916**

Read at least one of the Ishi volumes: *Ishi. Last of His Tribe*, *Ishi In Two Worlds*, or *Ishi. The Last Yahi* . . . all by Theodora Kroeber.

General Aboriginal Skills **-** As fashionable as it may be to be overly critical of the works of earlier teachers and authors as "outdated" or "behind the times", Larry Dean Olsen's *Outdoor Survival Skills* still stands as a classic work in the field of experiential primitive skills instruction, and is considered required reading. Readily available in most book stores and libraries . . . check out used book stores and flea markets as well. (By the way, Watts will pay well for a first edition copy.)

Most are familiar with John and Geri McPherson's series of books . . . all are good general introductions to aboriginal skills. Required reading from this series is Tools . . . not only for its specific technical info, but for the whole approach to the manufacture of simple tools in the field. Three dollars (plus shipping) direct from the McPhersons (P.O. Box 96, Randolph, Kansas, 66554) . . . or you can borrow from Watts.

Highly recommended but not required is Errett Callahan's *Primitive Technology: Practical Guidelines for Making Stone Tools, Pottery, Basketrv, The Aboriginal Way.*

Experimental Archaeologv **-** The requirement in this category is to take a look at at least one of the following volumes. These are available from most good libraries. Check one of them out and take it home. "Taking a look" may mean browsing, skimming or thoroughly reading. Reading some about the systematic approach to primitive technology will go a long way in inspiring and informing you about the subject..especially as it relates to your IRP (and its fun stuff to boot!). They are: two by John Coles, *Experimental Archaeology* and *Archaeology By Experiment:* and "Part 2" (Time Bandits: Living History as Research) of Jay Anderson's, *Time Machines: The World of Living History*. If you get hooked, Watts can supply you with lots more references.

continued . . .

IRP References - Once your IRP has been approved, many references related to that specific technology can be suggested. Assistance in obtaining them is also a part of Supportive Services. In the process of your research, you may discover new references which can then be shared with Watts, and which may ultimately be shared with all when your IRP takes written form. That way we all dine higher on the information chain.

General Non-Aboriginal Outdoor Skills- Check out at least one of the classics of traditional woodslore by Horace Kephart, Dan Beard, Ernest Thompson Seton, or Bernard Mason. Although not "stone age" they are filled with invaluable information for those seeking to apply these skills.

Inspiration - This is a big category . . . could include damn near anything: poetry (Whitman, Snyder, Emerson, Dillard, etc.), fiction (Auel and her devotees), Techno/experiential/scientific articles (*Bulletin of Primitive Technology,* etc.), news articles from the popular press, films and videos, etc. You get inspiration where you find it. Hunt and gather for words and images that help you in your quest for mental/emotional preparation. Highly recommended is *Voyage Of The Ant* by Jim Dina . . . a beautiful blend of abo info and philosophical meanderings.

Michael Eldredge

Grinding seeds in the field, Applied Primitive Skills, 1991.

David Wescott

Steve at Rivercane Rendezvous. National gatherings of primitive skills enthusiasts provide one of the best sources of skill development available today.

The Burial Mound Project

During the Neolithic in Western Europe (6,000BC-2,000BC), farmers and herders turned their bone, stone and antler agricultural tools to the task of building burial mounds, tombs and monuments. Some were single-chambered affairs completely covered with earth ("barrows") or with stone ("cairns"). Others were long gallery graves or passage graves similarly covered and designed to house many interments. Some were ossuaries where the bones of many individuals were housed. Others contained intact burials or urns filled with cremated remains.

During the weekend of September 6-8, 2002, thirty-five students gathered at the Schiele Museum of Natural History in Gastonia, North Carolina to explore the technology of these mounds and closely examine a part of our stone age heritage often overlooked.

The Burial Mound Project was a part of the museum's Aboriginal Studies Program series of on-going primitive technology workshops which began in 1985. This intensive course offered participants a unique opportunity to participate in the construction of a small burial mound demonstration site. This site will serve as a public education exhibit and as a living laboratory of experimental technology.

Participants examined information related to the late prehistoric cairns, barrows and burial mounds found around the world. Then using primitive tools and techniques, they constructed a chambered burial mound suitable for the interment of a single intact burial or the cremated remains of a family or clan.

A secondary goal of the course was to provide instruction and experience in the collection and interpretation of experimental/experiential data. Simple projects take on greater meaning when well documented and evaluated. Such data collection can prove itself useful beyond just the experience of those involved in any particular project.

The project was divided into four stages:

Stage I: Site Preparation

Photo 1 - Mound building in the past (and the present) required a group effort. The stages of the project are reviewed and work crews were organized.

Photo 2 - The site is cleared using antler rakes, unhafted scapula tools and hands. An 11' 10" diameter circular floor plan was then laid out using a rope and antler compass. While the site crew prepared the area, another crew carried and dragged stones to the site perimeter in preparation for Stage II.

Photo 3 - Data is collected at each stage of the project. Notes and field sketches were augmented with video and still photography.

Stage II: Chamber Construction

Photo 1 - The interior chamber construction begins, working from the center of the ground plan to the perimeter. Stones were dry-stacked. Footings were dug with antler picks where necessary.

Photo 2 - The completed stone chamber. (Entrance viewed from the east.)

Measuring the interior of the finished chamber.

Stage III: Mound Building

Photo 3 - Staff archaeologist Dr. Alan May records exterior and interior measurements of completed chamber.

Photo 1 - The mound floor was covered with a layer of sand carried from a nearby stream.

Aboriginal Studies Program

Schiele Museum of Natural History
Gastonia, North Carolina

The Burial Mound Project
September 6-8, 2002

Welcome to the "Burial Mound Project." More than a workshop, this course will feature an introduction to experimental archaeology data recovery techniques and will result in a public experimental site providing educational opportunities for years to come.

We will be constructing a chambered burial mound suitable for the interment of cremated remains. This mound will be built in an old world (British) style.

All of this will be put into context with discussions of late prehistoric cairns, burrows and burial mounds found around the world. This is part of our stone age heritage often ignored yet common to us all.

"Camp Cairn"

Monumental stone and earthworks required the cooperation of communities. They were not built by small bands of mobile hunter-gatherers. So for this course, we have assembled a large tribe. You may want to bring a tent or other shelter to set up in the woods or along the back of the property. Your site, the mound site and the ceremonial/social sites (the hearth and the stone circle) all together form "Camp Cairn".

Project Director: Steve Watts
Project Assistant: Jessica Hoffmire
Site Foreman: Michael Eldredge
Staff Archaeologist: Dr. Alan May
Procurement Officer: Mike Peters

The Burial Mound Project is part of the Schiele Museum Aboriginal Studies Program primitive technology workshop series for 2002. This intensive course offers a unique opportunity to participate in the construction of a small burial mound demonstration site. This site will serve as a public education exhibit and as a living laboratory of experimental technology.

Participants will examine information related to the late prehistoric cairns, barrows and burial mounds found around the world. Then, using primitive tools and techniques, a chambered burial mound suitable for the interment of cremated remains will be constructed on site. Instruction in the collection and interpretation of experimental data will also be an integral part of the course.

Burial Mound Project Construction Sequence

Stage 1: Site Preparation
Site is cleared using appropriate Neolithic-style tools
Circle ground plan is laid out with primitive compass
Measurements are made and recorded with contemporary tools

Site Plan View

Stage 2: Chamber Construction
Chamber floor is prepared
Stone chamber and passage are constructed
Measurements are made and recorded

Site Plan View

Stage 3: Earth Working
Baskets are used to transport earth to mound site
Baskets are loaded using appropriate Neolithic-style tools
Basket loads are recorded and tabulated
Mound is tamped (in progress)
Measurements are taken and recorded
Site is dedicated

Earth Working Record
Commercial agricultural produce baskets were used to standardized volume and weight tabulations.

*Basket Volume*___________
*Average Weight (per basketload)*________
*Basketloads by worker number*_______

Total Number of Basketloads _______

Total Volume of Earth_______

Total Approximate Weight of Earth _______

Commercial agricultural baskets were used to insure uniformity of loads for documentation purposes. Each basket held approximately 1/4 cubic foot of soil weighing 16 lbs, (good, heavy, southern, red clay).

Photo 2 - Earth moving begins on the afternoon of the first day. Loaders filled baskets from barrow pile using hands, bone and antler tools. Carriers stand ready for their loads.
Photo 3 - Carriers transported basket loads over 100 feet to the mound site. Each carrier and their load was documented.

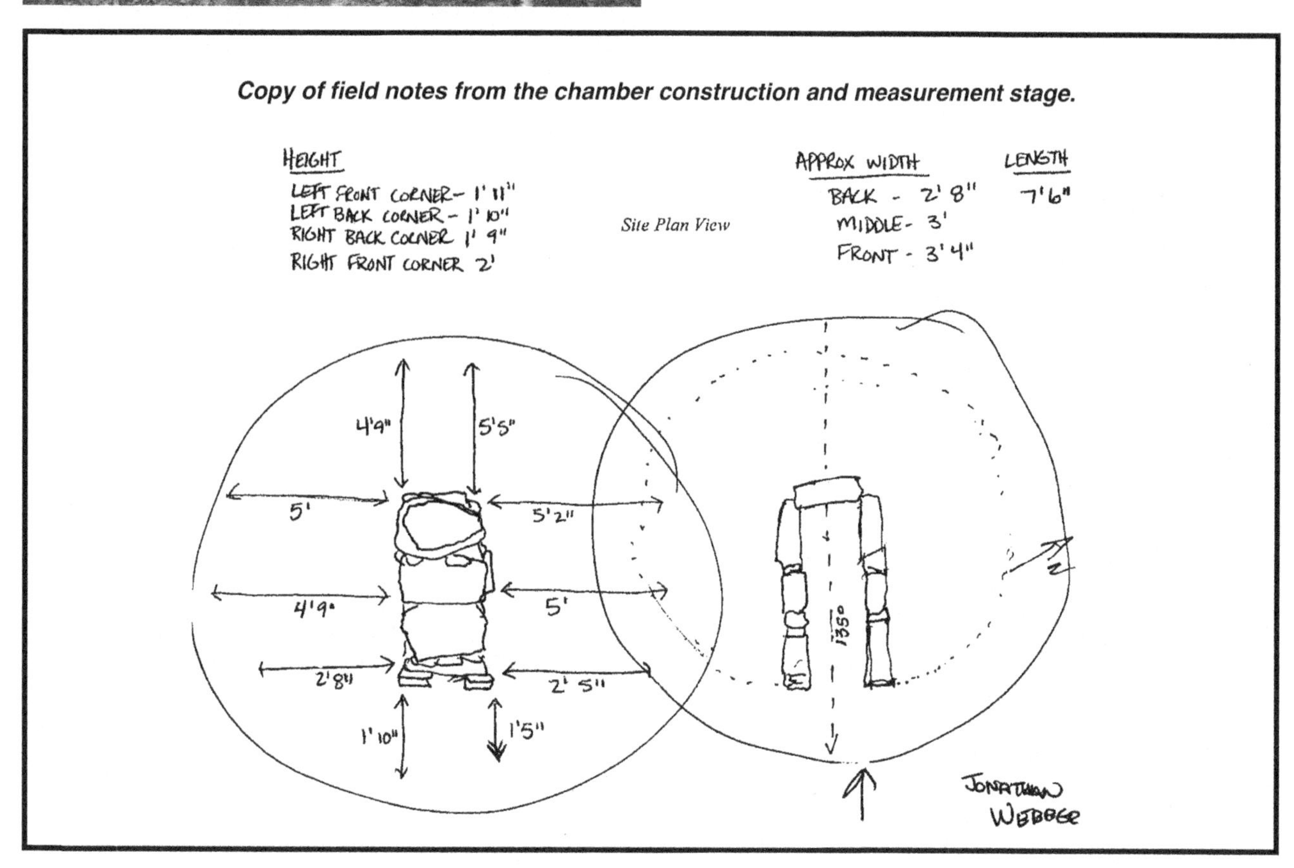

Copy of field notes from the chamber construction and measurement stage.

Photo 4 - Carriers dump basketloads on site as the site foreman directs, and pack the soil firm.

Photo 5 - Work continues on the morning of day two. Carriers return for new loads.

Photo 6 - The mound is complete. It required 1,031 basket loads of soil. That comes to 16, 496 pounds. The total volume of earth in the mound is approximately 275.75 cubic feet.

Photo 7 - Exterior mound measurements are recorded. The mound diameter is 14' 10". The height is 44 3/4". The planned diameter was 12' and the planned height, 48".

A view from the north with antler and bone tools displayed.

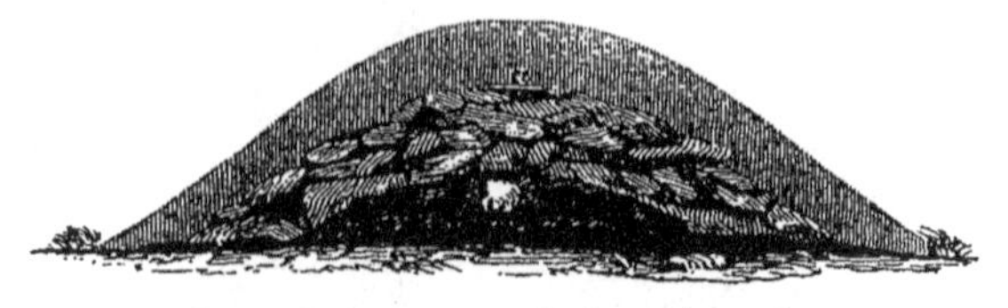

Completed mound-elevation view.

Stage IV: Interpretation, Monitoring and Maintenance

An interpretive sign will be developed to inform visitors of the project, including data collected and a cut-away diagram of the mound. The site will then be monitored periodically to note conditions and changes. The monitoring schedule includes documentation at three months, six months, one year, two years and four years.

Final Notes

The research questions most relevant to this project had to do with volume not time. We kept strict records of earth moved and by whom, but no records of how long it took. Volume is a fixed quantity, but time carries a lot of cultural baggage. Neolithic peoples perhaps worked faster than we did. Or, perhaps they worked slower. We can never know. Perhaps the rate of work was directly affected by ceremony or cultural taboos beyond our knowledge.

Yet, we could not help but notice (informally of course) that the total time actually spent carrying almost eight and a quarter tons of soil by our team of 35 was probably less than three hours. Also note that we were carrying loads from a site where the soil was previously excavated. I suspect that the actual digging of the dirt, would take much more time than the transporting of it in a prehistoric situation similar to ours.

Our team took advantage of the relaxed work atmosphere, working and playing together to accomplish a common goal. The evenings were spent with food (a meal which included only Old World Neolithic style ingredients), music, conversation and the firing of Watts' personal burial urn. Was it so in the past? Perhaps the labor was forced by a tyrannical clan chief. And, surely burial mound construction was overlain with sadness, grief and fear. That is a part of the past we cannot know.

We can however revisit the technology of our ancestors through imitative experiences such as these. We cannot recreate the time, but we can recreate some of the process. With primitive tools and processes...we touch a part of our lineage. With a burial mound....we bring to life a part of our heritage.

This project is dedicated to John White,
Ancient Lifeways Institute, Michael, Illinois.
John's inspired teaching planted the seed for this project way back in 1985.
Sorry, John, it takes me a while sometimes.

Project director, Steve Watts, at the end/beginning. After covering the mound with pine needles and dedicating the site, the real afterlife of the project begins.

The Megalithic

Steve's latest passion is the moving of big rocks. This series is from a workshop held at Rabbitstick, 2003, in Idaho, and shows the process of moving, lifting, setting, and enjoying a big standing rock.

Photos by David Wescott and Hal Farneman

The rock was a 700+ lb. piece of Idaho travertine from a local quarry. Although it took manpower to achieve the task, it wasn't a matter of brute force. Loads were well distributed and mechanical advantage was used in all phases of the project.

After Word

Suzanne Simmons

Sometimes . . . in the ashes . . . an ember is found.
Sometimes . . . from the ember . . . a fire is born.
Sometimes . . . by the fire . . . a story is told.
Sometimes . . . in the story . . . a lesson is learned.

Time is asymmetrical. We can know about the past, but cannot change it. We can influence the future, but cannot know it. We are all locked together in the split, split-second that is the present. The literal time machine of our dreams still waits for its own invention.

Yet, as prehistorians we are all virtual time travelers. Virtual not in the joy stick-roller ball-3-D-headset-cyberspace sense, but in the space between our own ears sense...that natural, folded, gray-matter space that helps to define us as a species and wherein resides our own inner net. There we are fed by archaeology, ethnology, history, linguistics, ethno-botany, folklore, paleo anthropology, forensics, geology, oral traditions, comparative studies, evolutionary biology and archeo-fiction.

"Time is a stream I go a-fishing in" said Thoreau. So, to sustain ourselves we move out from that place to pull catches large and small from that stream of times past. Like hunters and gatherers, we track down information here and pick up data there. Our weapons and tools are research, experience, experiment, recreation, study and curiosity. We return from our foraging to share our bounty with others. And, by the fire of Primitive Technology, we recall the stories of our hunt—the hunt for that link to our Ancestral Past.

The stories are told. Are there lessons within?

It is often said that we study the past in order to learn not to repeat its mistakes. Well, that is yet to be proven. Perhaps it is simpler than that. Perhaps we study the past just to get a stronger sense of who we are...To feel some kinship with our ancestral family...To break through that thin veneer of civilization and travel to the deeper, older, more sustainable part of our species' experience.

The fire grows dim.
The ashes grow cold.

Yet, sometimes in the ashes . . . an ember is found.
And, sometimes from the ember . . . a fire is born.
And, sometimes by the fire . . . the stories are told.
And, sometimes in the stories . . . lessons are learned.

"If it's not in context, it's just arts and crafts."
Steve Watts

About the Author

Steve Watts

Prehistorian Steve Watts directs the Aboriginal Studies Program at the Schiele Museum of Natural History in Gastonia, North Carolina (since 1984). There he offers a series of Southeastern Native American programs for school students and an annual series of primitive technology workshops for museum professionals, teachers, archaeologists and other interested adults.

Steve is a founding board member and current president of the international Society of Primitive Technology, which publishes a biannual journal, *The Bulletin of Primitive Technology.* He presents workshops and aboriginal skills demonstrations throughout the US and replicates prehistoric tools for display and experiential education programs. His replicas are on display in more than a dozen museums throughout the Southeast and Gulf regions.

He is the author of many articles dealing with culture and technology, served as a consultant on the Twentieth Century Fox movie *Cast Away,* and is currently involved in the development of an experimental archaeology program designed for long-term study and analysis. Steve completed his undergraduate education at Appalachian State University in 1969 and received his masters degree from Duke University in 1971.

Steve Watts and David Wescott, the editor of this publication, met in 1988 and are still great friends.

The Society of Primitive Technology

The Society of Primitive Technology was founded in 1989 by pioneer experimental archaeologist Dr. Errett Callahan to "promote the practice and teaching of aboriginal skills, foster communication between teachers and practitioners, and set standards for authenticity, ethics and quality".

The SPT publishes a biannual journal, *The Bulletin of Primitive Technology* and has produced two volumes devoted to the subject:
Primitive Technology:A Book of Earth Skills and
Primitive Technology II: Ancestral Skills
(Gibbs Smith, Publisher, Salt Lake City, Utah).

To find out more, contact:
Society of Primitive Technology
you can contact David Wescott
at the SPT office,
PO Box 905, Rexburg, Idaho 83440
or on the web at *www.primitive.org*

Schiele Museum Aboriginal Studies Program

The Aboriginal Studies Program at the Schiele Museum of Natural History in Gastonia, North Carolina was established in 1984. Programs include aboriginal technology workshops and field courses; experimental archaeology projects; Native American and Early Human study-tour programs for school students; displays, demonstrations and lectures for educational institutions and the general public.

An annual schedule of adult workshops is published each fall. These courses are designed for teachers, museum personnel, students of anthropology, and others interested in increasing their knowledge and understanding of ancient lifeways and technologies.

Aboriginal skills are not taught for skill's sake. An attempt is always made to place these skills within an anthropological matrix, providing participants with information drawn from archaeology, history, ethnology, linguistics, experimental studies and living oral traditions.

For more information contact:
The Aboriginal Studies Program,
Schiele Museum of Natural History
1500 E. Garrison Blvd.
Gastonia, NC 28054

"z-z-z-Z"
"Flint Knapping"
WATTS-85

SW - 2004